EX AUDITU

An International Journal for the Theological Interpretation of Scripture

Volume 20   2004

Ex Auditu is published annually by Wipf & Stock Publishers, 199 West 8th Avenue, Eugene, Oregon 97401, U.S.A.

Subscriptions

    Individuals:
        U.S.A. and all other countries (in U.S. funds) - $20.00
        Students - $12.00

    Institutions:
        U.S.A. and all other countries (in U.S. funds) - $30.00

This periodical is indexed in the ATLA Religion Database, published by the American Theological Library Association, 250 S. Wacker Dr., 16th Flr., Chicago, IL 60606, Email: atla@atla.com, WWW: http://www.atla.com/; *Internationale Zeitschriftenshau für Bibelwissenschaft*; *Religious and Theological Abstracts*; and *Old Testament Abstracts*.

Please address all subscription correspondence and change of address information to *Wipf & Stock Publishers*.

©2004 by Wipf & Stock Publishers
ISSN 0883-0053

EX AUDITU

An International Journal for the Theological Interpretation of Scripture

Klyne R. Snodgrass, *Editor*

North Park Theological Seminary
3225 West Foster Avenue
Chicago, Illinois 60625-4987
USA

Tel. (773) 244-6243
Fax: (773) 244-6244
email: ksnodgrass@northpark.edu
Website: http://www.northpark.edu/sem/exauditu

EDITORIAL BOARD

Terence E. Fretheim, *Luther Seminary, St. Paul, MN*
Richard B. Hays, *The Divinity School, Duke University, Durham, NC*
John E. Phelan, Jr., *President of North Park Theological Seminary, Chicago, IL*
Jon R. Stock, *Wipf & Stock Publishers, Eugene, OR*
Miroslav Volf, *Yale Divinity School, New Haven, CT*
John Wipf, *Wipf & Stock Publishers, Eugene, OR*

THE EDITORIAL BOARD MEMBERS AND CONSULTANTS represent various disciplines and denominations. Theological Interpretation of Scripture is a task to be taken seriously by scholars who are committed to the Christian faith and tradition. However, as one editorial consultant stated: "let people gradually get used to the idea that a sane hermeneutics is both oriented in advance toward agreement/consent and is simultaneously exigent, discriminating, critical."

EDITORIAL CONSULTANTS

RICHARD BAUCKHAM
University of St. Andrews
St. Andrews, Scotland

M. DANIEL CARROLL R.
Denver Seminary
Denver, Colorado

JAN DU RAND
Rand Afrikaans University
Johannesburg, South Africa

WILLIE JENNINGS
The Divinity School
Duke University
Durham, N. Carolina

ROBERT JOHNSTON
Fuller Theological Seminary
Pasadena, California

R. WALTER L. MOBERLY
University of Durham
Durham, England

KATHLEEN M. O'CONNOR
Columbia Theological Seminary
Decatur, Georgia

IAIN PROVAN
Regent College
Vancouver, B.C.

GRAHAM STANTON
University of Cambridge
Cambridge, England

ANTHONY THISELTON
University of Nottingham
Nottingham, England

AUGUSTINE THOMPSON
University of Virginia
Charlottesville, Virginia

MARIANNE MEYE THOMPSON
Fuller Theological Seminary
Pasadena, California

KEVIN J. VANHOOZER
Trinity Evangelical Divinity School
Deerfield, Illinois

GEOFFREY WAINWRIGHT
The Divinity School
Duke University
Durham, N. Carolina

SONDRA WHEELER
Wesley Theological Seminary
Washington, D.C.

WILLIAM H. WILLIMON
Bishop
The North Alabama Conference
The United Methodist Church
Birmingham, Alabama

N. T. WRIGHT
Bishop of Durham
Durham, England

EX AUDITU

Volume 20   2004

CONTENTS

Announcement of the 2005 Symposium	v
Abbreviations	vi
Introduction *Klyne Snodgrass*	viii
Judgment in the Book of Revelation *Richard Bauckham*	1
The Judgment of God in the Old Testament *J. Gordon McConville*	25
Response to McConville *Terence E. Fretheim*	43
The Nature of Hell *Clark H. Pinnock*	47
Response to Pinnock *Michael A. Van Horn*	60
Revelation, Empire, and the Violence of God *John E. Phelan, Jr.*	65
Response to Phelan *Grant R. Osborne*	85

Justice and Judgment in the Book of Jeremiah: Discerning
      the Boundaries of God's Wrath
        Pamela J. Scalise   89

Judgment: By Whose Authority? Who Will Come to
      Judge the Quick and the Dead?
        D. Stephen Long   106

Response to Long
        D. Lyle Dabney   124

The Implicit "Judgment of God" in the Narrative
      Theology of Mark: Some Postcolonial Reservations
        Emerson B. Powery   129

The Unity of Judgment and Love
        Randall C. Zachman   148

A Goat's Perspective: Matthew 25:31–46
        Paul Scott Wilson   162

Annotated Bibliography on Judgment   166

Presenters and Respondents   176

Persons in Attendance   178

Ex Auditu – Volumes Available   180

ANNOUNCEMENT OF THE 2005 SYMPOSIUM

North Park Theological Seminary in Chicago, Illinois, is pleased to announce that the twenty-first Symposium on the Theological Interpretation of Scripture will take place September 22–24, 2005. The symposium will start at 7:00 p.m. on September 22 in Nyvall Hall and will extend through a Saturday afternoon worship service on September 24. The theme in 2005 will be Health and Healing. The following persons have agreed to make presentations:

- James Bruckner, North Park Theological Seminary, Old Testament
- Warren S. Brown, Fuller Theological Seminary, Psychology
- Mary Chase-Ziolek, North Park Theological Seminary, Health Care
- Michelle Clifton-Soderstrom, North Park Theological Seminary, Theology
- Fred Gaiser, Luther Seminary, Old Testament
- Dwight Peterson, Eastern University, Preaching
- Joel Shuman, King's College, Theology
- John Christopher Thomas, Lee University, New Testament
- Alan Verhey, Duke University Divinity School, New Testament and Ethics

Persons interested in attending the sessions should write before September 1 to:

Ms. Guylla Brown
North Park Theological Seminary
3225 W. Foster Avenue
Chicago, Illinois 60625

Meals may be taken at North Park and assistance can be provided in finding nearby lodging.

ABBREVIATIONS

ABD	*Anchor Bible Dictionary*
ExAud	*Ex Auditu*
HBT	*Horizons in Biblical Theology*
Heb.	Hebrew
JBL	*Journal of Biblical Literature*
JSNTSup	Journal for the Study of the New Testament: Supplement Series
JSOT	*Journal for the Study of the Old Testament*
JSOTSup	Journal for the Study of the Old Testament: Supplement Series
L.A.B.	*Liber antiquitatum biblicarum*
LXX	Septuagint
MT	Masoretic Text
NIDOTTE	*New International Dictionary of Old Testament Theology and Exegesis*
NIGTC	New International Greek Testament Commentary
NIV	New International Version
NovTSup	Novum Testamentum Supplements
NRSV	New Revised Standard Version
NTS	*New Testament Studies*
PRSt	*Perspectives in Religious Studies*
SBL	Society of Biblical Literature

SJT	*Scottish Journal of Theology*
WBC	Word Biblical Commentary
WUNT	Wissenschaftliche Untersuchungen zum Neuen Testament
WW	*Word and World*

INTRODUCTION

Hardly anyone discusses judgment any more, which is one reason we thought it should be treated. The assumption of the church and the whole society is that everyone—except for the likes of Adolf Hitler and Saddam Hussein—go to heaven and continue doing there what they did here, surely a facile assumption. Part of the problem in modern society is that few think they will be held responsible for anything.

The truth is that we know very little about the details of judgment, but lack of knowledge about specifics does not mean the subject is unimportant. If there is no judgment, there is no need for salvation. If there is no judgment, God is not a righteous God, for this world is filled with evil. If there is no judgment on what people do, then it does not matter what people do, and there is little basis for ethics. If there is no judgment, this life is meaningless. People rightly speak of God's present judgment (as in Rom 1 or John 3:18–19), but any present judgment is uneven and often visited on innocent victims rather than on the perpetrators. Talk about present judgment is irrelevant—and surely brings forth a Job-like protest—if it is not followed by future judgment.

Wrath and judgment are not inherent aspects of God's character but reactions to something outside God, unnecessary without the evil reacted against. Judgment is not essentially what God is about; rather, salvation and loving relations are eternally demonstrative of the character of God. While we may not know details about judgment, we can take comfort in Abraham's question: "Will not the Judge of the earth do what is right?" (Gen 18:25; cf. Rom 3:4). If we cannot trust that God will be just and true, the rest of the discussion is useless. The expectation that the punishment fits the crime is significant as well, partly because it exposes evil for what it is.

One recurring theme in the articles that follow is that judgment is not merely for the other people. Much of the biblical discussion of judgment is directed at *Christians*. Both the articles on the book of Revelation urge that *we* read the book as "Laodiceans." The church does not escape judgment, a shocking idea to many Christians. People—Christian or otherwise—have little sense that they may face a crisis. What may we legitimately say? No one should want a return to a focus on fire and brimstone, but is judgment even on the radar screen? A gospel of escapism is juvenile, but do we even need good news about God's deliverance? The triumphalism of the "left behind" theology must be countered with the real triumph of the Lamb. Judgment sayings are not merely about negative judgment; they focus on God's twofold coming to bring both salvation and retribution. And, while this throws humans on the mercy of God, these sayings have the purpose of leading people to repentance.

The *lex talionis* is mentioned in several articles as one of the bases for judgment. The origin of the *lex talionis* was not revenge but the assurance that evil would be dealt with and that justice would prevail. But, in relation to judgment the *lex talionis* raises a question, one implied in Clark Pinnock's article: if the punishment must fit the crime, what implication results for understanding eternal judgment? Does any crime merit eternal suffering?

Thanks is expressed once again to the presenters and respondents who made a significant investment in the life of North Park. The friendship of these people is a privilege. The authors were given a chance to edit their papers after the symposium, but the responses are as presented there. As is obvious, the views expressed are those of the authors and not necessarily those of the journal or North Park. We also thank all those in attendance for their interest and contribution to the discussions.

With this issue we begin a new relation. Pickwick Publications, the former publishers of the journal, has been purchased by Wipf and Stock. Thanks and recognition must be expressed to Dikran and Jean Hadidian, the owners of Pickwick, for their years of friendship and collaboration with North Park and for what they established with the journal. They will be missed. We look forward to working with the new publishers, John Wipf and Jon Stock, who have already demonstrated their depth of commitment to the task. We also are in the process of reframing our editorial board and our editorial consultants. We express our gratitude to those who have served before, to those who are continuing, and to those who join us for this new phase of the journal.

As has been the case in recent years, this journal was typeset using the word processor *NotaBene*, and gratitude is expressed to the good people at *NotaBene* for their continued, generous help. Special thanks is expressed to Rebekah Eklund, who proofread the journal, and to Guylla Brown from North Park's staff, without whom the symposium would not be possible.

Klyne Snodgrass
The Editor

JUDGMENT IN THE BOOK OF REVELATION

RICHARD BAUCKHAM

In order to explore the many-sided richness of the theme of judgment in Revelation, my method will be to deal with a series of aspects of the topic, approaching it from a variety of angles. There will be seven such aspects.

I. GOD'S JUDGMENTS ARE JUST

The desire for justice in an unjust world or—better—the desire for a just world is a central concern of the book of Revelation. It is axiomatic for Revelation that God, the universal Judge, is perfectly righteous and judges with absolute justice. He is the judge whose justice must prevail in the end. The hope for a just world would be futile were there not this universal Judge who is willing and able to implement justice universally. Revelation therefore makes a point of praising the justice of God's judgments: "Just (*dikaiai*) and true are your ways" (15:3); "your judgments (*kriseis*) are true and just (*dikaiai*)" (16:7); "his judgments (*kriseis*) are true and just (*dikaiai*)" (19:2); "in righteousness (*dikaiosunē*) he [Jesus Christ at the parousia] judges (*krinei*)" (19:11). In the first three of these statements the conjunction of the word "true" (*alēthinai*) with "just" is notable (cf. also 6:10). Justice is about exposing the truth of things. God's judgments are true in that they correspond to reality. They establish truth, sweeping away the lies and illusions in which evil cloaks itself. Thus the themes of judgment and justice are closely connected with another central set of themes in the Revelation: truth and deceit.

The justice of God's judgments is especially emphasized in relation to those that effect the final judgment of Babylon and her adherents (16:5–7; 18:6–7; 19:2). When the third of the bowls of God's wrath is poured out on the waters, turning them to blood (16:4), John hears the angel, whose sphere of authority is the waters, address God:

> You are just (*dikaios*), O Holy One, who are and were,
> for you have judged (*ekrinas*) these things;
> because they shed the blood of saints and prophets,

> you have given them blood to drink.
> It is what they deserve (*axioi eisin*)! (16:5–6)

This is an example of the *lex talionis* (or "measure for measure") principle of justice, found throughout early Jewish and Christian literature.[1] The general principle is well stated in Obad 15: "As you have done it shall be done to you; your deeds shall return on your own head." The basic idea is that the punishment should fit the crime. This can take many forms, some of which seem highly artificial to us. In this case, blood is the factor that corresponds in both crime and punishment: they have shed blood and so they must drink blood. In this surreal visionary context we should not be too concerned that the correspondence of crime and punishment does not really insure that the severity of the punishment is appropriate to the seriousness of the crime. The point is rather a graphic way of claiming that strict justice is being done, a point emphasized in the added insistence that those judged deserve what they get. It is not for nothing that this passage embodying the *lex talionis* principle is one of the rather few in which the act of judgment is explicitly attributed to God as the subject of the verb (cf. 18:8, 20; 19:2).

Another instance of the *lex talionis* is in 11:18:

> The nations raged,
> but your wrath has come,
> and the time for judging the dead,
> for rewarding your servants . . .
> and for destroying the destroyers of the earth
>   (*diaphtheirai tous diaphtheirontas tēn gēn*).

The correspondence of crime and punishment here depends on a wordplay, exploiting the double meaning of *diaphtheirō*, which can mean both "destroy," in the sense of causing to perish, and "ruin," in the sense of corrupting with evil. The destroyers of the earth are the powers of evil who are ruining God's creation with their violence, oppression, and idolatrous religion (cf. 19:2). There is an allusion to the equivalent wordplay in the Genesis story of the flood (Gen 6:11–13, 17, where *šḥt* has the same double meaning). In both cases God's wholesale destruction of those who are ruining his creation is justified as necessary for the preservation of his creation and its salvation from the evil they are doing to it.

The *lex talionis* reappears in relation to the fall of Babylon in 18:6–7a,[2] where a voice from heaven calls on the agents of divine justice (presumably angels):

> Render to her as she herself has rendered [cf. Ps 137:8],
> give her the exact equivalent (*diplōsate ta dipla*) of her deeds
>   [cf. Isa 40:2];
> and in the cup she mixed mix for her the exact equivalent (*diploun*).

> To the extent that she glorified herself and lived luxuriously,
> so give her an equal measure of torment and mourning.[3]

Here the usual English translation of lines 2–3 (e.g., NRSV: "repay her double for her deeds; mix a double draught for her in the cup she mixed") suggests a grossly unjust punishment by the standard of the *lex talionis*, expressly contradicting lines 1 and 4–5. Fortunately, this usual translation is wrong. The point again is that what Babylon receives is precisely what her iniquities deserve.

Intrinsic to the idea of "measure for measure" judgments is that this is the best kind of justice because its justice should be obvious even to the criminal. To receive something equivalent to what one has done is to find, as it were, one's own sin boomeranging back at one. As Obadiah puts it, the sinners' deeds return on their own head. As the Psalms sometimes have it, they fall into the pit they have dug for another. A contemporary newspaper story may help us to see the point. A local medical center was troubled by young vandals putting bricks through the windows, and so they installed toughened glass. Soon afterwards a mother came into the center to complain about what had happened to her son. He had suffered a cut on the head when he threw a brick at a window and it bounced back and hit him on the head. Probably most people's reaction would be to feel that this is justice of the sweetest and most appropriate kind: the sin itself rebounding on the sinner. No court of law would prescribe this punishment for this crime, but it appeals to the imagination as more just than any punishment the court might impose.

Elisabeth Schüssler Fiorenza is right when she claims that in Revelation "justice is understood as the conviction that each act brings about consequences which must be faced responsibly."[4] We should not, however, set up a false antithesis between the acts bringing about their own punishment and God acting in judgment. The two belong together, as in the poetic parallelism of Ezek 22:31: "Therefore I have poured out my indignation upon them; I have consumed them with the fire of my wrath; I have returned their conduct upon their heads, says the Lord YHWH." As Schüssler Fiorenza continues, "It is God who has the power to make sure that all people have to bear the consequences of their actions."[5] Whereas human systems of justice must always to some degree be conventional (and therefore contestable), God's judgment brings to light the evil intrinsic in the act itself. God's judgment is not an external authority imposing its will on people, but the light of truth exposing evil for all to see. This is the case even when, as in the judgments of the bowls in Rev 16, the perpetrators of evil themselves refuse to acknowledge it. The "measure for measure" judgment (16:4–7) should have brought the truth home even to them, but in fact they curse God and refuse to repent (16:9–11, 21). They refuse the truth which therefore shows them to be people who choose to live a lie.

Many readers of Revelation recoil with horror from its lurid depictions of judgment, which seem to them the actions not of the just God but of a wantonly cruel deity. The first step in dealing with this reaction must be to recognize that Revelation itself insists emphatically on the justice of God and his dealings with the world. An interpretation of Revelation that is faithful to its own priorities must surely give this affirmation of divine justice hermeneutical priority.[6] We should not from our reading of the visions of judgment conclude that the God of Revelation is a cruel monster, but recognize Revelation's fundamental confession of the God of absolute justice and read the visions of judgment in the light of that confession.

II. GOD'S RELATION TO THE JUDGMENTS

It has not often been noticed that Revelation rarely states unequivocally that it is God who acts when judgments occur. In fact, this occurs only in ascriptions of praise and thanksgiving to God for his acts of judgment (16:5–6; 18:8, 20; 19:2; cf. also 14:7; 16:7).[7] In the actual accounts of the judgments there is a remarkable reticence about exactly how they are related to God.

On the one hand, there is no doubt that they issue from God's heavenly throne room, as John depicts it in ch. 4. This is made clear in the cases of all three septenaries of judgments. It is the four living creatures, who belong to God's throne, who summon the four riders of the first four seal-openings (6:1, 3, 5, 7). The seven trumpets are blown by the seven angels who stand in God's presence (8:2, 6). The seven angels who are to pour out the bowls of God's wrath, the final plagues with which "the wrath of God is ended" (15:1), emerge from the heavenly throne room or temple (15:5–6), and it is one of the living creatures who gives them the bowls (15:7). Then, in the picture of smoke filling the temple (15:8), there is an echo of Isaiah's throne vision (Isa 6:4) that completes the allusion to this vision begun in the depiction of the throne room in Rev 4:8 (cf. Isa 6:3). The command actually to pour the bowls comes from the temple (16:1). Most significant of all, however, in connecting all the septenaries of judgments with the vision of God on his throne in ch. 4, is the literary link between 4:5a and the seventh of each of these series of judgments. The words of 4:5a recall both Ezekiel's vision of the divine throne (Ezek 1:13) and the Exodus account of God's appearance on Sinai (Exod 19:16; 20:18): "Coming from the throne are flashes of lightning, and rumblings and peals of thunder." This formula appears again at the opening of the seventh seal (8:5), at the sounding of the seventh trumpet (11:19), and the pouring out of the seventh bowl (16:18–21). Each time the formula appears it is expanded, such that what began in 4:5a as a depiction of God's fearful holiness becomes also a depiction of final judgment, while the progressive expansion of the formula corresponds to the progressive intensification of the judgments in the three series. In this way the whole course of the judgments is represented as the manifestation of the same divine holiness that is revealed in the theophany of ch. 4.

The judgments issue from God's presence, but, on the other hand, in none of these cases is it directly said that God commands or executes them. For the most part the descriptions of the judgments themselves use the passive voice so that the agent of the events is unstated even where the verb clearly requires that there be an agent: the first rider *"was given"* a crown (6:2), the second *"was given"* a sword (6:4), "hail and fire . . . *were thrown* to the earth" (8:7), "something like a great mountain . . . *was thrown* into the sea" (8:8), the star *"was given"* the key to the abyss (9:1), and so forth (8:2, 3, 12; 11:1, 2; 13:5; 18:21).[8] Are these instances of the so-called "divine passive," a practice found often in the words of Jesus in the Gospels?[9] The expression "divine passive" refers to the Jewish reverential habit of protecting the transcendence of God by not stating his agency in the world directly but only as the implied agent of verbs in the passive. Reverential circumlocution certainly occurs in the final judgment of the bowl series, the climax of all three septenaries, the judgment of Babylon. First, there is "a loud voice . . . from the throne, from the temple, saying, 'It is done!'" (16:17). Though the voice comes from the throne, the anthropomorphism of "God said" is carefully avoided.[10] Then comes the theophany-judgment formula expanded from 4:5a. Then, in 16:19b, a literal translation would be: "And Babylon the Great was remembered before God to give her the cup of the wine of the fury of his wrath." The implied meaning is that God remembered Babylon and so gave her the cup, but the need to avoid directly stating God's agency results in a rather awkward circumlocution.[11]

These anti-anthropomorphic linguistic devices are almost entirely confined to God's actions in judgment.[12] It is therefore very significant that they are abandoned when the talk is rather of God's eschatological action in salvation, beyond the judgments. It is not merely a voice from the throne, but unequivocally the one seated on the throne who declares, "See, I am making all things new!" (21:5). This is the first speech said directly to be that of God since 1:8. The divine self-description of 1:8 is echoed as God continues to speak in 21:6, but also noteworthy is that this continuing speech of God begins with the triumphant "It is done!" (21:6). The plural verb (*gegonan*, a contracted form of *gegonasin*) might be better rendered, "All things are now accomplished!"[13] Since Revelation regularly varies repeated expressions, it is difficult to tell whether the plural is meant to contrast with the singular *gegonen* ("It is done!") in 16:17. But there is certainly a contrast between the fact that in 16:17 it is a voice from the throne that pronounces the completion of judgment on Babylon and her adherents, whereas in 21:6 it is the one seated on the throne who pronounces the new creation accomplished.

One is reminded here of Martin Luther's distinction between God's strange work (of judgment) and his proper work (of salvation). The book of Revelation distances God from his judgments—both linguistically and actually (by the intermediation of angelic agents)—but not from his acts of salvation. The latter are precisely a matter of God's unparalleled closeness to his creation: he will make his home with humans; he will be with them; he himself will wipe every tear from their eyes; he himself will give them the water of life to drink; he will be their God and they will be his children; they will see his face (21:3–4, 6–7; 22:3; cf. also 7:17). However precisely we should interpret this difference, it is clear that for Revelation God is not related in the same way to judgment as he is to salvation.

Finally, we should notice that, among the passive verbs that characteristically describe the judgments, there is a special use of the expression "was given" (*edothē* + dative + infinitive), either in this simple form (6:4; 7:2; 13:7, 14, 15; 16:8)[14] or in the fuller form "authority was given" (*edothē exousia* + dative) (6:8; 9:3, 5; 13:5, 7; cf. 17:12).[15] Probably the former (often translated "was allowed" or "was permitted") is merely a short form of the latter ("was given authority over" or "to"). Both are used of the supernatural agents of calamity and horror (whether these agents themselves are good servants of God or evil powers): the riders; the four angels; the demonic locusts; the beasts. The meaning is that these evils do not happen without the knowledge and authority of God. They are in some sense authorized by him, but again there is the distancing use of the passive. Only once is this expression used with the passive with reference to something good, some aspect of salvation (19:8). In other cases, when what is authorized is good, God or Jesus is the explicit subject of an active form of the verb "to give," as in, for example, 2:7: "to the one who conquers I will give (authority) to eat of the tree of life" (cf. 2:26; 3:9, 21; 11:3). The contrasting ways of speaking of God's relation to the judgmental and the salvific are the same in this case as in the others we have discussed.

We should probably not think of the majority of the judgments in Revelation as special divine interventions. They are simply the regular evils of human history, escalated over the course of the three septenaries to exceptional proportions. The terrors the four riders bring to the world at the openings of the first four seals—imperialism, war, famine, and disease—are history's "business as usual." In our time they are, to take merely some of the best known examples, Darfur, Beslan, 9/11, the Asian tsunami and the AIDS epidemic in Africa. God's relation to such evils is, of course, the age-old and ultimately unanswerable question of theodicy. The book of Revelation has its own way of treading the very fine line between making God the direct cause of such vast human misery and denying that the world has got out of God's control. That God does not prevent such things, that God leaves humanity to the consequences of its own ways, is a form of judgment. After the extreme horrors of twentieth-century history, which show no sign of abating in the twenty-first, it is naive to complain that Revelation wallows in doom and disaster. It depicts the world as we know it. It recognizes

God's strange work without denying its strangeness, its disturbing difference from God's proper work of salvation.

III. JESUS CHRIST'S RELATION TO THE JUDGMENTS

I differ from the majority of scholars who see the septenaries of judgments as a series of consequences of the victory Jesus achieved by his bloody witness to God, the victory of the slaughtered Lamb (5:6, 9). They take this view because they correctly understand the sealed scroll to contain a revelation of the way in which the Lamb's victory will work out in the course of history up to the end, but also, incorrectly in my view, suppose that when the Lamb opens the seals, part of the content of the scroll is revealed each time a seal is broken. But it is impossible to imagine a scroll to which this could be done. Only after all seven seals have been released could any of the content of a scroll sealed with seven seals become visible. In my view the scroll of chs. 5–8 is the same as the scroll of chapter 10. It is opened in seven stages, and then, when it is open (10:2), an angel brings it from heaven to give to John, who eats it (10:8–10) and then reveals its content in the following chapters of his apocalypse. We are given a short version of its contents in 11:1–13, then a fuller version in the chapters that follow. The series of seal-openings (6:1–17 and 8:1) are preliminary to the revelation of the content of the scroll. They are a literary device that enables John to fill in for us some of the background we need to learn first if we are to appreciate the content of the scroll.[16]

In this case, there is a story of judgment that derives from the revelation of the holy God in ch. 4 and runs through the three septenaries of judgments to the fall of Babylon. But there is also another story that derives from the victory of the slaughtered Lamb in ch. 5, interrupts the septenaries of judgment (in ch. 7, in 10:1–11:13, in chs. 12–14, and in 15:2–4), and reaches its culmination in the coming of Jesus to judge in 19:11–21. The significance of distinguishing these stories is as follows. The reason why the judgments are strung out through three series of seven, with the severity progressively increasing, is that time is left for humanity to take heed of them, to repent and to worship the true God. But this does not happen, a point made emphatically in 9:20–21, summing up the (non)effect of the first six trumpets, and throughout the series of bowl pourings (16:9, 11, 21). As a strategy for bringing humanity at large to repentance, judgments fail. This story can only lead to the destruction of the great mass of unrepentant humanity. But what the scroll reveals is that God has another strategy for the salvation of the nations, one that is the outworking of the Lamb's sacrificial victory. This is truly a revelation, not something that could be known (except in hints) from the OT revelation. The followers of the Lamb are to follow him in his costly witness, even to the point of death, and this suffering witness will win the nations to God (11:13; 15:3–4; 21:3, 4–6).[17]

This story of the Lamb's victory does lead to a kind of judgment of its own, described in 19:11–21. I do not think (as some have argued) that this passage itself describes the victory of the cross, where Jesus himself trod the winepress of the wrath of God so that others need not.[18] Rather I think this passage describes the consequences of the witness of Jesus and his followers for those who do not accept it. The same witness that is salvific for those who heed it necessarily becomes evidence against those who do not. Like much of Revelation, this passage deploys the imagery of holy war, but the only weapon wielded by the divine warrior is the sharp two-edged sword that projects from his mouth (19:15, 21; cf. 1:16; 2:12, 16; the image derives from Isa 11:4). This is the word of his faithful and true witness to God (cf. 19:11; 3:14), now turned into judgment on those who reject the witness. Its power is that of truth to destroy illusion and lies. In the form of Jesus' suffering witness and that of his followers, truth has been demonstrated in the face of the lies of the dragon and the beasts, such that people can recognize the truth and turn away from lies (i.e., repent). But when the truth is finally established and all illusion dispelled, then those who persist to the end in refusing the truth must perish with the lies they will not relinquish. This is what happens in 19:11–21. It constitutes a quite different kind of judgment from that of the three septenaries, which are natural and historical cataclysms and have no power to bring repentance. The judgment at the parousia presupposes the suffering witness of Jesus and his followers, which can and has brought many to repentance and worship of the true God. This judgment is final confrontation with the truth of God in Jesus Christ. It is the paradoxical judgment of the gospel of salvation, the same judgment of which the Gospel of John speaks in different images (John 3:17–21; 12:46–49; cf. also 2 Cor 2:14–16).[19]

IV. THE RELATION OF THE PRAYERS OF THE SAINTS TO THE JUDGMENTS

Although I think the idea of two stories—one of judgments on evil, the other of the Lamb's victory—is useful, we should not separate out the two stories as though they were unrelated to each other. In fact, they are closely interwoven in this narrative of the coming of God's kingdom. The three septenaries of judgments do lead to the coming of the kingdom of God (at the seventh seal opening, the seventh trumpet, and the seventh bowl pouring, which is the fall of Babylon), just as the victory of the Lamb does (with the conversion of the nations and the parousia). Babylon must fall if the new Jerusalem is to come, just as the nations must repent and worship God if they are not to perish with Babylon but bring their glory into the new Jerusalem. The people of God, the followers of Jesus, have a role in both stories. In the story of the Lamb's victory they must bear witness to the nations by their costly testimony even to the point of death. But in the story of the judgments they also have a role, which is probably rather more problematic for many readers. This is the role their prayers play in bringing about the judgments that lead to the final destruction of historical evil.

We first encounter the prayers of the saints in 5:8, where they are figured as incense (on the basis of the imagery of the Jerusalem temple). At this point the prayers are merely held in readiness by the heavenly priests, not yet offered to God on the altar of incense (that is, the heavenly equivalent of the altar of incense in the temple). This offering takes place at 8:3–5 (at the opening of the seventh seal), where "the prayers of all the saints" are offered by an angel on the altar and ascend with the incense before God. Then the angel takes fire from the altar and throws it on the earth. There follows the theophanic manifestation of God's holiness in judgment that always signals the end (8:5; cf. 11:19; 16:18–21). It seems clear that this culmination of judgment is the answer to the prayers of the saints. We should probably understand that these "prayers of all the saints" (8:3) are for the coming of God's kingdom (the second petition of the Lord's Prayer), which entails the destruction of evil. The saints in these texts do not pray for judgment as such, but for the kingdom whose coming must be a judgment on evil.

Rather different are the prayers of "the souls of those who had been slaughtered for the word of God and for the testimony they had given" (6:9). At the opening of the fifth seal John sees these souls under the altar—not here the altar of incense, but the altar of burnt offering, on which these saints have been offered in sacrifice. Like the blood of the animal sacrifices in the temple, their blood has poured down from the altar, and so John sees their "souls," their sacrificed lives, at the foot of the altar. We should not think too literally of the "souls" of these martyrs. The scene is a figurative depiction of the idea that the blood of the martyrs cries to God to be avenged. But the prayer is important: "Sovereign Lord, holy and true, how long will it be before you judge and avenge our blood on the inhabitants of the earth?" (6:10).

This is not an expression of personal vindictiveness. God is invoked as the perfectly just judge who in his judgments enacts the truth (note the recurrence here of the connection we noticed earlier between the justice of God's judgments and the term "true" [*alēthinos*]). The martyrs pray for vindication in which the truth of things will come to light. They ask for justice understood in a positive way that is common in Scripture: justice for the oppressed, which is necessarily justice against their oppressors. Hence the call to the saints to rejoice at the fall of Babylon: "For God has given judgment for you against her" (18:20). An answer to the prayer of the martyrs for vengeance is not denied but postponed in 6:11. The answer is clearly indicated in 16:5–7 (where the response in v. 7 is from the altar, i.e., the same altar of burnt offering on which the saints have been slaughtered) and 18:2 (the word "avenge" [*ekdikeō*] occurs in Revelation only in 6:10 and 18:2, forming a kind of *inclusio* linking the prayer with its answer).

The reason why the prayer of the martyrs occurs at the opening of the fifth seal is not, as some commentators think, because they are the victims of the conquest, war, famine, and disease brought by the four riders at the first four seal openings. It is rather because the judgments brought by the riders are disappointingly limited. They do not seem to be leading very rapidly to the final judgment for which the martyrs long and pray. The message is much as in the Synoptic apocalypse, which this part of Revelation is probably intended to recall:

> When you hear of wars and rumours of wars, do not be alarmed; this must take place, but the end is still to come. For nation will rise against nation, and kingdom against kingdom; there will be earthquakes in various places; there will be famine. This is but the beginning of the birthpangs. (Mark 13:7–8)

The martyrs' cry of "How long?" echoes the cries of the oppressed people of God down through the biblical centuries (Pss 6:3; 13:1–2; 74:9–10; 79:5; 80:4; 94:3; Hab 1:2; Dan 8:13; 12:6; cf. also 4 Ezra 4:33; 6:59; 2 Bar 21:19; 81:13). It expresses the thirst for justice in an unjust world. The book of Revelation is to reveal why its fulfillment has to be delayed—a delay symbolized by the lengthy interruptions within each of the first two septenaries, dividing the sixth judgment, at which the end seems imminent, and the end itself, the seventh of the series. The end is deferred so that the suffering witness of the followers of Jesus may persuade the nations to repent, rather than to face judgment. This is a better way for the kingdom to come. The prayer of the martyrs for justice will be answered, but faithful witness to the nations, at the cost of the deaths of many more of God's witnesses (6:11), takes precedence in God's purpose. The same innocent blood that cries for justice is itself the price of the Lamb's victory.

On the prayer of the souls under the altar, Schüssler Fiorenza comments:

> Exegetes, who generally do not suffer unbearable oppression and are not tormented by God's apparent toleration of injustice, tend to label this outcry for justice as unchristian and contrary to the preaching of the gospel. One can adjudicate the central quest of Revelation in theological terms, however, only if one comprehends the anguish that fuels this outcry for justice and vindication, for divine revenge and restitution for so many lives taken, and so much blood unnecessarily shed.[21]

This is generally right, but I am not sure that this desire for justice is "the central quest of Revelation." I think we appreciate Revelation more fully when we recognize that, important as this theme of justice is, the prophecy in fact defers this concern by giving priority to another: the conversion of the unjust and the oppressors. Insofar as the latter is successful, the desire for justice is satisfied without the judgment of the unjust.[22]

V. PROPHETIC DISCERNMENT OF EVIL

Friedrich Nietzsche called Revelation "the most rabid outburst of vindictiveness in all recorded history."[23] In order to appreciate how wide of the mark this is we need not only to see that the desire of the martyrs for justice is not personal resentment but is subject to the judgment of the perfectly just God to whom they appeal. We need also to recognize that Revelation condemns the earthly powers of evil—the beasts and Babylon—not only, and not even primarily, because of what they do to Christians. Revelation exposes the Roman Empire as a system of violent oppression, founded on conquest, maintained by military brutality. It is a system both of political tyranny (the beast from the sea) and of economic exploitation (Babylon). The imperial cult, represented by the beast from the land, is an idolatrous absolutizing of political and military might. The prophetic vision of Revelation sees through the ideological propaganda of the *Pax Romana* according to which Rome's gift to the world was peace, security, and prosperity. It may indeed be advantageous to the privileged local elites of the empire, whose power was bolstered by Rome's and who profited from Rome's prosperity—this is why the "kings of the earth" and the "merchants of the earth" mourn for Babylon in ch. 18: Rome's downfall is also their own.

However, we should note that the condemnation and judgment is visited primarily not on persons but on the systems of military, political, and economic power that the beasts and the whore represent: "systemic evil and structural sin."[24] Persons fall under the same condemnation and judgment insofar as they identify with these systemic evils, worshipping the beast and fornicating with the whore. Hence the call to God's people to disassociate from the evil Babylon represents: "Come out of her, my people, so that you do not take part in her sins, and so that you do not share in her plagues" (18:4). When the saints are invited to rejoice over Babylon's fall (18:20), it is the destruction of an evil system they are to celebrate, much as, for example, many people rejoiced over the fall of apartheid in South Africa or "the collapse of communism."

According to Schüssler Fiorenza, 18:24 is "the theological key to the whole Babylon series of judgments":[25] "[In Babylon] was found the blood of prophets and saints, and of all who have been slaughtered on earth." It is not just for the martyrdom of Christians that Rome will be judged, but also for the slaughter of all her innocent victims. This verse, at the climax of Revelation's whole indictment of Rome, expresses a kind of solidarity between the martyrs and all of Rome's victims—indeed, all the victims of the many murderous powers of which Babylon is the consummation. The use of the word "slaughtered" (*esphagmenōn*) even suggests a solidarity of the slaughtered Lamb himself with all the victimized and oppressed of the earth. Revelation condemns Rome for its treatment of all of these, but the death of the Lamb and those of his followers bring to light what is finally at stake in Rome's tyranny, since in their deaths they bear witness to the one true God, the only true absolute, to whom all power is subject. Thereby they expose Rome's idolatrous self-deification for what it is. The importance Revelation gives the martyrs and their vindication in the judgment of their oppressors cannot be understood within a narrow context merely of the hostility between the early Christian communities and the pagan societies within which they lived. It is of such importance because it crystallizes the much greater world-historical issue of power and oppression, the issue of justice for "all who have been slaughtered on earth."

VI. A HERMENEUTICAL APPROACH FOR TWENTY-FIRST-CENTURY FIRST WORLD CHRISTIANS: READING REVELATION "AS LAODICEANS"

There are many ways into Revelation. The book itself provides seven different approaches for readers in different situations. The messages to the churches are seven introductions to the rest of the book, providing the readers in each of the churches (as well as readers elsewhere or later but in analogous circumstances) with their own way into the rest of the book. The acute prophetic analysis of the spiritual strengths and weaknesses of each church provides that church with the starting-point from which its members may find their way as "conquerors" through the rest of the apocalyptic drama to the new Jerusalem, or, should they refuse to heed the prophecy, their path to sharing Babylon's fate. Specific themes and images in each message are echoed and taken up later in the book, so that each church should recognize material of special relevance to it as its people read from their message on through the subsequent visions until they find the promises to the conquerors at the end of each of the seven messages finally recurring in the closing scenes of the book. Thus, for example, the Christians of Thyatira will find in the vision of the whore of Babylon a large-scale equivalent of their own false prophet "Jezebel" and so learn to see the latter as the representative of Babylon within their own community. The theme of wealth and poverty, prominent in the messages to Smyrna and Laodicea, echoes through chs. 18 and 21.

Proper attention to the seven messages to the churches should be enough to dispel the still all too common claim that the function of Revelation (and other Jewish and Christian apocalypses) was comfort, consolation, and hope for Christians suffering persecution and oppression. Some of its first readers were suffering, and this would have been part of its function for them, but the seven messages to the churches show that Christians who were already suffering for their uncompromising faith were in a small minority. Compromise and complacency seem more common among the seven churches. To most of his readers, sadly failing in their loyalty and witness to Jesus, John's message is a call to repentance. The conflict with the powers of evil that the visions portray is not, for the most part, already happening, because for the most part the Christians in these churches do not recognize the evil in which they are themselves too closely implicated. If only they do recognize it, if only they adopt the standpoint of prophetic resistance to evil that is this book's understanding of the role of Christians in God's world, then there will indeed be the great conflict Revelation predicts, in which faithfulness and endurance to the point of death are required, and in which Christians will share in the Lamb's victory only by following him in his witness as far as death. As Harry Maier aptly puts it, the problem John perceives for many of his readers is "not too much persecution, but too little."[26]

Commentators have a tendency to excuse what they see as the vindictiveness and excessive character of the judgments in Revelation by pointing to the circumstances of extreme suffering in which the readers are imagined to be. Adela Yarbro Collins, shocked by so much material that cannot, in her view, be reconciled with Christian love, argued that the book's function is catharsis, providing a kind of safety-valve for the expression of all the hostility and resentment Christians had accumulated against their pagan neighbours.[27] Alternatively, commentators of a liberationist perspective, for whom Revelation offers a theology of justice for the oppressed,[28] tend to argue that the book can only be appreciated from the standpoint of the poor, the oppressed, and the persecuted today, whether by readers in such situations themselves or by others able to put themselves in empathetic solidarity with the oppressed. This approach is certainly more valid than one that can deal with the judgments only by somehow excusing the author and the readers for indulging such repulsive fantasies. Some of Revelation's first readers, such as the Christians at Smyrna, were certainly suffering for their faith in a variety of ways, from material poverty and social exclusion to the threat of judicial execution. Revelation does speak powerfully to such readers—and always has done through the centuries. We have also noticed that there is an important sense in which the prophecy does express solidarity not only with oppressed Christians but with all victims of oppression and injustice throughout the horrors of history, not least those of the twentieth and twenty-first centuries. We cannot appreciate the book's condemnation of Babylon and the beasts—for murderous military force, brutal political repression, and economic exploitation of the poor—unless we recognize the fate of the victims of history (surely the majority in any age) and their claims to justice. Of course, the judgments will seem excessive to those taken in by the propaganda of the beasts because they themselves profit from Babylon's prosperity. Such people cannot see the violent and foul underside of their own history until their eyes are opened by such prophetic vision as Revelation provides. This is precisely one of the functions of the book. Perhaps more than at any other group of readers, it was aimed at the complacent and the compromising among its first readers, and the portrayals of judgment were there precisely to shock and even to scare such readers into an understanding of where they stood in the spiritual crisis of their time. For such readers the judgments were not simply on *other* people, their enemies rightly or wrongly characterized as such, but the fate for which they themselves were headed, unless they took urgent action to end their complicity with the evils of their society and to take instead the costly road of faithful testimony to Jesus.

If all too comfortable and complacent Christians, enjoying the benefits of relative power and prosperity, read Revelation as though they were persecuted and oppressed, the result can be disastrous. The message they hear is promise without cost and a kind of amoral partisan triumphalism that entirely evades the book's concern for justice—in short, a "Left Behind" theology. Harry Maier, in his stimulating book, *Revelation Recalled: The Book of Revelation after Christendom*, makes a different hermeneutical choice. Concerned as he is with "Revelation's challenge to a sleeping and culturally assimilated church,"[29] he finds it most appropriate to "read as a Laodicean":

> For where is a first-world white male of privilege to find himself described in the Apocalypse if not in this seventh message—rich, not needing anything, neither hot nor cold, but lukewarm—the typical citizen of a reigning order that keeps the majority of the planet's inhabitants in servitude to furnish me with my comforts? Who if not me needs persuasion that I am naked, blind, pitiable, and wretched, I who walk down golden-lit streets in my expensive clothing with the jingle-jangle of money in my pocket, window shopping as recreation beneath jewel-colored neon lights urging me to buy? Who if not me should be frightened if there is a knock at the door—maybe a thief to steal my riches or even my life away? Who if not I should be offended at the suggestion that a stranger should invite himself over to eat in *my* house, challenge me with shortsightedness, and invite me to a new economy of scale? Who if not I needs salve for my eyes and to be rescued at last "from single vision and Newton's sleep"? [a quotation from William Blake] And who should tell me, seduced as I am by the beauty of my weapons, that there is another way to conquer and be conquered?[30]

From this perspective Maier takes on the visions of judgment as indispensable to Revelation's power to challenge:

> Most often interpreted as a book of comfort to the persecuted, [Revelation] must be listened to as a letter of challenge to the culturally comfortable and ecclesially indolent. Amid the ruins of Christendom, Revelation—the full and bloody version—is the book of the hour.[31]

I conclude this section with some reflections on what it might mean to read Revelation's septenaries of judgment as twenty-first-century Laodiceans, complicit as prosperous citizens of the first world in a system of political, military, and especially economic domination of the world, which functions both to create an ever-widening gap between rich and poor in the world and also to destroy the environment, threatening unprecedented damage to God's creation.

First, for original Laodicean readers basking in the beneficent sunshine of Roman rule, the four riders of the first four seal-openings (6:1–8) would constitute an initial deconstruction of the myth of the *Pax Romana*—Rome's claim, as the eternal city destined to rule forever, to have brought peace, security, and prosperity to the world. The description of the four riders says: Look no further than what is happening all around you. Imperial conquest (probably the Parthian threat to Rome is especially in view), war, famine, disease—these are ravaging the earth as we speak. *Pax Romana*! What *Pax Romana*? The comfortable and the complacent, the cultural optimists of any age, find a form of realized eschatology, such as the *Pax Romana* was, very attractive. A new world order, destined to last forever, is what they already enjoy and want to continue, oblivious to the oppressive underside of their peace and prosperity, the reality that impels others to long for a truly just world that is very far from realized already. It now seems astonishing to many of us how plausible Francis Fukuyama's claim that history had ended seemed just a few years ago. Since then we have seen the four apocalyptic horsemen ride triumphantly through our world once again, shattering the illusion of the *Pax Americana* with its fragile façade of world peace and increasing prosperity for all. We need not think of the mission of the riders as judgment in the punitive sense (Revelation does not in fact say this of them), but more as shocking reminders that for world history, beyond its alleged end and in spite of the new world order, it is still "business as usual."

With the trumpet blasts and the bowl pourings, the evils of the seal openings are progressively intensified, conjuring nightmare visions of a terrifying future that spirals rapidly towards "apocalypse" (in the current contemporary usage of that word), though the spiral is also importantly interrupted. As well as images from OT history and prophecy—images of holy war such as the plagues of Exodus, the trumpets at Jericho, the locust-army of Joel—these depictions of judgment play on the realistic fears of Revelation's contemporaries, magnified in accordance with the principle of apocalyptic hyperbole "such as has never happened before" (cf. 16:18).[32] With these judgments we move more clearly into the sphere of retributive justice, that, as we have seen, is particularly highlighted by the expression of the "measure for measure" or *lex talionis* principle at 16:5–6. These judgments are not evidence of the cruelty of some divine monster, a wishful projection of his world-hating followers, but reminders that "human acts cause human downfall."[33]

Schüssler Fiorenza helpfully compares their rhetorical function to that of "today's literature warning against ecological and atomic destruction":

> Present-day futuristic accounts portraying atomic warfare, ecological devastation, or scientific cloning do not intend to predict or accurately describe the future. Rather, they offer a fictional projection of what might be if the industrialized nations do not halt their military expansion or their technological exploitation of the earth. The terrible visions of such literature that portray a totally manipulated and dehumanized future seek to shock us out of our current lethargy.[34]

She is right that there is a parallel in rhetorical intention, but there is perhaps rather more material difference than she allows. The visions of Revelation work by imaginative evocation of Scripture and contemporary experience, whereas scientific projections of the effects of global warming, for example, are based on science, though limited by bounds of present knowledge and, importantly, conditional on human actions in the future. However, it is true that in this latter respect they function like the visions of Revelation to call for repentance by warning of consequences.

The effects of nuclear war, ecological disaster, or global epidemics are retributive in the straightforward sense that they are the consequences of human actions. They are the boomerangs that rebound on our own heads. Like all the horrors of history they fall on the innocent as well as the guilty; they have victims who are not their perpetrators. (So they are less discriminating than the demonic locusts of Rev 9:4.) Some, perhaps all, would have far more innocent victims than perpetrators. No one should therefore wish them on humanity as though they were a desirable form of justice. But the solidarity of humanity is unavoidable. The activities of the prosperous and powerful affect the poor and vulnerable—either negatively if the powerful persist in not recognizing this, or positively if the powerful do recognize their responsible solidarity with the poor and act accordingly, heeding the warnings and averting the consequences of their thoughtless greed and irresponsible use of power.

In an article called "The Seven Bowls of Wrath: An Ecological Parable," Richard Woods has drawn attention to the highly suggestive parallel between the judgments of the trumpets and the bowls in Revelation and the ecological destruction now happening, in consequence of human behaviour—more precisely, in consequence of the rampant consumerism and waste of the powerful nations of the first world:

> It does not take a great stretch of the imagination to recognize that the richly prophetic symbolism of Revelation ably describes the inevitable destruction of the biological systems of the earth whenever human foolishness, greed, selfishness and waste take precedence over justice and mercy.[35]

But it needs to be added that this is not just a perennial truth. The modern technological dominance of humanity over the rest of creation on this planet is creating an escalating spiral of destruction and threatened cataclysm that closely corresponds to the progressively intensifying movement of Revelation's judgments towards a "worse than has ever happened before" scenario. The apocalyptic hyperbole is an all too imminent danger.

In Revelation the warning judgments do not—at least by themselves — succeed in turning the mass of humanity to repentance. This task is given instead to the suffering witness of the Lamb's followers. Maier's account of what this would mean for early twenty-first-century first world Christians—repentant Laodiceans—is pungent:

> My diagnosis of our cultural condition is that the Book of Revelation is indispensable to mainstream first world churches of the historic confession struggling to come to terms with their institutional mortality. Indeed, it may be the most important book of the Bible for this task. Too often muzzled by the strict separation of church and state, North American Christians have for too long been silent and willing participants in a consumer culture that degrades us all. John urges us to be troublemakers by teaching us the power of public confession of belief. I later insist, with Martin Luther, that the church must be a *Mundhaus,* a "mouthhouse," or house of proclamation ringing with confession of the gospel of God's action in the life, death, and resurrection of Jesus Christ. If the churches are looking for transformation, here they will find it. Only then will we find the courage to envisage new ways of being in society and face the fact that we [i.e., the "mainstream first world churches of the historic confession"] no longer inhabit the halls of privilege. More seriously still, such courage may lead us to repentance for the idolatrous misapprehension that we could ever have comfortably sat in halls of economic pragmatism even as they brought us into direct contradiction with our gospel identity of God's lavish expenditure for the world. . . . The Book of Revelation's demand is to learn to be more marginalized, edgier disciples leading lives of costly testimony.[36]

VII. JUDGMENT OF THE DEAD

With the rest of the NT Revelation shares the conviction that God's justice is not fully achieved within history but must be finally and definitively enacted for every human individual at the last judgment. Revelation places this judgment at the pivot of its narrative turn from the old creation to the new (20:11–15). The flight of the old heaven and the old earth from the awesome presence of the almighty Judge (20:11) effectively makes this judgment the end of the whole created order of things in its present, provisional, and sin-damaged form, settling all the unfinished business of this world so that the new heaven and the new earth may take its place (21:1).

The judgment is based on the records in two sorts of books: the book of life which contains the names of the redeemed (3:5; 13:8; 17:8; 21:27; cf. Dan 12:1; 1QM 12:2–5; Luke 10:20; Phil 4:3; Heb 12:23), and the books that record all the deeds of all people (cf. Dan 7:10).[37] Judgment of all is according to the criterion of their deeds (20:12–13), a formulaic expression for God's just judgment of individuals (cf. 22:12; Ps 62:12; Prov 24:12; Job 34:11; Jer 17:10; Sir 16:14; *L.A.B.* 3:10; Matt 16:27; Rom 2:6; 1 Pet 1:17; Did 16:8; 1 Clem 34:3; 2 Clem 11:6; 17:4).[38] In view of the emphasis we have placed on the fact that, for readers of Revelation, judgment is not simply impending on other people but a real danger to themselves, we should note that it is possible to have one's name erased from the book of life (3:5; similarly 22:19; cf. Exod 32:32–33; Ps 69:28; Jub 30:22).[39]

For the fate of those whose names are not found written in the book of life Revelation uses three graphic and traditional images. As always in Revelation it is vital to realise that we are dealing with *images*, which *as images* need not be consistent with one another. One image, not often give much attention, is that they will be "outside" the new Jerusalem (22:15; cf. 21:27). We are reminded of similar parabolic images in the Gospels (Matt 8:12; 22:13; 25:10–11, 30; Luke 13:25). This negative image of exclusion from the destiny for which human beings were made is in reality as terrible as the images of positive punishment that Revelation deploys more frequently.

Another image, that of "the second death" (2:11; 20:6, 14; 21:8) is, surprisingly, found outside Revelation only in the Targums, though Jude 12 makes a rather clear allusion to it in the course of a different image (twice-dead trees). The image of the second death has a special appropriateness in Revelation, which urges its readers not to fear the first death. That death, ordinary death in this world, they must be prepared to suffer at the hands of the beast for their loyalty to God and in imitation of Jesus Christ. The slaughtered Lamb has made death the means of victory over the beast, not the defeat it is in the eyes of people in general. What is to be feared is not this first death, but the second, the death that all those not raised to eternal life must die (cf. 20:6, 14–15). The first death is the opposite only of mortal life, and so its sting is drawn by the Lamb's transformation of it into the way to eternal life. But the second death is the opposite of eternal life. It is what must happen when God leaves the finally unrepentant to the evil they have chosen. Without the life which only God can give they perish eternally.

The second death is the death that "Death and Hades" (the personified powers of death; cf. 6:8) themselves will die in the end (20:14; cf. 21:4; Isa 25:8; 1 Cor 15:54–55). Having surrendered all their dead, the dead they have held in safekeeping until the judgment (20:13), they have no further function in God's purpose. It is in this "death of death" that the wicked also die finally (20:15). They belong in the old order of things with its mortality rather than in the new order of eternal life.

A third image is "the lake of fire" (19:20; 20:10, 14 [*bis*], 15; 21:8; cf. 14:10), which is identified with the second death (20:14; 21:8) but is a distinct image of final judgment. That it burns not only with fire, a very common biblical image of God's judgment, but also with brimstone (sulphur) (19:20; 20:10; 21:8; cf. 14:10) makes an allusion to the judgment on Sodom and Gomorrah virtually certain. (For "brimstone" in this connection, see Gen 19:24; Deut 29:23; Luke 17:29; Philo, *Mos.* 2.56.) This had long been treated as the paradigmatic case of God's judgment (see Jer 49:18), such that other judgments were also depicted in terms borrowed from the story of Sodom and Gomorrah: fire, brimstone, and smoke rising (Ps 11:6; *Sib. Or.* 3:504–507; Isa 30:33; 34:9–10; Ezek 38:22). It was believed that the fate of these Cities of the Plain continued to be in evidence in the form of the smoking wasteland to the south of the Dead Sea (Wisd 10:7; Josephus, *War* 4.483; Philo, *Mos.* 2.56). For this reason language indicating that the judgment continues forever could be used: "its smoke shall go up forever" (Isa 34:10); the cities "are exhibited as an example by undergoing the punishment of eternal fire" (Jude 7). This last example from Jude seems to mean that the still burning site of the cities is a warning picture of the eternal fires of hell.[40] But we should note that in this whole tradition rooted in Genesis and the prophets the idea that the punishment is long-lasting or eternal refers to its *finality*. The still smoking site signifies that the cities will never be rebuilt. Their *destruction* lasts forever.

This is clearly the significance when Revelation borrows this imagery to describe the fate of Babylon: "The smoke goes up from her forever and ever" (19:3). Presumably the meaning is the same when Death and Hades are thrown into the lake of fire (20:14): these powers of death will be finally eliminated from God's world (cf. 21:4). Is more than this meant when the dragon, the beast, and the false prophet—Revelation's satanic trinity—are said to be "tormented day and night forever and ever" in the lake of fire (20:10; cf. 19:20)? The implication of eternally enduring torment seems also to be present in the description of the fate of unredeemed humans in 14:10–11. We need to look more closely at this passage:

> Then another angel, a third, followed them, crying with a loud voice, "Those who worship the beast and its image, and receive a mark on their foreheads or on their hands, they will also drink the wine of God's wrath, poured unmixed into the cup of his anger, and they will be tormented with fire and sulfur in the presence of the holy angels and in the presence of the Lamb. And the smoke of their torment goes up forever and ever. There is no rest day or night for those who worship the beast and its image and for anyone who receives the mark of its name." Here is a call for the endurance of the saints, those who keep the commandments of God and hold fast to the faith of Jesus. (14:9–12, NRSV)

Like all of Revelation the passage is carefully composed. Reference to the worship of the beast both opens and closes the angel's message, making it unequivocal that it is the fate of these sinners, those who have thrown in their lot with the pretended divinity of the power that tries to rival God, while the descriptions of the punishment create significant cross-references within the text of Revelation. We should note first how the punishment of these sinners is described in terms that align it with that of the nonhuman powers of evil. They are identified with the fate of Babylon in that they are "tormented" with fire (Babylon tormented: 18:10, 15; fire: 17:16; 18:9, 18), as also by the fact that "the smoke of their torment goes up forever and ever" (Babylon: 19:3). That they will be tormented with "fire and sulfur" corresponds to the fate of the devil, the beast, and the false prophet (20:10), as does the eternally enduring punishment (20:10), said to be "day and night" (20:10). Of course, it is appropriate that those who worship the beast (and thereby the devil: 13:4) should share the beast's judgment. Those who worship the beast are also those who shared in Babylon's evil and so must share the judgment of Babylon which the second of the three angels has just announced in the immediately preceding context of this passage (14:8).

The thought is not far from that of the parable of the sheep and the goats, where the blessed are invited to "inherit the kingdom prepared for you from the foundation of the world" (Matt 25:34) but the damned are told to "depart from me into the eternal fire prepared for the devil and his angels" (Matt 25:41). Whereas the redeemed inherit the destiny designed for them, the damned share a fate designed for the powers of evil. It is not their own true destiny but the result of culpably missing their true destiny. In Rev 14 the damned are those who have rejected the message of the first angel (14:7: "Fear God and give him glory") and so share the judgment of Babylon announced by the second angel.

The passage also contains two key examples of *lex talionis*. When we are told that the sinners "will also drink the wine of God's wrath (*thymou*), poured unmixed into the cup of his anger" (14:10), we are reminded that the judgment of Babylon, as just announced, takes place because "she has made all nations drink of the wine of the wrath (*thymou*) of her fornication" (14:8). The word *thymos* denotes passion, whether intense desire or intense anger. As used of God's wine here, the meaning is clearly "wrath," but "passion" would be a more appropriate translation in relation to Babylon's wine (as also in 18:3). However, the use of the same word is precisely designed to underline the correspondence between crime and punishment. In reward for drinking the wine of Babylon's passion, the sinners will have to drink the wine of God's passion.[41]

The second instance of *lex talionis* can only be seen when we notice the parallelism between 14:11b and 4:8. The former says that for those who worship the beast "there is no rest day or night" (*ouk echousin anapausin ēmeras kai nyktos*) from the torment, while 4:8, part of John's vision of the worship of God in heaven, says that the four living creatures, the paradigmatic worshipers of God, sing their hymn "day and night without ceasing" (*anapausin ouk echousin ēmeras kai nyktos*).[42] Because they have chosen to worship the beast rather than God, instead of joining the ceaseless worship of God in heaven, the damned will share the ceaseless torment of the powers of evil (20:10: *ēmeras kai nyktos*).

We should further notice that the fate of the worshipers of the beast is contrasted with that of those who refuse to worship the beast, as described in the immediately following context of our passage. Whereas the former "have no rest" from torment, the latter "will rest" (*anapaēsontai*) from their labours (14:13). Probably there is also another such contrast between the eternal futures of the worshipers of God and those of the beast in this passage. The latter are said to be tormented "in the presence of the Lamb," while the redeemed are also to be in the presence of the Lamb as his worshipers (22:3; cf. 7:15–17). (Torment in the presence of the Lamb is not, of course, for the sake of the Lamb's pleasure in observing their judgment, but, as in the reference to "the wrath of the Lamb" in 6:16, to point up the nature of their sin as rejection of the sacrificial love of God.)

The exquisitely careful formulation of this passage, tying it into the contrast between true and false worship that runs through the whole book and is at the heart of its message, shows that this picture of the punishment of the worshipers of the beast is no impulsive outburst of hatred and anger on John's part. On the contrary, it is very considered. However, once we have seen how the imagery works to convey parallels and contrasts, there is no more need to read this imagery literally than there is to read literally the rest of the imagery of this exuberantly imaginative book. What is depicted is emphatically the outworking of God's perfect justice, not only in this world but also in eternity. Moreover, we must once again observe that Revelation's readers are not encouraged to view the scene as the punishment coming to *other people*, their enemies, but as the judgment they themselves risk if they give way to the enticements of Babylon and the threats of the beast by participating in the worship of the beast.[43] It is this that makes the passage "a call to the endurance of the saints" (14:12). The parallels and contrasts that are so integral to the imagery make visible the stark and decisive alternatives that lie before Revelation's readers (cf. 22:14–15). Like the historical judgments of God in this book, the function of these truly terrifying images is to lay bare the real truth of things, and, like the material treated in section six above, these images of judgment may find their proper place, a properly limited one, in a "Laodicean" reading of Revelation.

ENDNOTES

1. R. Bauckham, *The Fate of the Dead* (NovTSup 93; Leiden: Brill, 1998), 212–218.
2. There is one other occurrence of the *lex talionis* principle in Rev 22:18–19.

3. This is my own translation based on the discussion in G. K. Beale, *The Book of Revelation* (NIGTC; Grand Rapids: Eerdmans, 1999), 900–902, who follows M. G. Kline's demonstration that *diploō* does not mean "double" but "duplicate."

4. E. Schüssler Fiorenza, *Revelation: Vision of a Just World* (Edinburgh: T. & T. Clark, 1993), 95. Similarly D. L. Barr refers to "John's basic understanding that human acts cause human downfall" ("Doing Violence: Moral Issues in Reading John's Apocalypse," in *Reading the Book of Revelation,* ed. D. L. Barr; Atlanta: SBL, 2003, 102).

5. Schüssler Fiorenza, *Revelation,* 95.

6. Schüssler Fiorenza *(Revelation,* 122) states that her "liberationist reading of Revelation's rhetoric subordinates the book's depiction of cosmic destruction and holy war to its desire for justice." However, I do not think that this hermeneutical subordination is merely a choice the interpreter makes, as though it would be just as true to the text itself to read it otherwise. It seems clear to me that the structure of the book itself gives priority to its vision of God.

7. Rev 22:18–19 is a perhaps rather surprising exception to this rule, but it occurs outside the visions of judgment.

8. Note also the passive ("was trodden") in 14:20, with the active ("he will tread") superseding it in 19:15.

9. J. Jeremias *(New Testament Theology,* trans. J. Bowden; London: SCM, 1971, 9–14) treats it as "one of the ways of speaking preferred by Jesus," and counts about one hundred occurrences in the sayings of Jesus. Jeremias' claim that it is characteristic of apocalyptic literature is supported only by the evidence of Revelation, with no evidence to show that Revelation is in this respect typical of apocalyptic literature. Evidence from Jewish apocalyptic literature is required if this claim is to be sustained. Dan 7 offers the most striking parallels to Revelation's usage.

10. Comparison with other voices from the throne (6:6; 19:5) leave the reader in some doubt whether any of these are actually the voice of God. One might compare the rabbinic notion of the *bat qol* (daughter of a voice), the voice from heaven that speaks for God but is presumably at one remove from the divine voice itself.

11. With "was remembered before God," cf. the even more circumlocutory expressions in Luke 15:7, 10. The possibility that Rev 14:10 also uses such a circumlocution should be considered, but Revelation seems only rarely to use such circumlocutions when speaking of the Lamb's actions (only in 14:20?).

12. Rev 12:5 and 14 seem to be instances where protection rather than judgment is in view, but note the noncircumlocutionary "prepared by God" in 12:6. In 6:11 there is a close connection with the judgments.

13. Cf. D. E. Aune, *Revelation 17–21* (WBC 52C; Nashville: Nelson, 1998), 1126.

14. This expression should be distinguished from cases where *something* (a crown, a sword, a mouth, etc.) is given: e.g., 6:2, 4, 11; 9:1; 11:1; 12:14; 13:5; 20:4. The usage in 17:17 is somewhat different again.

15. The expression in the passive form probably derives from Dan 7:6, 14. For the data see Beale, *The Book of Revelation,* 700–701, but he does not sufficiently distinguish this specific idiom from cases where something other than authority is given.

16. For detailed argument for the position outlined here, see R. Bauckham, *The Climax of Prophecy: Studies on the Book of Revelation* (Edinburgh: T. & T. Clark, 1993), 243–266; idem, *The Theology of the Book of Revelation* (Cambridge: Cambridge University Press, 1993), 80–84.

17. See Bauckham, *The Climax of Prophecy,* ch. 9; idem, *The Theology of the Book of Revelation,* 84–104. Because I have been misunderstood on this point, I should make it clear that

when I refer to the conversion of the nations in Revelation, I do not mean the salvation of every human individual.

18. M. Bredin offers the most persuasive recent reading partially along these lines, but he does not deny that the passage depicts judgment; see his *Jesus, Revolutionary of Peace: A Nonviolent Christology in the Book of Revelation* (Carlisle: Paternoster, 2003), ch. 15.

19. On this understanding of the parousia in Revelation, see further Bauckham, *The Theology of the Book of Revelation,* 104–106.

20. See R. Bauckham, "Prayer in the Book of Revelation," in *Into God's Presence: Prayer in the New Testament* (ed. R. Longenecker; Grand Rapids: Eerdmans, 2001), 252–271.

21. Schüssler Fiorenza, *Revelation,* 64.

22. Essentially Schüssler Fiorenza recognizes this later, when, reading 11:13 rather literally, she comments, "It is crucial that Revelation's rhetoric of judgment expresses hope for the conversion of nine-tenths of the nations in response to Christian witness and preaching. Otherwise, one will not understand that the author advocates a theology of justice rather than a theology of hate and resentment" (*Revelation,* 79).

23. Quoted in H. O. Maier, *Apocalypse Recalled: The Book of Revelation after Christendom* (Minneapolis: Fortress, 2002), 167.

24. Schüssler Fiorenza, *Revelation,* 87.

25. Ibid., 95.

26. Maier, *Apocalypse Recalled,* xiii, 34.

27. A. Y. Collins, *Crisis and Catharsis: The Power of the Apocalypse* (Philadelphia: Westminster, 1984).

28. Schüssler Fiorenza, *Revelation;* P. Richard, *Apocalypse: A People's Commentary on the Book of Revelation* (Bible and Liberation Series; Maryknoll, N.Y.: Orbis, 1995); W. Howard-Brook and A. Gwyther, *Unveiling Empire: Reading Revelation Then and Now* (Bible and Liberation Series; Maryknoll, N.Y.: Orbis, 1999).

29. Maier, *Apocalypse Recalled,* 13.

30. Ibid., 38.

31. Ibid., 29.

32. Bauckham, *The Climax of Prophecy,* 207.

33. Barr, "Doing Violence: Moral Issues in Reading John's Apocalypse," 102.

34. Schüssler Fiorenza, *Revelation,* 72.

35. R. Woods, "The Seven Bowls of Wrath: An Ecological Parable," *Ecotheology* 7 (1999): 14.

36. Maier, *Apocalypse Recalled,* 29.

37. On these two kinds of books see D. E. Aune, *Revelation 17–21,* 223–225.

38. Bauckham, *The Fate of the Dead,* 195–198.

39. The argument of Beale (*The Book of Revelation,* 279–282) that this is not really the case seems to me strained.

40. R. Bauckham, *Jude, 2 Peter* (WBC 50; Waco, Texas: Word, 1983), 55.

41. The operation of the *lex talionis* principle in the use of these images is a creative development of Revelation's OT sources for them (Ps 75:8; Jer 25:15–16; 51:6–8). Note that Jer 51:6, which calls for *lex talionis* judgment on Babylon, is echoed in Rev 18:6. On these images, see also Bredin, *Jesus, Revolutionary of Peace,* 210–211.

42. See further Bauckham, *The Climax of Prophecy,* 28.

43. But I am not persuaded by the argument of D. Powys (*"Hell": A Hard Look at a Hard Question,* Carlisle: Paternoster 1998, 366–367) to the effect that the "torment" of 14:10–11 is modeled on the tortures used by the imperial authorities to coerce Christians to deny Christ and worship the emperor. On this view, readers who risk becoming apostate are assured that the

tortures inflicted on them by God after death will be far worse than those they face at the hands of the beast. But this ignores the links with references to torment in 18:10, 15; 20:10, and the fact that Revelation never depicts the beast or the false prophet using torture. The word is used of the effect of the monstrous locusts in 9:5, but the intended contrast between this reference and 14:10–11 is probably that 9:5 depicts one of the limited judgments of God (the torment is for five months only) and is aimed at repentance (9:20–21), whereas 14:10–11 depicts the final, unlimited judgment of the finally unrepentant.

THE JUDGMENT OF GOD IN THE OLD TESTAMENT

J. GORDON McCONVILLE

The judgment of God in the OT is inseparable from the love and mercy of God. This needs to be said at the outset, in order to avoid the typical misconception that the OT is all law and wrath, while grace and mercy are the province of the New. Such a polarization misconstrues the picture of God and the world in both Testaments and runs the risk of residual Marcionism and implicit anti-Semitism.[1] On the contrary, the close intertwining of judgment, mercy, and salvation will appear from each part of this essay and is its central point.[2] As we proceed to consider closely the nuances of judgment, we should be aware that Yahweh is at the same time creator and redeemer. The metaphors of "judge" and "king" should not overwhelm the larger picture of Yahweh's person and activity in the OT by importing ideas from the ancient Near Eastern environment wholesale. This picture is dominated by Yahweh's resolve to enter into a relationship of mutuality with a community that manifests the characteristics of peace, love, and justice. Judgment in the OT is subject to this purpose.

This said, the idea of God as judge is one of the most pervasive metaphors applied to God in the OT. Perhaps only that of kingship lies deeper as the root metaphor, since in the ancient world it is characteristically kings who judge or who authorize judgment. Kingship and judgeship, therefore, are never far apart; it is the sovereignty of God in all the affairs of heaven and earth that makes his court the universal court of appeal. Individuals seek God's judgment, Israel both benefits and suffers from it, and in the end the nations are all subject to it. Much of the literature of the OT may be said to relate precisely to the premise of God's judgeship. His remembered actions, which form the core of Israel's confession, are acts of judgment, archetypically on heart-hardened Pharaoh and his forces, drowned in the returning waters of the Reed Sea. "Salvation history" is from another perspective "judgment history," and these are in reality one. God's expected attention to the business of judging justly between human beings gives rise to those lamentations which appear when deserts are not meted out as anticipated. The frequent characterization of parts of the OT as "theodicy" alludes to just such expectations and the attempt to understand their disappointment while sustaining the belief in the premise of God as judge.

Judgment, therefore, does not translate directly into the wrath of God but rather is complex and nuanced, being represented by no single term in the vocabulary of the Hebrew Bible. The vocabulary of judgment is a semantic field in which the concept is constructed by the way in which key terms are brought into relation to each other in the Bible's literary contexts. This means, of course, that we can only understand the idea by close attention to texts. And then we must take another step, namely to trace the activity of God as judge by unfolding the OT story, not merely at the level of its surface narratives, but more deeply, as it can be fathomed, for example, in the theological structure of the prophetic books. It is a story that issues in thoughts of forgiveness and restoration through and beyond judgment, as in the newness of new covenant, yet in such a way as to continue to pose questions about the relationship between the two (judgment and forgiveness), as indeed about the relationship between divine grace and human freedom. We begin, then, by looking more closely at the metaphor of God as judge.

GOD AS JUDGE: A LEADING OLD TESTAMENT METAPHOR

In Ps 82 we read that God (*ĕlōhîm*) takes his place in the assembly of God (*ēl*) among the "gods" (*ĕlōhîm*). The picture is of a divine assembly in which God presides. The background is furnished by the widespread ancient Near Eastern concept of a divine council in which a chief god dominates a pantheon, as El at Ugarit. As the psalm proceeds it transpires that those who are addressed as "gods" are in practice human bearers of authority, charged with dispensing justice in favour of the poor and needy. As God takes his place to "judge" (*šāpaṭ*), so he requires that human rulers do likewise (v. 3). Yet the essential picture is crucial: the God of Israel (by whatever name) is the supreme judge in heaven and earth. The reach of his judging is by no means parochial, for the psalmist's final plea is that God should arise and judge the earth, "for all the nations belong to you" (v. 8). The same understanding (though a different concern) informs Abraham's interrogation of God in Gen 18 and his rhetorical question: "Shall not the judge (*šōpēṭ*) of all the earth do what is just (*mišpāṭ*)?" (Gen 18:25, NRSV).

Where does this concept arise? I ask the question not in a strict historical sense but rather in relation to the religious understanding of the ancient world. There, the right of God to judge resides in his sovereignty, demonstrated in his power to create and order the universe. At Ugarit El is variously called king, creator, and judge.[3] The epithet "judge" is not limited to El, but is also applied regularly to the sea-god Yam, especially in the name Judge Nahar (River). It seems that judgeship is regarded as an attribute of deities, perhaps as an aspect of kingship. (The relationship between royal and judicial functions may be conventional when applied to gods in this way.)

In the prologue to the Babylonian Laws of Hammurabi, the cosmic deities Anum and Enlil appoint Hammurabi "to cause justice to prevail in the land."[4] There is therefore a connection between establishing justice in the social order and harmony in the created order generally. This is expressed in the ancient Near Eastern myths of origins, with their progression from the creation of order in the universe to the establishment of a political order with the mandate for maintaining justice. As Marduk overcomes Chaos and takes up his reign in Babylon,[5] so the Canaanite Baal overcomes the god Yam ("sea") and consequently is installed in his palace as guarantor of order in the world.[6]

In the OT there is a parallel story stretching from God's creation to the enthronement of David in Jerusalem. The creation is an ordering act, as evidenced by the separating decrees of Gen 1 (e.g., light from darkness), and the harmonies produced between the elements of God's work, with only an echo of Chaos in the background ("the deep," Gen 1:2). As God pronounces each part "good," we meet the divine rationality, finding (or "judging") this good and, by implication, that bad. The story makes this distinguishing examination explicit: (to the serpent) "Because you have done this, cursed are you above all animals" (Gen 3:14); (before the flood) "The Lord saw that the wickedness of humankind was great in the earth. . . . So the Lord said, 'I will blot out from the earth the human beings I have created . . .'" (Gen 6:5–7).

God's intention for order has not only cosmic but also social and political aspects. The man and the woman are in God's "image" (Gen 1:26), with the royal connotations of that metaphor, and are to "rule" (*rdh*) in the earth. The nature of the "ordering" for which humans are responsible takes shape when Noah, the flood survivor, is found "righteous" and "blameless" (*ṣaddîq, tāmîm*). The ordering of God's world proceeds through divine "judgments" (expulsion from the garden, flood, scattering at Babel, deliverance of Israel from Egypt through "sea" [*yām*], now historicized) which are driven by a purpose that human beings should live on earth in harmonious relationship with each other and with Yahweh according to a standard of righteousness. By virtue of Noah's character righteousness is set as the goal in the key primeval event of the flood. This fundamental "judgment" underlies all others.

As the ancient Near Eastern deities entrust lawgiving to the king, so too Yahweh gives laws to his people Israel in the context of his act of deliverance in the exodus and the covenant he makes with them through Moses. Here, Yahweh himself is "king" in a "kingship" defined by his will to save. As such, he gives laws more directly than do ancient Near Eastern deities, albeit through the mediator Moses. The people do not remain under Moses at Sinai, however, but the narrative takes them into the land which ultimately has a temple city at its heart, where a king rules as "son of Yahweh" (Ps 2:7), and where Yahweh himself has his "footstool" and "resting-place" (Ps 132:7–8). The obligations of the king under Yahweh are clearly set out in Ps 72:1–2:

> Give the king your justice (*mišpāṭêkā*), O God
>   and your righteousness (*ṣidqāṯěkā*) to a king's son
> May he judge your people with righteousness (*ṣedeq*),
>   and your poor with justice (*mišpāṭ*). (NRSV)

The same note of deliverance of the weak is struck that we noticed in Ps 82. And here again we see the connection between God's own desire for merciful righteousness in the world and the king's responsibility to enact it. The "justice and righteousness" entrusted to the king belong to God, as do the "poor" for whom they are to be practised. Indeed, as other texts make clear, the king's throne itself is also (or primarily) God's (e.g., 1 Chr 17:14).[7] The prayer "Give the king your justice" might be taken as "Give the king your *laws*" in accordance with the common deuteronomic usage (and in Ps 119). In that case the king's responsibility would be closely analogous to that of Hammurabi, according to the prologue to his law code.[8]

The OT story, therefore, tells of a progression from creation, itself an act of love with an inbuilt propensity towards social and political order, to the establishment of actual structures in which responsibility for such order devolves mainly upon the king. This story, I have suggested, is at the same time a story of God's "judgment" in the sense that it displays God's desire to produce a condition of being in the world that he judges good, in distinction from conditions that he judges evil. It also becomes a story of judgment in the sense that Israel in its attempt to be a people of "justice and righteousness" is found wanting, and God acts in judgment repeatedly, in time removing from them land and kingdom, never to be restored in the same way. That, of course, is not the end of the story. The continuation also says much about the nature of God's judgment, for divine resumptions in the OT are always grounded in grace, as we shall see. Next, however, we must turn to the vocabulary of judging.

THE VOCABULARY OF JUDGMENT

So far I have considered the metaphor of God as judge (Ps 82) and in a preliminary way the narrative portrayal of God's enactment of justice in the world and the ancient Near Eastern analogues to this. I have not yet attended directly to questions of definition and terminology, although we have begun to use the key terms. The reason for this is that narrative and metaphor play a very important part in drawing the picture of God's judgment in the OT. So indeed does certain typical vocabulary. However, there is no single word in biblical Hebrew which is always correctly translated as "judge" and none that always means "judgment." An entrée to the subject via the vocabulary, therefore, can be misleading, for it is essential to observe how the key terms interact with each other in actual contexts.

We have by now met the terms *šāpaṭ* ("judge," "deliver," Ps 82), *mišpāṭ* ("judgment," Hos 6:5; "justice," "law," Ps 72), and *ṣedeq/ṣĕdāqâ* ("righteousness," "justice," "salvation," Ps 72; 65:5[Heb. v. 6]; Isa 16:5). It is clear already from these multiple translations of the terms that an interpretation of judging has to be alert to issues of translation.[9] The verb *šāpaṭ*, while it often means "judge," often has the connotation of "deliver" or "liberate," and indeed this is its typical meaning in the Book of Judges (where the term *šōpēṭ*, "judge," is a participial form of the verb); Gideon and others are "deliverers" from oppressors. A connection is immediately evident, of course, between this political usage and the judicial activity of God in Ps 82 where he commands human judges to judge *for* the poor and weak, that is, to liberate them from oppression in the social sphere. Furthermore, some find in *šāpaṭ* an underlying meaning of "rule" because the noun *šōpēṭ* sometimes occurs in parallelism with words for ruler, including *melek* ("king") and *śar* ("prince") (e.g., Pss 2:10; 148:11; Prov 8:15–16; Isa 40:23; Amos 2:3; Hos 7:7).[10] A study of *šāpaṭ*, therefore, leads us to a similar connection of thought to that which we found in the OT narrative: authority to judge is an entailment of the authority to rule. Ruling, judging, and delivering from oppression are once again closely bound up with each other. This deliverance is also close to "justice," a concept which is hard to disentangle from judgment, and which in many cases is the best translation of *mišpāṭ*. *Mišpāṭ*, indeed, can bear a range of meanings within the field of law and justice, including "law" itself (as we saw in Ps 72:1), "legal case," "cause" (1 Kgs 8:49), "verdict," and "vindication" (e.g., Ps 17:2, NRSV).

Having seen the semantic range of *šāpaṭ/mišpāṭ*, we now turn to the semantic field of judgment, that is, the vocabulary with which *šāpaṭ/mišpāṭ* are typically associated (as we have already begun to observe) and which fill out the biblical understanding of God's judgment. According to Knierim, the "word field" of *mišpāṭ* includes not only the most important term *ṣedeq/ṣĕddāqâ*, often translated "righteousness," but also words meaning "faithfulness," "truth," "steadfast love" (*ḥesed*), "equity," "peace" (*šālôm*), "law," "command," (*tôrâ*), "discipline," "perfect" (*tām*).[12] To these Schultz adds another verb meaning "judge" (*dîn*), and a noun meaning "lawsuit," or "contention (*rîb*).[13] These associations are based in actual collocations in biblical texts. For example, judgment (in human courts) is to be carried out righteously (with *ṣedeq/ṣĕdāqâ*; Deut 16:18), truthfully (Ps 96:13; Isa 59:4), and equitably (Ps 58:1 [Heb. v. 2]). Some of these collocations reflect the Old Testament's predilection for parallelism (or "seconding"), that is, the near repetition of a phrase or idea in slightly different terms (this is the case with "truth" and "righteousness" in Ps 96:13b). Parallelism is one example of how concepts in Hebrew are illumined precisely by this juxtaposing of vocabulary elements, with the effect of opening the meanings of words on to each other.

The clearest example of this, in our study, is the common pairing of *mišpāṭ* and *ṣedeq/ṣĕdāqâ* (often translated "justice and righteousness"), as in the portrait of the just king in Isa 9:7 [Heb. v. 6]. The latter term has a wide range of its own, and "righteousness" is not always the best translation. It can have the sense of "justification," or even "salvation" (e.g., Judg 5:11[14]), and like *mišpāṭ*, its range includes "justice."[15] It follows that in the pairing of the terms neither has a fixed content. It is not possible to separate out the connotations of each, and each is in a sense informed by the other.[16] The pairing means the practice of justice in society by those who have the authority and responsibility for it.

The use of the phrase may be exemplified by Isaiah's famous Song of the Vineyard (Isa 5:1–7). There, as in other places (e.g., Amos 5:24), the pair is broken up into parallel lines, with powerful rhetorical effect:

> [Yahweh] expected justice (*mišpāṭ*), but saw bloodshed (*miśpāḥ*)
> righteousness (*ṣĕdāqâ*), but heard a cry (*ṣĕʿāqâ*)! (Isa 5:7)

The absence of "justice and righteousness" in the society of Israel becomes the ground of Yahweh's action in punishment. Such action rests upon a "judgment," for the hearers of the Song, the inhabitants of Jerusalem and the people of Judah (v. 3a), are invited rhetorically to "judge (*šāpaṭ*) between me and my vineyard" (v. 3b). This invitation is ironic, of course, for these are the very ones against whom the Song is directed. In reality the judgment is being made by Yahweh, using a form of logic frequent in the prophets in which he proclaims publicly as in a court his own faithfulness to his covenant people, while accusing them of failure to meet their responsibilities. (The rhetorical pattern is sometimes referred to as the *rîb*, or "lawsuit" pattern; cf. Hos 4:1–6; Mic 6:1–4.[17])

THE JUDGMENT VOCABULARY AND THE CREATED ORDER

In judging Israel Yahweh appeals to standards which, it is implied, are or ought to be widely known. The lawsuit pattern has, no doubt, a specific background in the relationship between God and Israel, but even so, it casts its appeal broadly. The graciousness of God in preparing the vineyard can be understood in terms of ordinary experience, the poetry of Isa 5:1–7 being designed to evoke a sympathetic understanding on the part of any reader.[18] Or again, God's deliverance of Israel from Egypt and his gift to her of good laws can be admired by other nations as something desirable (Deut 4:6–8). In this text the nations can see that the laws given to Israel (*ḥuqqîm ûmišpāṭîm*, and these together as "this entire tôrâ") are "just" (ṣaddîqîm), a remarkable and unique application to the Mosaic laws of this adjective related to ṣĕdāqâ. God's justice, therefore, can be recognized by nations from a standpoint outside the covenant; ṣĕdāqâ is universal and needs no special revelation to disclose it. The same assumption, I think, underlies some prophetic texts. Amos's accusations of nations other than Israel (Amos 1:1–2:3) are probably based on a belief that certain basic standards of behaviour among nations are commonly known and should be commonly applied.[19] Nations that do not do what they know to be right are subject to judgment. Finally, we should observe texts in which God calls heaven and earth as witnesses to what he has to say in judgment contexts (Deut 32:1; Isa 1:2). Such invocations take the place in the Hebrew Bible of those made to the gods in polytheistic contexts. But the universality of the appeal is unmistakable.

There is a theological rationale for these assumptions of universality. For, in the OT the idea of justice is attached first to God himself and then to the creation. If God's tôrâ is "just" (ṣaddîq), this is because first God is "just" (ṣaddîq, Deut 32:4; Ps 119:137). The origin of ṣĕdāqâ is in God, and this is transmitted to his law and the creation. The closeness of "righteousness" to "judgment" is evident here in the phrase: "All his ways are justice/judgment" (mišpāṭ, Deut 32:4). The close relationship between ṣĕdāqâ and the creation itself has been noted by a number of writers. In his much-quoted article on creation as "the broad horizon" of OT theology, H. H. Schmid argued for a "close connection between the cosmic and ethical social order."[20] Describing the concept of ṣĕdāqâ ("righteousness") he says, "In (certain) instances 'righteousness' is not understood narrowly as a legal matter, but as universal world order, as comprehensive salvation."[21] Knierim too writes of the restoration of world-order as a work of divine justice, citing for example Pss 65 and 67.[22] A number of poetic texts illustrate the connection between creation and justice (ṣĕdāqâ), albeit allusively (Isa 45:8; 51:6, 8; 61:11; cf. Ps 36:5–6 [Heb. vv. 6–7]; 71:19; 72:3; 111:3; 119:142).

This foundation of justice in the created order should not be misconstrued. On one hand lies the danger of a "mechanistic" worldview in which actions necessarily produce consequences which are somehow inevitably built into them. This view is sometimes advocated on the basis of certain Hebrew vocabulary. For example, the term ʿāwôn is variously rendered "sin," "guilt," and "punishment."[23] However, as Miller rightly argues, the correspondences between sin and punishment frequently drawn out by the prophets do not necessarily imply inevitable consequence. Rather, such correspondences are based on a talionic way of thinking taken from the judicial sphere and are therefore harmonious with the idea of God's retributive justice, as with his specific decisions and actions in history.[24]

On the other hand, the foundation of the justice of God in creation does not preclude the application of his judgment in history. Knierim, who argued for a recovery of creation thology to counter the dominance in OT theology of a model too influenced by history (represented broadly by von Rad), was wary of reintroducing an erroneous dichotomy between "cosmos" understood mythologically and "history." Rather, "Both cosmos and history are understood nonmythologically under the aspect of Israel's theology of creation."[25] Zenger has protested against the silencing of the imprecatory psalms in Christian usage, arguing that the psalmists' conviction that God is at work in history and society challenges "a Christianity whose belief in God has exhausted its historical potential in soteriology or postponed it to an afterlife by a privatist and spiritualizing attitude."[26]

It follows from this study of vocabulary and usage that justice and judgment are inextricably related. God's "judgment is for the sake of justice," and "the purpose of this judgment is to restore everything 'as it should be.'"[27] The broadest context of this divine purpose is the created order itself. But to say this is not to remove justice from the historical sphere. On the contrary, the OT portrays God's quest for justice in the story of Israel and the nations and in his acts in judgment and salvation in order to carry that purpose forward. It is to this story that we now turn.

JUDGMENT IN THE "DEEP STRUCTURE" OF THE OLD TESTAMENT STORY

The OT story is ultimately one of grace, as we have seen. Yet there is a strong element of judgment as God's rejection of sin and evil. The first human beings are judged unworthy to remain in the Eden following their misguided bid to become "like gods" (Gen 3). In the flood God destroys humanity because sin, typified by increasing murderousness and fundamental disregard for the created order (6:1–4), has become endemic (Gen 6:5–7). The climactic moment of covenant-making at Sinai is undermined by Israel's breach of the first commandment, even while Moses is still on the mountain, and is met by a severe punishment (Exod 32:25–29, 35). The covenant itself sets up a choice of two ways, between the blessing in the case of faithfulness and the curse in the case of unfaithfulness (Deut 28). A pattern of recurring idolatry leads to a pattern of withdrawal of blessing (Judges). The deepest cut in Israel's history, the double exile to Assyria and Babylon, comes as a consequence of the sins identified by the prophets: idolatry (Hos 2:5), disregard of God and his law, and especially a disjunction between worship and social ethics (Isa 1:10–17; Amos 5:21–25). Israel is punished not least because it was "known" (or "chosen") by God; that is, it had a special commission to realize in itself a community that both knew God and embodied his justice (Amos 3:2). The story of judgment is one of a purpose for *justice* thwarted by covenantal failure.

Alongside the erratic progress of Israel, however, a more general pattern emerges, in which the proud, the powerful, and the tyrannical are brought low, and the salvific character of judgment appears. This tendency gains vivid symbolic expression in the encounter between the young David and the Philistine giant Goliath (1 Sam 17). God's judgment on the overbearing is the theme of Hannah's famous prayer (1 Sam 2:1–10, cf. Mary's Magnificat; Luke 1:46–55). The histories and prophetic books tell of the rise and fall of empires. The scattering of the Assyrian army before the walls of Jerusalem (2 Kgs 19:35–37//Isa 37:36–38) is an object lesson in Isaiah's message about God's "day" against "all that is proud and lofty, against all that is lifted up and high" (Isa 2:12). God's use of Assyria against Judah as the "rod of his anger" (Isa 10:5) does not preclude his acting against Assyria in due course, because its motives in coming against Judah were self-seeking (Isa 10:12–19). The book of Jeremiah, in its masoretic form, is structured so as to climax in extended and terrible words of judgment against Babylon, which, though in its turn God's instrument of punishment, would also finally suffer for its overweening pride (Jer 50–51).

The punishment of the tyrants answers to the consistency and universality of God's justice. It is Habakkuk who makes of judgment an issue of theodicy. How can it be that Israel in its due punishment should suffer at the hands of an enemy that was unsurpassed in its own wickedness (Hab 1, esp. v. 13)? God's answer is that the righteous, when they faithfully wait, will see his vengeance on these and be vindicated themselves (Hab 2:2–5).

The story of God's judgment is not fully told, however, when it is noted that all the sinful are finally brought low. For there is no final withdrawal of God from the world or the history with which he has engaged. The punishment of sin always gives way to some renewal. So it is when Noah finds favour with God, and a creation begins again after the flood, though the cause of the original punishment does not seem to have diminished (Gen 8:21). So it is when Moses is given two new tablets of the law to replace the first, so that God might continue to go with the people "although it is a stiff-necked people" (Exod 34:9). And so it is when God commits himself again to Israel after the exile.

This pattern of judgment with its trajectory of punishment and renewed favour may be illustrated by turning again to Deut 32. What is predicated of God, "all his ways are justice/judgment" (*mišpāṭ*, v. 4), is demonstrated by the unfolding logic of the song. The song tracks the movement within Deuteronomy up to this point; that is, it portrays an Israel redeemed by a loving God into a close "father-child" relationship (v. 6, cf. 14:1–2), unable to keep faith with him, suffering God's punishment in consequence (vv. 19–27), yet finally knowing again his renewing, reviving "judgment" (vv. 36–43). (The sequence punishment-salvation, or curse-blessing, in Israel's covenantal history is explicit in Deut 30:1, together with the following discourse on redemption in 30:1–10). It is Deut 32:36 that characterizes this reversal in Israel's fortunes as a "judgment" with the verb *dîn* ("judge," cf. Isa 3:13; Ps 72:2), which is paralleled by *nḥm* ("have compassion"). Judgment as punishment is now directed against God's enemies (v. 41, *mišpāṭ*, in parallel with *nāqām*, "vengeance," and *šillēm*, "requite"; cf. v. 35).

We may notice in passing the universal scope of judgment here. This is established in 32:8–9, in which God as ʿ*elyôn* ("Most High") created the nations in their respective territories, and then as Yahweh takes Jacob for his special portion or inheritance.[28] This universality is maintained in the song when it is said that other nations could only overcome Israel at the behest of God himself, since "their rock is not like our Rock" (v. 31).

More importantly for our immediate purpose, however, judgment in ch. 32 in its full expansion embraces mercy. The turn to mercy in Yahweh's dealings with Israel belongs to his ways that are justice/judgment (v. 4). There is an undercurrent of apologetic or theodicy in the argument. The rhetorical appeal in vv. 30–31 corresponds to the perplexed questions posed by Habakkuk, and the claim that only Yahweh has power to act in history echoes the argument of Isa 40–55. The works of Yahweh are shown to be just. And the purpose of God's acts in judgment, expressed in the textually contorted 32:43, is that God should finally create a people beyond corruption (and not identified narrowly with empirical Israel), in a cleansed land (or earth), worthy of universal praise.[29] God's whole act, universal and gracious, is *mišpāṭ*, and he acts as one who is *ṣaddîq*.

The story of judgment illustrated here in Deut 32 is also in the "deep structure" of the major prophetic books. The book of Jeremiah with its sustained accusation of Judah heralds close to the outset God's intention to show mercy when he says: "I will heal your faithlessness" (3:22b). The book rises to its great midpoint climax in its theology of the new covenant with its vision for a newly righteous people beyond the cataclysm of exile (31:31–34; 32:37–41). The new covenant idea is located within the so-called "Book of Consolation" (Jer 30–33), in which the reversal of fortunes from wrath to salvation is emphasized with great rhetorical effect. This is clearest in Jer 30:4–17, where the incurable nature of Israel's wickedness, formerly the ground of punishment, now becomes the ground of salvation. The illogicality of the line of thought (e.g., 30:12–17) is reminiscent of that which we also find in the narratives of the flood and the Golden Calf.

Such illogicalities in these various OT narratives (including the prophetic "narrative" that we meet in Jeremiah) give the impression that God is determined ultimately to save his chosen people in spite of their wickedness. This indeed according to the song of Moses is an intrinsic part of justice. But can such a divine intention really be regarded as just?[30] If a mechanical relationship between actions and rewards and punishments is regarded as ethically crude, it may be no improvement to sever any link between merit and outcome, especially if the rewards are distributed with partiality. Yet surprisingly perhaps, the OT portrays the imbalance between moral character and the gifts of God's blessing almost as a matter of principle. The chosen people, who are to enter the land God gives them and take on covenantal obligation, are depicted rather brutally as thoroughly incapable of doing so (Deut 9:6–24)—yet they are given the land anyway! (The inability of Israel to keep covenant is also a major theme in Ezekiel, especially Ezek 20; and see Josh 24:19.) When in the fullness of time Israel loses the land because of their (anticipated) failure to keep covenant, it is only to receive it again. While some texts relate this to their repentance (Deut 30:1–3), the song of Moses explains the turn to mercy as being for the sake of Yahweh's own reputation (Deut 32:26–27), a concept also espoused in Ezek 20:8–9. The "vindication" of Israel (Deut 32:36) is predicated in this case only on their known association with the name of Yahweh, not on their righteousness, or at least not on a righteousness already achieved.

The story of judgment, then, has unexpected aspects, almost self-contradictory, arising from the inseparability of wrath and love. For some, the Old Testament's theologies of wrath and mercy are antithetical and unreconciled. Brueggemann, taking Exod 34:6–7 as a key text, argues that Yahweh's inclination to be "for Israel" is never harmonized within the OT with his inclination to be "for Yahweh's own self":

> As a consequence, in any moment of Israel's life with Israel, Yahweh has available more than one alternative response to Israel, and Israel is never fully, finally certain of Yahweh's inclination towards it.[31]

In this analysis Yahweh's "love and care" appear on one side of the balance sheet, while on the other stand "holiness, wrath, and rage," with Israel caught permanently between the two, never quite knowing what to expect from Yahweh, but rather faced with the conundrum of trying "to bring Yahweh to adequate speech."[32] Brueggemann is merely one among many modern voices that regard theologies of grace and wrath as incompatible, the former wholesome and good, while the latter is negative, violent, and dangerous.[33]

JUDGMENT AND FORGIVENESS

Is there an answer to these perceptions of acute disjunctions between concepts of justice and judgment in the OT? We can look first to the authors of the OT themselves, for they are aware of the issues and offer several answers. The book of Jonah displays with humour and irony the discomfiture of one Israelite prophet who imagined that the relationship between a people's wickedness and God's judgment on them was simple and direct. What if God had acted towards

Israel in the way that Jonah wanted him to act against Nineveh? If such logic had applied without qualification, then the dreadful covenantal curses (Deut 28:15–68; Lev 26:14–39) could only have fallen irrevocably on Israel and Judah when they persistently rebelled against God, without hope of forgiveness and redemption. In fact, God gave Nineveh time to repent and avoid God's wrathful judgment. And Israel too benefited from his decision not to implement the terms of the covenant in a mechanical way (as we have seen in Deuteronomy and Jeremiah), but in due course to enjoy his forgiveness.

The case of Nineveh in Jonah helps us understand how the unity of God's judgment and his saving righteousness may be maintained. For while these are in principle a unity, they are artificially set apart in the history of Israel—and the nations—in order to allow both judgment against sin and forgiving mercy to come to full expression. It is from this perspective that the illogical sequences we have observed in Deuteronomy and Jeremiah make sense. Amos, with its unexpected and much disputed turn to salvation at the end (9:11–15), may be called in evidence too. In all these books, we see an awareness that what seems irreconcilable has a unity in God's purpose.

However, it is in the book of Isaiah that the polarities of wrathful judgment and forgiving mercy are given the fullest independent expression and are also brought into conjunction with each other. We have observed already the importance of "justice and righteousness" (*mišpāṭ ûṣĕdāqâ*) as a theme in Isaiah. But in the latter part of the book, as Rendtorff has shown, the correlation of the two concepts tends to express powerfully the closeness of judgment and salvation. While the pairing of *mišpāṭ ûṣĕdāqâ* in contexts of accusation is typical of Isa 1–39, *ṣĕdāqâ* is regularly paired with forms of *yēšaʻ/yĕšûʻâ* (salvation) in Isa 40–55 (45:8; 46:12–13; 51:6, 8; cf. 45:23–25; 54:14, 17), while in Isa 56–66 all three terms are brought together, as in its opening verse, 56:1.[34] This schema is instructive, if not perfect. The idea of God as judge and saviour already appears in a key text in the heart of the book, Isa 33:22, and 48:1 is more like the usage in chs. 1–39. Rendtorff's observation broadly corresponds to the development of the book's underlying narrative in which Israel first suffers God's wrath, then is restored because it is regarded as having paid sufficiently for its sins (Isa 40:2). Yet thereafter Israel is once again held accountable for actualizing a society that exhibits *ṣĕdāqâ* (chs. 56–66). The book of Isaiah resists a neat division of history into a time of judgment for sin followed by a time of renewed salvation for Israel while its enemies receive their just deserts. The transition from chs. 36–39 to ch. 40 with its account of Assyria's demise, its elided narrative of Babylon's rise and Judean exile, and its turn to "comfort" merely sets the stage for a more complex dénouement. In it, the picture of a restored exilic community, already troubled in passages such as ch. 48, mutates into a picture of a divided people, subject to prophetic accusation and exhortation as in the days before the exile (e.g., chs. 57–

58), and in which a fundamental distinction is reasserted between the faithful and the wicked, rising to a climax in chs. 65–66 (cf. 1:27–31).

The tensions in this portrayal of a people that has known God's saving judgment are expressed clearly in ch. 59, where the distribution and connotations of *mišpāṭ* and *ṣĕdāqâ* are revealing. *Mišpāṭ* is paralleled with *ṣĕdāqâ* (59:9, 14), *yĕšûʿâ* ("salvation," 59:11), *šālôm* ("peace," 59:8), and *ʾemet* ("truth," 59:15). In these juxtapositions the closeness of judgment and salvation emerges clearly. *Mišpāṭ* is thus salvation, which implies in turn a condition of justice, peace, and truth. Here is the judgment that is desired, as in those psalms in which the psalmists seek deliverance from oppression. But Isa 59 is important for the way in which this understanding of judgment is woven into a prophetic discourse. In it the hearers are accused of not practicing justice. The legal process is corrupt: "No one brings suit justly (*bĕṣedeq*), no one goes to law (*nišpāṭ*) honestly"; v. 4, NRSV. *Mišpāṭ* and *ṣĕdāqâ*, together with truth and uprightness, are kept out of public life (59:14–15).

But *mišpāṭ* refers not only to the justice incumbent on a society to do, but to the *judgment* as salvation that a beleaguered community awaits. This is clearest in v. 11, where the speech of accusation in the third person has changed to a plural first person voice in a tone of lamentation.[35] The disappointed hope of *mišpāṭ* as salvation ironically echoes the failure of the society to practise *mišpāṭ* as justice (and also Yahweh's disappointed hope of *mišpāṭ* as justice in Isa 5:7)[36]. (There is a certain ironic ambiguity in 59:9a, the beginning of the "we" passage, between *mišpāṭ* as the justice that is far from the community's practice and *mišpāṭ* as God's saving judgment that is far from their experience. However, it is most logically taken in the same way as v. 11, with *mišpāṭ* as desirable judgment, and *ṣĕdāqâ* as salvation, because of the parallel v. 9b, with its expression of longing for light, an Isaianic metaphor for salvation; see 9:1–2 [Heb. 8:23–9:1]).[37]

The line of thought then turns back to Yahweh's reaction to the lack of *mišpāṭ* as justice (59:15b). Full vent is given to his vengeance, retribution, and anger against his "enemies" (vv. 17b–18). But now another unexpected reversal: this venting of anger stands in parallel to *ṣĕdāqâ* and *yĕšûʿâ*, a pairing that connotes salvation. With this last twist, the paradoxes involved in the Isaianic concepts of justice/judgment and righteousness/salvation are complete.

The culmination of the discourse in ch. 59 is the universal acknowledgement of Yahweh, his name, his glory (v. 19, cf. 40:5), and his coming "to Zion as redeemer" (v. 20a). In this way the dominant theme of chs. 40–55 (redemption of Zion) is resumed, but now subject to the theological developments contained in 59:1–19. And it is further qualified with the gloss on "Zion" as "those in Jacob who turn from transgression" (59:20b).[38] The discourse in Isa 59 culminates in the great divide with which the book itself ominously ends (66:18–24).

The careful composition of Isa 59 shows the extent to which the biblical authors engage in delineating the contours of the divine judgment. A number of other passages might be cited in support of this general point. The fourth Servant Song (Isa 52:3–52:12), for example, explicitly pits the false "judgment" (*mišpāṭ*) of the Servant's enemies (Isa 53:8)[39] against the judgment of Yahweh. In the view of Yahweh, the servant was not just another sinner who rightly incurred the punishment of death; rather, through his suffering as an offering for sin (*ʾāšām*, v. 10) he would prolong his days, and as "the righteous one" (*ṣaddîq*), he would "make many righteous" (*yaṣdîq*, v. 11). The vindication of the servant is Yahweh's judgment on false judgment. The meditation on right judgment continues in ch. 54, a song of Zion's vindication. Yahweh, having hidden his face from her in wrath "for a brief moment," now shows her everlasting love and compassion (54:8). Her vindication in the face of those who thought they could destroy her is a vindication (*ṣĕdāqâ*) against false *judgment* (*mišpāṭ*, v. 17).[40]

Finally, in Hos 11:8–9 Yahweh speaks in highly anthropomorphic terms of his compassion, expressing his revulsion of any idea of the final destruction of Ephraim. Here the tension between wrath and mercy is expressed as belonging within Yahweh himself (cf. Jer 31:20). For Brueggemann these bold evocations are a new thing, an "emergence of spousal parental pathos" which implies some derogation from Yahweh as judge-king: "The judge-king speaks now as mother-father, who in this moment acknowledges that the relationship counts for more than self-regard, and that sovereignty is decisively qualified by pathos."[41] In this perspective Yahweh as judge is caught up in Brueggemann's characterization of Yahweh's sovereignty and wrath as his "self-regard," this whole tendency being regularly regarded as "negative." Brueggemann's language tends towards finding a dualism in the biblical God. However, it is clear from our review that the biblical writers are not caught unaware by these tensions. Rather, maintaining their belief in the unity of God, they see what appear to be illogicalities as subject to higher divine rationality.

FINAL JUDGMENT?

To think, then, that mercy somehow replaces justice is misconceived. The placement of Isa 56:1 immediately after 55:13 counsels otherwise. Yahweh the judge continues to seek justice and righteousness, even after the great deliverance from exile, though it was depicted as a virtually definitive salvation. Indeed in Isa 56:1 salvation has again become future, as if once more contingent. The biblical storyline, therefore, resists being read as a triumphal march from wrath to mercy, or even from judgment understood as wrath to judgment understood as mercy. The jarring ending of Isaiah makes the point, as do parts of the post-exilic prophetic books: Haggai, with its severe criticism of the returned exiles' neglect of the temple; Malachi's excoriation of corrupt priests and people; images of an all-encompassing judgment yet to come (Zech 14; Joel 3[4]:9–21).

But do these "endings" really point to some finality? It is not straightforward to piece together a picture of final judgment in the OT writings. Yahweh's universal reign in justice is pictured symbolically as rule from Zion (Isa 2:2–4). But is this peaceful vision definitive? If swords are in one place beaten into ploughshares and spears to pruning-hooks, there is a time for the reverse process (Joel 3[4]:9–10). When the nations rouse themselves and come to the valley of Jehoshaphat, there, Yahweh says, "I will sit to judge (*lišpôṭ*) the nations" (Joel 3[4]:12). Is it finally a story of an inviolable Zion where Yahweh dwells forever, his enemies subdued under his feet (as Joel 3[4] might lead us to think)? The great finale of Joel 3[4] is apparently qualified, according to the usual canonical order of the Book of the Twelve, by Amos, which follows Joel and in 1:2 picks up the phrase "the LORD roars from Zion" (Joel 3[4]:16) and proceeds quickly to the sting in the tail for Israel and Judah in the Oracles against the Nations (Amos 2:4–3:2). Canonical readings of the prophetic books produce mutual qualifications of this sort, which seem to leave certain questions open. Is "the day of the LORD" not after all darkness instead of light (Amos 5:18)? Is "that day" a day of mourning in Jerusalem over "the one whom they have pierced" (Zech 12:10–11), or the day of victory, when Yahweh will stand on the Mt. of Olives to fight against the enemy nations, when there will be continuous day, and when "living waters shall flow out from Jerusalem" (Zech 14:4–5, 6–7, 8)? The day of the LORD cannot readily be restricted to either pole, not a single day, but perpetual possibilities. Is it possible that the refraction of the judgment-righteousness-salvation unity into a history that exhibits both polarities leads to an infinite cycle of judgments followed by new mercies followed by new judgments? (Some have seen the new covenant as nothing more than a recrudescence of a failed Deuteronomistic covenant ideology.[42]) Is there a way off this treadmill?

It is preferable to see the balancing message in the Book of the Twelve as a function of the Old Testament's situation "between salvations." In its "day of small things" (Zech 4:10) it looks back to deliverance from exile in the past and forward in hope of a greater salvation yet to come. Particularly in the Christian canonical form, with the forward look of the prophetic corpus closing the canon, the Old Testament's final word is not final, but expectant.

There are, of course, significant pointers to a finality in the sense of perfection or ultimate renewal. The Isaianic image of new heavens and a new earth (Isa 65:17) has the unmistakable force of something entirely new. The Book of Daniel offers a view of history which sees it moving towards a "time of the end" (Dan 12:4, 9), when the kingdoms of the world give way to the kingdom of God and God's people are finally vindicated. The foreshadowing of the resurrection of the righteous in this passage (12:2–3) and the repetitive stress on an "everlasting" destiny indicate a future reality that is definitively new. The book of Isaiah has something analogous, with its picture of a feast for all peoples on Mt. Zion, death having been swallowed up forever, and this as part of the culmination of a series of oracles of judgment against the nations (Isa 13–27). Perhaps too the ending of Malachi has special canonical significance because of its placing at the end of the prophetic collection (in the Christian canon) and because of its summative call to keep the commandments of Moses, together with its promise of the return of Elijah "before the great and terrible day of the Lord comes" (Mal 4:4–5[3:22–24]). It should be added, however, that in these cases as in others, the purpose of such a judgment is to create a new beginning, in which righteousness (ṣĕdāqâ) will prevail (Dan 12:3; Mal 4:2[3:20]). Thus the obligation to do justice and righteousness is never lost in the Old Testament's pictures of the end.

It is important also to note those passages in which God is involved personally in the issue of judgment and salvation. Hos 11:8–9 is paramount here. Whatever "finality" may be postulated in thinking about the Old Testament's theology of judgment is bound to be expressed in terms of the suffering of Yahweh, and indeed of his Servant (Isa 52:13–53:12).[43] In Christian theology the trajectory of divine suffering culminates outside the OT in the cross, with its correlatives in resurrection and ascension. The new heavens and the new earth are brought to pass finally by the creator's own gift of himself, in an act of judgment whose purpose is that he might remain in the midst of his human creatures.

Meanwhile the servant people of God wait for the perfection of God's judgment-salvation and show by prophetic word and action, and readiness for suffering, how the righteousness of God might be done in the world.

ENDNOTES

1. See Erich Zenger, *A God of Vengeance? Understanding the Psalms of Divine Wrath* (Louisville: Westminster John Knox, 1996), 13–22.

2. I am grateful to Professor Terence Fretheim, who responded to my paper at the symposium. I have given greater emphasis to this point in consequence of some of his remarks.

3. See F. M. Cross, *Canaanite Myth and Hebrew Epic* (Cambridge, Mass.: Harvard University Press, 1973), 15–21. For "judge" see p. 21; the term used is a cognate of the Hebrew šōpēṭ.

4. "The Laws of Hammurabi," in *The Context of Scripture: Monumental Inscriptions from the Biblical World 2* (ed. William W. Hallo and K. Lawson Younger; Leiden: Brill, 2000), 336. Marduk, conqueror of Chaos and supreme god in Babylon, is also named in the prologue, his destiny determined by Anum and Enlil. And it is Shamash, the sun-god, who is depicted on the Hammurabi stele as handing him the law. However, it is the "cosmological deities" who are ultimately responsible for this entrusting of justice to the earthly king. H. H. Schmid, "Creation, Righteousness, and Salvation: Creation as the 'Broad Horizon' of Biblical Theology," in *Creation in the Old Testament* (ed. B. W. Anderson; Philadelphia: Fortress/London: SPCK, 1984), 102–117, here 104–105.

5. "The Epic of Creation," in *The Context of Scripture: Monumental Inscriptions from the Biblical World 1* (ed. William W. Hallo and K. Lawson Younger; Leiden: Brill, 1997), 390–402.

6. "The Ba'lu Myth," in *Monumental Inscriptions 1*, 241–274; here 253–262.

7. 1 Chr 17:14 transposes the phrase "your kingdom," addressed to David in 2 Sam 7:16, to "my kingdom," that is, God's. Note also Deut 33:5, where it is not wholly clear whether the king who shall "arise in Jeshurun" is Yahweh or the Davidic king.

8. The role of the king in the story as outlined here does not prejudge the question, aired in the OT itself, about whether kingship is the only or best form of rule in human society.

9. T. Leclerc criticises E. J. Young (*Isaiah vols 1-3*; repr. Grand Rapids: Eerdmans, 1992) because he translates 40 of the 42 occurrences of *mišpāṭ* in Isaiah as "judgment"; see his *Yahweh is Exalted in Justice: Solidarity and Conflict in Isaiah* (Minneapolis: Fortress, 2001), 181, n. 1.

10. E.g., R. Schultz, "שפט" (*špṭ*), *NIDOTTE* 4, 213–220, here 218; see also H. Niehr, *Herrschen und Richten: die Wurzel spt im alten Orient und im alten Testament* (Forschungen zur Bibel 54; Würzburg: Echter, 1986).

11. Leclerc's study of Isaiah (*Yahweh is Exalted*) is essentially a study of God's *mišpāṭ* as justice.

12. R. Knierim, *The Task of Old Testament Theology: Substance, Method and Cases* (Grand Rapids: Eerdmans, 1995), 86–87. The terms in Hebrew are *'ĕmûnâ, 'ĕmet, ḥesed, mêšārîm/mîšôr, šālôm, ḥōq, miṣwâ, tôrâ, mûsār, tām*.

13. Schultz, 214.

14. Here in the plural; see D. J. Reimer, "צדק" (*ṣdq*), *NIDOTTE* 3, 744–769, here 762.

15. Leclerc (*Yahweh is Exalted*, 182, n. 9) points out that several studies of "justice" in the OT take *ṣĕdāqâ* as their base term.

16. M. Weinfeld (*Social Justice in Ancient Israel and in the Ancient Near East*, Minneapolis: Fortress, 1995, e.g., p. 29) described the phrase as a hendiadys meaning "social justice."

17. See Kirsten Nielsen, *Yahweh as Prosecutor and Judge* (JSOTSup 9; JSOT Press, Sheffield, 1978) for an account. The idea of a lawsuit pattern has been critiqued by Michael DeRoche, "Yahweh's *rîb* Against Israel: a Reassessment of the so-called 'Prophetic Lawsuit' in the Preexilic Prophets," *JBL* 102 (1983): 563–574.

18. It is commonly argued that the lawsuit pattern is not required to be understood against a covenantal background but that it rests on more common assumptions about justice; e.g., R. E. Clements, *Prophecy and Tradition* (Atlanta: John Knox, 1978). However, see in contrast P. D. Miller, *Sin and Judgment in the Prophets: a Stylistic and Theological Analysis* (Chico: Scholars Press, 1982), 3–4, for the view that Hos 4:4–6 has its background in the covenant; citing N. Lohfink, "Zu Text und Form von Os 4, 4–6," *Biblica* 42 (1961): 303–332.

19. See John Barton, *Amos's Oracles against the Nations* (Cambridge: Cambridge University Press, 1980).

20. H. H. Schmid, "Creation, Righteousness, and Salvation," 105.

21. Ibid.

22. Knierim, *The Task of Old Testament Theology*, 112.

23. See Miller's concession to this point, advocated by K. Koch: Miller, *Sin and Judgment*, 125. He refers to K. Koch, *Um das Prinzip der Vergeltung in Religion und Recht des Alten Testaments* (Darmstadt: Wissenschaftliche Buchgesellschaft, 1972), 433.

24. Miller, *Sin and Judgment*, 134–136.

25. Knierim, *Task of Old Testament Theology*, 184 and note.

26. Zenger, *A God of Vengeance?* 74.

27. Zenger, *A God of Vengeance?* 64.

28. Commentators sometimes see in the occurrence of ʿelyôn here a memory of the idea that the high god apportioned nations and lands to lower gods in the pantheon; e.g., M. Barker, *The Great Angel: A Study of Israel's Second God* (London: SPCK/Louisville: Westminster John Knox, 1992), 6. It is preferable, however, to see ʿelyôn and yhwh in parallel, as also in Gen 14:21 (MT). Elyon was the Canaanite high god worshipped in Jerusalem (cf. Pss 46:4[5]; 47:2[3]); the name was assimilated to Yahweh in the OT, yet here appears to retain the connotations which make it appropriate to speak of him as universal creator.

29. The LXX and Qumran witnesses diverge considerably from the MT in this verse, and the NRSV represents the longer forms found in the former. The MT is in line with Deuteronomy's theme of the nations as witnesses to God's benevolence to Israel, while Qumran locates the praise of God's justice in heaven. (The LXX has elements of both.) All forms attest the universal demonstration of God's justice. The textual hesitations may betray reflection on the identity of the finally vindicated people; i.e., is it empirical "Israel"?

30. Knierim is critical of the type of "justice" that is based on Israel's election. In his view justice in election theology is what serves this election by and covenant with Yahweh "rather than and regardless of a principle of justice that is the same for all nations" (*The Task of Old Testament Theology*, 97). He also finds the idea of justice based on election incompatible with the concept of act-consequence justice, and indeed it eclipses it in the OT story; *ibid.*, 99.

31. Walter Brueggemann, *Theology of the Old Testament* (Minneapolis: Fortress, 1997), 227; see also 270–271, 276, 307–311.

32. Ibid., 227–228.

33. See, for example, Regina Schwartz, *The Curse of Cain: the Violent Legacy of Monotheism* (Chicago and London: University of Chicago Press, 1997).

34. R. Rendtorff, "The Composition of the Book of Isaiah," in idem, *Canon and Theology* (Edinburgh: T. & T. Clark, 1994), 146–169.

35. Cf. Leclerc, *Yahweh Is Exalted*, 149.

36. Ibid.

37. Differently from Leclerc, who takes mišpāṭ and ṣĕdāqâ in 59:9a as "justice and righteousness"; see *Yahweh Is Exalted*, 148.

38. The oracles in 59:18a, 20 are examples of what P. D. Hanson calls "the salvation-judgment oracle"; see *Dawn of Apocalyptic* (Philadelphia: Fortress, 1979), 119–120; cf. Leclerc, *Yahweh Is Exalted*, 152.

39. The text of Isa 53:8a is difficult. I follow NRSV, "By a perversion of justice." B. S. Childs has "Through oppressive judgment"; see his *Isaiah* (Louisville: Westminster John Knox, 2001), 408, but see 416; see also Leclerc, *Yahweh Is Exalted*, 123.

40. Leclerc, *Yahweh Is Exalted*, 123–126.

41. Brueggemann, *Theology of the Old Testament*, 301.

42. See R. P. Carroll, *From Chaos to Covenant* (London: SCM, 1981), 215–225; e.g., 217: "What a triumph of hope over experience! [The New Covenant] is a good example of a certain kind of ideological thinking which, when in trouble, retreats to advocating the principle: 'If something has failed, what is required for its success is more of the same.'"

43. See T. E. Fretheim, *The Suffering of God: an Old Testament Perspective* (Philadelphia: Fortress Press, 1984); also E. Otto, "Die Überwindung der Dialektik von Gewalt und Gegengewalt durch den Schmerz Gottes im Hoseabuch," in idem, *Krieg und Frieden in der Bibel und im Alten Orient* (Stuttgart: Kohlhammer, 1999), 77–86.

RESPONSE TO McCONVILLE

TERENCE E. FRETHEIM

Professor McConville's paper is clearly written, with a strong theological focus, and with much helpful detail. I especially appreciated his refusal to set grace/mercy and judgment/wrath in opposition to each other. I could quibble with some details, but I choose to lift up several overarching theological concerns generated by the paper.[1]

As I see it, judgment is a form of agency, in this case divine agency (not a divine attribute), which may have various effects ranging from mercy to disaster. But it is the latter aspect of judgment that is most in play in current conversations about these matters, on which I focus this response.

McConville seems not to present an argument on behalf of a single thesis but considers various facets of judgment. If anything is an argument, it is the defense of an ongoing judgment-mercy rhythm of life, the "cycle of judgments followed by new mercies followed by new judgments." The purpose of judgment is "to create a new beginning." But, even in that newness the importance of justice and righteousness remains. In referring to this reality, I much prefer McConville's use of the word "polarity" to the puzzling word "illogicality." But why call this judgment-mercy rhythm a "treadmill"? Is there no movement toward a divine goal, no final judgment? McConville opens up the question in his discussion of the new covenant, but then seems to close it down. In his view, the new covenant (and other texts, such as Jer 32:40) "seems to bring closure to the story of Israel's moral life." And McConville does not want to go there. I would claim that these texts are a grand witness to a new heaven and earth in which sin is no longer possible (in traditional language, *non posse peccare*). That witness should not be undercut, for then there would indeed be a treadmill, just more of the same—forever. Some day God's will *will* be done on earth as it is in heaven, and sin will be no more. Then we will be beyond freedom, or a new kind of freedom beyond moral choice.

On another issue, McConville begins his paper on judgment by placing it within the context of kingship; indeed, among the metaphors for God, "only that of kingship lies deeper." Sovereignty images for God are pervasive in the paper (though not in the OT). I think that juridical or royal metaphors do not sufficiently comprehend the workings of divine judgment. In a paper on judgment, with talk about "root metaphor," a word such as "relationality" seems far more basic. Divine judgment is understood fundamentally in relational terms: a relationship is at stake, not an agreement or a contract (and, by the way, "covenant" must not be equated with relationship, as Eichrodt's *Theology* already shows).

And so I would begin with Exod 34:6–7 (and its numerous echoes), perhaps the most basic creedal statement about God in the OT—a God gracious, merciful, slow to anger, and abounding in steadfast love and faithfulness, forgiving iniquity and transgression and sin. Only then, from within those kinds of claims about God and those kinds of metaphors, is the word about judgment stated: yet by no means clearing the guilty, but visiting the iniquity of the parents upon the children and the children's children to the third and fourth generation (and, in later formulations, repents concerning judgment; Joel 2:13; Jon 4:2). It is the language of divine steadfast love, grace, and mercy that constitutes the theological matrix within which the OT itself places the language of judgment, and I think these creedal texts show us the way. This is not to say that sovereignty language for God is inappropriate, but it cries out for definition. The Exod 34 text invites us to think about kingship and judgeship in ways more like that of the NT where the king wears a crown of thorns and reigns from a tree.

I agree that to speak of God as judge is to use metaphoric language drawn from the court of law. But it is important to recognize that to speak of Judge as a metaphor for God is to claim, as with all metaphors, both a "yes" and a "no" regarding the use of this language. God is in some ways like a human judge; in other ways, God is unlike a human judge (or a king). One of the basic tasks of OT theological work is to sort this out. Erich Zenger, in thinking about God as judge, is helpful in showing that "the public system of justice remains only an analogue for what is at stake in talk about God." God is not at all "a neutral representative of an independent court of justice."[2] For example, human judges, when they are doing their job well, dispense sentences with dispassionate objectivity. (What would courtrooms be like if judges displayed their personal anger and anguish?) God, on the other hand, is not cool and detached. God has a binding relationship with those at whom the divine judgment is directed, is openly anguished over present and future possibilities (e.g., Hos 6:4, "What shall I do with you?"), and is personally caught up in the situation.

Such features of the portrayal of God, particularly in the prophets, constitute a "no" in the use of the metaphor of God as judge (or *any* "official" divine role) that must stand alongside any "yes." One might also cite here the creedal witness to God as one who is open to changing the divine mind—both before and during the time that the judgment is exercised. In other words, the more personal/relational dimensions of divine action, more evident in, say, the parental or marital metaphors for God, qualify any legal or juridical understandings. God's judgment is never simply justice; in terms of straightforward legal thinking God is much too lenient. The personal and political senses of divine judgment must remain linked, but not collapsed, and each must qualify the other. When thinking of God as judge, remember that the judge behind the bench is the spouse of the accused one in the dock. I might note that, if justice is fundamentally what kings and judges do, then human responsibilities are lessened, if not eliminated altogether.

Another dimension of this understanding of judgment in predominantly personal and relational terms can be seen in the language of separation. In terms of the marital imagery, the closer and more intimate the relationship, the deeper the effects of brokenness should something go wrong (see Amos 3:2). Hence, it is not uncommon for texts to speak of God's judgment in terms of withdrawal, hiding, or forsaking, though these metaphors do not imply actual divine absence (e.g., Isa 54:7–8; 59:2; Jer 7:29; 12:7; Ezek 39:23–29). As people remove themselves from relationship, God engages in massive efforts to heal the breach, because God wants life not death (Ezek 18:23, 32). But, finally, God withdraws from closeness, and all the forces that make for death and destruction inherent in the wickedness itself are allowed to have their way. The images drawn from the marital metaphor are often played out in graphic and violent terms as a rhetorical strategy to impress upon readers what unfaithfulness might entail in terms of their own experience (e.g., Jer 3:1–5; 13:20–27; Hos 2).

Yet, while God may give the people up to their sinfulness and its effects (cf. Rom 1:24–28), God does not finally give up on them. In other terms, judgment as the circumstantial will of God is always in the service of the ultimate will of God to save. To that end, God will *use* already existing judgmental effects for a variety of salutary purposes (e.g., refining, cleansing, insight, discipline).

These various formulations show that God mediates the consequences of that which is already present in the wicked situation. The people's sin has had a significant level of "negative fallout," given the interrelatedness of all creatures; God brings those consequences to completion. This is never simply a "what goes around, comes around" perspective. God is a real subject, but God does not introduce or impose anything new on the situation. Rather, the divine agency is real and effective, mediating the consequences of sin; the created moral order is a divine agent. Though the agency issues cannot be factored out with precision, some helpful claims are made in various texts (e.g., Hos 8:7; 10:13–15; 13:7–9, 16). Ezekiel 22:31 states the matter clearly; what the divine declaration "I have consumed them with the fire of my wrath" entails is immediately stated: "I have returned *their* conduct upon their heads." Israel's sin generates certain snowballing effects. At the same time, God is active in the interplay of human sinful actions and their effects, and "third parties" are used by God as agents for that judgment (e.g., the Assyrians). Both divine and creaturely factors are interwoven to produce the judgmental result.

In modern terms, our own sin as well as the sins of our forebears presses in upon us, but no less does the hand of God. For history is our judgment, and God enables history—carrying the world along, not in mechanistic ways but with a personal attentiveness in view of a relationship of consequence. God's salvific will remains intact in everything, and God's gracious concern is always for the best; but in a given situation the best that God may be able to offer is burning the chaff to fertilize the field for a new crop.

ENDNOTES

1. In what follows I make use of several of my articles, including "Divine Judgment and the Warming of the World: An Old Testament Perspective," in *God, Evil, and Suffering* (ed. T. Fretheim and C. Thompson; St. Paul, Minn.: Word and World Supplement 4, 2000), 21–32; "Theological Reflections on the Wrath of God in the Old Testament," *HBT* 24 (2002): 1–26; "God and Violence in the Old Testament," *WW* 24 (2004): 18–28.

2. E. Zenger, *A God of Vengeance? Understanding the Psalms of Divine Wrath* (Louisville: Westminster/John Knox, 1996), 72.

THE NATURE OF HELL

CLARK H. PINNOCK

In this symposium we have in essence been exploring the Pauline dialectic recorded in Rom 11:22: "Note then the kindness and the severity of God." Both of these traits show up repeatedly in God's dealings. The tension holds too when it comes to consideration of the nature of hell, which is certainly a severe judgment yet laced with mercy. In the symposium Stephen Long registered an important distinction which can help us. He said that orthodox believers are certain about judgment being real but not as certain as to its precise nature. He wrote: "Following Hans Urs von Balthasar, we can distance ourselves from some of the harsh Augustinian elements of the doctrine of damnation. We do not know it is eternal. We do not know that it must be populated. We do not know that we have an obligation to delight in the punishment of the damned" (*infra*, p. 120). In other words, there is no orthodox dogma of the nature of hell per se; so we can relax and entertain possibilities, including my conviction that hell should be understood as destruction, a view favoured by a growing number. My proposal belongs to the spirit (I think) of John Phelan's chapter in which he too sees the need of improving our understanding of biblical symbols of judgment. In such matters, as in theology generally, it is wise to be critical realists, that is, to be seriously in the search for truth but modest about the extent to which we have grasped it. If my view about the nature of hell proves mistaken, the epitaph can read: "he tried to help."[1]

Christian belief in hell is (oddly enough) part of the good news when understood in the context of a relational theology. It safeguards the mystery that God wants us to love him freely.[2] We are not robots devoid of significance who end up in God's kingdom whether we want to or not. God loves us and wants to be loved in return. But love cannot be forced; it has to be freely given and hell represents the possibility of even saying "no" to God finally. Hell is not God's choice so much as it is ours. It is not something that God wants for us. God loves us but, like the father of the prodigal, lets his son make up his own mind, even if it means loss. The good news is that God made us free to choose good or evil. We can say "yes" to God's love, and there is the possibility of saying "no." Hell is more about refusing life than suffering punishment, because God loves us even in his judging of us. Miroslav Volf writes: "God will judge, not because God gives people what they deserve, but because some people refuse to receive what no one deserves. If evildoers experience God's terror, it will not be because they have done evil, but because they have resisted to the end the powerful lure of the open arms of the crucified messiah."[3]

Hell, however, cannot easily be considered good news so long as the traditional understanding of its nature is retained. Herein lies a great challenge. Given the fact that the traditional view of the nature of hell involves the everlasting conscious punishing of the impenitent in body and soul, it is hard to detect any kindness in it. Only horror and sadism remain. But this is, like it or not, the view of the historic churches and their theologians. It is and has been the "orthodox" view of the matter. It was the position of Augustine and of every orthodox theologian since him through the Reformation and beyond.[4] Queen Mary I, mincing no words, said: "As the souls of heretics are hereafter to be eternally burning in hell, there can be nothing more proper than for me to imitate the divine vengeance by burning them on earth."[5] What an inspiration it must have been to the inquisition to do its work of burning unhappy persons at the stake! The view is nicely summarised by John Gerstner in a study of Jonathan Edwards: "Hell is a spiritual and material furnace of fire where its victims are exquisitely tortured in their minds and in their bodies eternally according to their various capacities, by God, the devils, and damned humans including themselves, in their memories and consciences as well as in their raging, unsatisfied lusts, from which place of death God's saving grace, mercy, and pity are gone forever, never for a moment to return."[6] Harsh as it may seem, traditionalists see any challenge to this position as diminishing the glory of the divine judgment, taking away from the dignity of our immortality, and making hell less of a punishment than it actually is.[7] However gruesome the traditional view, there is resistance to a new model because it is not traditional. Some cannot easily accept that the orthodox teachers of the church erred in this matter.

At the same time there is decline occurring in belief in the traditional understanding of the nature of hell. The orthodox view is being challenged amidst changing views of punishment, questioning of natural immortality, the possibility that the suffering might be metaphorical not literal, and a general revulsion.[8] John Wenham, an Anglican, expresses his feelings boldly: "Unending torment speaks to me of sadism not justice. It is a doctrine that I do not know how to preach without negating the loveliness and glory of God. From the days of Tertullian it has been the emphasis of fanatics. It is a doctrine which makes the Inquisition look reasonable. I believe that endless torment is a hideous and unscriptural doctrine which has been a terrible burden on the mind of the church for many centuries and a terrible blot on her presentation of the gospel. I should indeed be happy if, before I die, I could help in sweeping it away."[9]

The way forward appears to lie in the direction of an alternative interpretation in which hell is seen as irreversible destruction. In the wake of the report in Britain of the Evangelical Alliance on the nature of hell, this alternative is becoming a legitimate opinion alongside the traditional views.[10] Paul expresses the new option: "The wages of sin is death but the gift of God is eternal life" (Rom 6:23). One road leads to life and another leads to destruction. After the first death there is the resurrection, but after the second death there is only destruction. The choices which the wicked have made in life will be respected such that they will have no part in the kingdom of God, and being severed from the source of life they will exist no more as persons.[11] Their torment will come to an end.

SCRIPTURAL FOUNDATIONS

Jesus was not what you would call a hellfire preacher. He shows little interest in what gehenna is like. He does not reveal truths about it. He does not talk about the torments of the damned as they are talked about in the apocryphal Apocalypse of Peter or in Dante's or Milton's work. Jesus does not try to satisfy our curiosity with regard to the hereafter. The heart of his message is "gospel," which is a joyful rather than a threatening proclamation. His words about hell are not elaborated upon but serve chiefly to admonish us. Hell chiefly serves as a warning that one can exclude oneself from the presence of God and suffer eternal loss. The language which is used is figurative and parabolic in nature because it deals with realities which lie far outside human experience: images like pitch darkness, eternal fire, feeding maggots, etc. The language is figurative and connotative rather than denotative and literal. (This is what makes it possible for others to work the images differently and stay closer to the traditional model.[12])

Texts about eschatology are notoriously difficult to interpret. A hiddenness hangs over them, and reliable information is in short supply. Yet the biblical basis supporting the idea of the nature of hell as destruction is pretty strong. We receive from Scripture the strong impression of a final and irreversible loss, of ruin and perishing, and of a fire that consumes rather than a fire that tortures. The Bible privileges the language of death, destruction, ruin, and perishing when speaking of the fate of the finally impenitent.[13]

The OT witness sets the stage and supplies the basic imagery for the NT. In Ps 37 we read that the wicked will fade like grass and wither like the herb (v. 2) and that they will be cut off and be no more (vv. 9–10). They will perish and vanish like smoke (v. 20) and will be altogether destroyed (v. 38). The prophet Malachi declares: "The day is coming, burning like an oven, when all the arrogant and all evildoers will be stubble; the day that comes will burn them up, says the Lord of hosts, so that it will leave them neither root nor branch" (Mal 4:1–2). It is true that the point of reference of such warnings is this-worldly and does not present the afterlife. Nevertheless, the basic imagery is unmistakable and sets the tone for NT doctrine.

Jesus' teachings about the destiny of the wicked is bold concerning their destruction but modest when it comes to precise descriptions. He does not dwell on the act of damnation or on the torments of the damned (unlike the Apocalypse of Peter) but on the importance of decision here and now. There is no speculation about the furniture of heaven or the temperature of hell. He wants us to feel the urgency of making a decision but does not dwell on the details of destruction. He warns: "Do not fear those who kill the body but cannot kill the soul. Rather fear him who can destroy both body and soul in hell" (Matt 10:28). The language echoes the language of John the Baptist who pictured the wicked as dry wood about to be thrown into the fire and as chaff about to be burned (Matt 3:10, 12). Jesus too sees the wicked as weeds to be bundled and burned (Matt 13:30).

The apostle Paul speaks in the same terms, as do the other apostles, warning of the "everlasting destruction" that will descend upon unrepentant sinners (2 Thess 1:9). They will reap corruption (Gal 6:8) and be destroyed (1 Cor 3:17; Phil 1:28). Concerning the wicked, Paul says plainly: "Their destiny is destruction" (Phil 3:19). This is the pattern of teaching elsewhere also. Peter speaks of the "destruction of ungodly men" (2 Pet 3:7) and of false teachers who will bring "swift destruction on themselves" (2 Pet 2:1, 3). He says that they would be like the cities of Sodom and Gomorrah that were burned to ashes (2:6) and that they would perish like the ancient world perished in the great flood (3:6–7). Jude too points to Sodom as an analogy to God's final judgment as the city that underwent "the punishment of eternal fire" (Jude 7). Similarly, the Apocalypse of John speaks of a lake of fire that consumes the wicked and of the second death (Rev 20:14–15). Following the lead of the OT the NT employs images of death and destruction to depict the end of the finally impenitent. Chris Marshall writes: "The overwhelming weight of biblical data favours annihilation or destruction as the fate of the wicked."[14]

COUNTER TESTIMONY

Alongside the large number of texts that depict hell as a place of death and destruction there is some counter testimony. There are three texts in particular to note, one in the gospel of Matthew and two in the Book of the Revelation. They require comment because they are cited as proof texts for the traditional opinion.[15]

First, there are the words of Jesus: "Some will go away into eternal punishment but the righteous into eternal life" (Matt 25:46). Does it not suggest that the punishment, like the eternal life, goes on forever? It certainly could mean that. But the question arises: Why take this text to be meaning what is denied earlier in Matthew—that "God can destroy both body and soul in hell" (10:28)?

The Nature of Hell

Why privilege Matt 25:46 over Matt 10:28? It might be that "eternal punishment" signifies the permanence of judgment rather than the everlasting continuation of it. The text teaches two destinies but leaves open the question whether hell involves a ceaseless conscious experience of torment or not. (There is a danger of interpolating "conscious" into the term "eternal punishment" where it may not belong.) In this parable Jesus teaches an end-time judgment which divides persons into two categories and sentences them to opposite conditions. The wicked are banished into the fire of judgment where they will be destroyed and burned to ashes (cf. Jude 7; 2 Pet 2:6).

Second, there are two passages in the Book of Revelation that must be visited also because they appear to support the traditional view of hellfire. We may want to approach them cautiously, given the genre of the book. It is a type of literature not often taken literally by either side, and it would be ironic if the argument turned on a few verses there. In Rev 14:9–11, the text speaks of those who worship the beast drinking from the cup of God's anger and being tormented with fire and sulphur in the presence of the holy angels and in the presence of the Lamb. It says that the smoke of their torment goes up forever and that they have no rest day or night. (I think that this may well be the most difficult passage for annihilationists to explain.) The main thrust is easy to handle. The imagery of smoke going up forever harks back to the fate of Sodom which ceased to exist as a city when it was judged (Gen 19:24). The smoke goes up as a reminder of its destruction, and the burning sulphur denotes destruction. The more difficult part is the wicked not having any rest day or night. This may simply indicate that they have no relief for as long as the situation lasts. Thus it could point either to hell as destruction or to the traditional view.

In Rev 20:10 we read: "And the devil who had deceived them was thrown into the lake of fire and sulfur, where the beast and the false prophet were, and they will be tormented day and night forever." None of them is a human being. G. E. Ladd remarks: "How a lake of fire can bring everlasting torture to nonphysical beings is impossible to imagine. It is obvious that this is picturesque language describing a real fact in the spiritual world: the final and everlasting destruction of the forces of evil which have plagued humankind since the garden of Eden."[16]

In Rev 20:14 we read further: "Death and Hades were thrown into the lake of fire. This is the second death. And anyone whose name was not found written in the book of life was thrown into the lake of fire." This too is the language of extinction, the defeat of all God's enemies and the destruction of persecuting civil government and corrupting false religion. As for the finally impenitent, the names not found in the book of life, they experience the second death and cease to be obstacles to the reign of God anymore.

THE ONUS PROBANDI

Scripture aside though, belief in the nature of hell as everlasting conscious punishment remains solidly traditional. It is the doctrine of the churches, which means that the burden of proof rests on the shoulders of the reformers. Let me register two points. First, the belief in hell as termination and destruction has been a minority conviction from day one. It is not a recent concoction to be dismissed and not taken seriously. *Didache* (for example) speaks of two ways: the way of life and the way of death. It makes no mention of unending torment (*Did.* 1:1; 5:1). This was true also of *The Epistle of Barnabus* and *The Epistle to Diognetus* and of the writings of Clement of Rome and of Ignatius of Antioch. Noteworthy is Irenaeus, who emphasizes the resurrection of the body and does not seem to have believed that persons are inherently immortal. Humans have immortality only through the resurrection of Jesus. As for the wicked, they will be destroyed. He writes: "It is the Father who imparts continuance forever on those who are saved. Life does not arise from us or from our nature. It is bestowed according to the grace of God" (*Against Heresies* II.34.3). Famously there was one Arnobius of Sicca who devoted much energy to denying Plato's doctrine of immortal souls. He concludes thus: "The wicked are cast into hell and, being annihilated, pass away vain in everlasting destruction which is man's real death" (*Adversus Nationes* 2:14).[17] There is a stream of testimony also from the Reformation times. Holding to the minority view were John Milton, John Locke, and Isaac Watts, and recent advocates include people such as John Stott, P. E. Hughes, John Wenham, H. E. Guillebaud, Basil Atkinson, and Michael Green. As a result it needs to be said that there has always been a minority report which deserves to be heard, even respected.

Second, there is a trend even in the ranks of the traditionalists these days that favours seeing the nature of hell as destruction. One detects a softening on the part of traditionalists. Some are rethinking the majority opinion while claiming to be traditional. I refer to attempts to take the hell out of hell while still claiming essential continuity with tradition. We find less emphasis being placed on physical torment and more on the mental. (They are sensing the problem of pain which the traditional view creates.) We see moves in the direction of a Sartre who imagined hell as a shabby hotel where three people torment each other mentally, where there is a pain of loss but not a pain of sense. It is reminiscent of C. S. Lewis who once pictured hell as a drab town from which one can take day trips into heaven. In such renditions one would find hell nasty but no lake of fire. I understand why they want to make hell more tolerable, but I cannot recognise this as the traditional view. Jerry Walls remarks: "It will be clear by now that the picture of hell I have presented is in essential continuity with traditional theology in holding that hell is a place of misery. It is not, admittedly, as gruesome an account of hell as that held by some notable classical theologians. If it were, I could not plausibly hold that some persons may freely choose it."[18]

Another move being made by traditionalists brings them close to the alternative view of the nature of hell as destruction. C. S. Lewis sometimes pictures hell, not as the beginning of eternal life in the fire, but as the end of a life of rebellion. He sees hell as "the outer rim where being fades away into nonentity."[19] He says of persons that to enter heaven is to become more fully human, while to enter hell is to be the "remains" of a man or even an "ex-man." People are like those who "used to exist" and are "very nearly nothing."[20] It sounds as if hell in this conception is very close to being nothing at all. In fact, its inhabitants will have chosen the Nothingness to which, in Barth's view, God had uttered a rejection. They will have embraced the nihil of annihilation.

What we have here is a good reform of the tradition, one very like my own, the soul of which they have embraced.[21] The two approaches should therefore not attack each other but form an alliance.

CONDITIONAL IMMORTALITY

Conditional immortality, the view that souls are not inherently immortal but acquire it on the condition of faith, should be mentioned. On one level, it is irrelevant. Whether or not we were created to live forever, the plan could always be scrapped. God would still be free to eliminate the finally impenitent if he chooses. Even an immortal soul is no match for the power of God who can reduce it to nothing. Admittedly, conditionalism is usually appealed to as the basis of the belief in annihilation, but the latter does not require it. God may remove immortality at the judgment with the result that souls perish. In earlier centuries it was thought that removing immortality would require an extraordinary act of God. Therefore, the destruction of the wicked was seldom entertained as a possibility. But today we are more likely to think (given the doctrine of the resurrection) that conservation in existence, rather than elimination from it, is what requires special divine action. John Cooper writes: "Plato argued that the soul is metaphysically indestructible because it is a simple spiritual substance and cannot undergo decomposition. It is true that some Christians, including Augustine and Aquinas, adopted this argument. But no Christian holds that the soul is necessarily immortal, can exist independent of God, and is impervious to destruction by God."[22]

On another level though, conditional immortality needs to be mentioned because belief in the natural immortality of the soul has doubtless contributed to the traditional view of hell. It drives the interpretation of Scripture in that direction with those who believe it. If souls are immortal, the expectation would be that the punishing would go on forever. But if souls are not immortal, the expectation would be that destruction would be final. Belief in human immortality has long attached itself to Christian theology and (among other things) has skewed the meaning of hell. If the soul cannot die, it must exist forever and must suffer the torment of hell forever. Nothing else can be done. But human souls are not everlasting like God and unlike God can cease to be. These are after all creatures made from dirt, breathed upon by God, and made mortal. This is not a being who cannot but exist. The psalmist says: "When you take away their breath, they die and return to their dust. When you send forth your spirit, they are created" (Ps 104:29–30). Our hope for life after death is based on God's promises and on the resurrection of Jesus Christ. Man is not immortal because he has a soul. He becomes immortal when God raises the dead. It was Platonic thought which made immortality an inalienable attribute of the soul, not the Bible. We need a biblical anthropology in which God gives life to the righteous as a benefit and does not compel the wicked to live forever.[23]

FOUR POSITIVE CONTRIBUTIONS

Although scriptural backing is what I value most, I welcome other support from various quarters. First, the elimination of the wicked, which we see in Scripture, seems philosophically to be a sensible way for God to deal with the finally impenitent. It would not be right for God to compel belief in them. He who seeks fellowship with us respects our choices and does not force his friendship. It would be wrong of him to use force to change that, even if he could, just because our choices are not to his liking. God allows us to become the sort of persons we choose to become, even if totally corrupt. In effect, he lets us damn ourselves. But what to do then? There would be no point in keeping the reprobate alive. The obvious place for the corrupt soul is on the scrap heap and in the garbage dump. God loves persons and does not choose death for them, but hell is nevertheless a possibility arising out of unbelief.[24] It might be argued that such a plan would diminish human freedom to a degree, by detracting from the seriousness of it. After all, freedom requires that we live out the consequences of our choices, and the choices would be more significant, if the consequences were eternal rather than only temporal. There is truth in that. But I think that God in his mercy draws back from imposing unending torment and does not let us hurt ourselves so badly. If the wicked refuse to belong to the coming order, better that they not be hanging around.[25]

Second, regarding the nature of hell as destruction helps us to deal with the moral problem, orthodoxy's problem of pain. In the traditional view God is pictured as acting in ways that contradict his goodness and offend the moral sense. The God revealed in Jesus Christ is boundlessly merciful and not a cruel and sadistic torturer. There is a powerful moral revulsion against the traditional doctrine. How can we even think of projecting a deity of such cruelty? How can we think for a minute that torturing people without end is the sort of thing that the God and father of Jesus would do? Would the God who commands us to love our enemies be planning to wreak vengeance on his own enemies for all eternity? What would we think of a human being who satisfied his thirst for revenge so implacably? It is morally repugnant. Would God sustain people in existence just in order to punish them unendingly? Is God two-faced? Is he boundlessly merciful on the one hand and insatiably cruel on the other?

Any doctrine of hell has to pass the moral test. Christian theology simply cannot depict God acting like a bloodthirsty monster who maintains an everlasting Auschwitz for his enemies whom he will not even allow to die. And what purpose would possibly be served by it? It is intolerable. One could, I suppose, fear such a God, but how could one love and respect him? Are we supposed to strive to be "like him" in this too? In his mercilessness? John Stott comments: "I find the concept intolerable and do not understand how people can live with it without either cauterizing their feelings or cracking under the strain."[26] Thinking of hell as the elimination of the finally impenitent satisfies the moral challenge. It does not envisage everlasting torture. God is morally justified in destroying the wicked because he respects their moral and spiritual choices. He cannot save them, if they refuse to be saved. He does not force his friendship on anyone. In the end, he allows us to become what we have chosen.

Third, principles of justice also pose a problem for the traditional doctrine of the nature of hell because it depicts God acting unjustly. What crimes could a person have committed on earth that would merit a punishment of such magnitude? One can assent to annihilation as (in a sense) being "deserved" by those who end up incorrigibly wicked, but no assent can be given to everlasting conscious torment with no hope for escape or remittance. This is too heavy a sentence. This treats people worse than they deserve. A just God would not punish a sinner with a punishment beyond his deserving. And what purpose would be served by endless and totally unredemptive suffering?

Ask yourself what set of actions would deserve the ultimate of penalties, unending torment in body and soul? Elimination seems appropriate for those who say "no" to God definitively, but not unending pain. The sentence is too heavy. The OT standard of justice was "an eye for an eye, a tooth for a tooth." Did a sinner ever visit everlasting suffering on God so as to justify unending pain? Did anyone ever cause God or his own neighbour everlasting pain and loss? Of course not. No human being has the power to do such harm. No finite set of misdeeds that the sinner has done can justify an infinite penalty, which is true without even considering the higher standard of Jesus. The tradition posits a serious disproportion between sins committed in time and the suffering experienced forever.

Anselm attempted to argue that our sins are worthy of an infinite punishment because they are committed against an infinite majesty. He thought that human guilt is proportional to the status of the party offended against and to the amount of the harm intended, not just the harm actually done. So, since God is infinite and the harm intended against his rule is infinitely serious, this would merit an infinite punishment. Such a "status" argument may have seemed plausible in the Middle Ages but does not work as any argument today. We do not accept inequality in judgment on the basis of the honour owed to the victim, as if stealing from a CEO is worse than stealing from a beggar, or as if killing a baby would be less criminal than killing an adult. The fact that we have sinned against an infinite God does not justify an infinite penalty. No judge today would calibrate the degree of punishment on a scale of the honour of the one who has been wronged. It would be the reverse: hurting a weak person seems to us more reprehensible than hurting a strong one.

Hans Küng writes: "Even apart from the image of a truly merciless God that contradicts everything we can assume from what Jesus says about the father of the lost, can we be surprised at a time when retributive punishments without an opportunity of probation are being increasingly abandoned in education and penal justice, that the idea not only of a lifelong, but even eternal punishment of body and soul, seems to many people absolutely monstrous."[27]

Elimination (on the other hand) makes good sense of hell. If people refuse God's friendship, one can see their elimination as the best remedy. Certainly it would not be right to visit on them a punishment beyond what was deserved and thus violate the biblical standard of justice. God judges us according to what we have done (Rev 20:12). We may safely say that his penalties are commensurate with what was done and are not disproportionate. His justice would never demand for finite sins the penalty of eternal pain.

Fourth, viewing the nature of hell as destruction also meets a metaphysical objection. If as Paul says, God is to be "all in all" (1 Cor 15:24), how can a reality opposed to God still exist eternally alongside him? It would make history end badly with good and evil existing alongside one another forever. Whatever became of the promise that "there shall be no more mourning nor crying nor pain any more, for the former things have passed away" (Rev 21:4). The idea of countless millions suffering unending torment (perhaps within view of the saved in heaven) is hideous and depressing. It would mean that the "new order" would be flawed from day one. Surely the victory of Christ means that sin, evil, and death are done away in the lake of fire, not to threaten us anymore. The Christian hope is that evil and rebellion will not continue to happen. They will not belong and will have no place in the new creation. The biblical picture is one where Jesus is victorious and where his enemies are consumed in the lake of fire. His is an unqualified victory. True, Saint Augustine thought that the unending torment of the wicked would add to the beauty of the picture as a whole, but this does not appeal. Metaphysically it seems best to think of the nature of hell as final destruction and a dwindling out of existence of the wicked, rather than positing a disloyal opposition existing eternally alongside God in an unredeemed corner of the new creation. Eternal torment would suggest an eternal cosmological dualism which cannot be reconciled with the victory of God. It would be easier to hold to the reality of hell and the victory of God, if hell meant destruction. Christopher Marshall writes: "The finality of God's victory over evil is fatally compromised by the notion of eternal existence in hell."[28] Only if the souls of the wicked are eventually annihilated would the victory of redemption bespeak an unqualified success.

CONCLUSION

Viewing the nature of hell as everlasting conscious punishing is unbiblical, likely fostered by a hellenistic view of human nature, and detrimental to the character of God. Viewing hell as destruction makes better sense biblically, anthropologically, morally, judicially, and metaphysically. It does not make hell an attractive option, but it does make it less of a torture chamber. To be rejected by God, to miss the purpose for which one was created, to pass into oblivion while others enter into bliss is an awful prospect. Hell remains a terrifying possibility, the possibility of using our God-given freedom to lose God and destroy ourselves.

In the current situation and given the difficulties that attend the traditional view of the nature of hell, it might be wise to consider theological revision. Rather than threatening the reality of hell, this proposal to see hell in terms of destruction may actually help preserve it. The fact is that the tradition is causing more and more people to deny hell altogether and to accept universalism instead just in order to avoid its sadistic horrors. Hell as destruction maintains the doctrine of hell but without the sadistic and unjust aspects. It retains the realism of some people finally saying "No" to God and going to hell but without turning the notion of hell into a monstrosity.

Admittedly there is so much that we do not know about eschatology. Humble agnosticism is a wise choice in such matters. Exactly how the destruction of wickedness and the redemption of all things are to be effected is known only to God. But thanks be to God that the final word is not going to be retribution but recreation, such that sin, suffering, sickness, and death will be no more.

ENDNOTES

1. My interest in this topic stems from the need I feel to lighten the burden which many churched and unchurched people carry around. If I can help any of them to negotiate this concept of the nature of hell better, I will rejoice and be glad.

2. Henri J. M. Nouwen, *Bread for the Journey: A Daybook of Wisdom and Faith* (San Francisco: HarperSanFrancisco, 1997), December 15.

3. Miroslav Volf, *Exclusion and Embrace: A Theological Exploration of Identity, Otherness, and Reconciliation* (Nashville: Abingdon Press, 1996), 193.

4. This is well documented in "The Road to Traditionalism" by Robert A. Peterson in *Two Views of Hell: A Biblical and Theological Debate*, co-authored by Edward W. Fudge and Robert A. Peterson (Downers Grove, Ill.: InterVarsity Press, 2000), ch. 7; and in Peterson's "Traditionalism and Conditionalism in Church History," in his *The Nature of Hell* (London: Acute, 2000), ch. 4.

5. Cited in W. R. Alger, *The Destiny of the Soul: A Critical History of the Doctrine of a Future Life* (Boston: Roberts Brothers, 1880), 515.

6. John Gerstner, *Jonathan Edwards on Heaven and Hell* (Grand Rapids: Baker, 1980), 53.

7. J. I. Packer, "The Problem of Eternal Punishment," CRUX 26 (1990): 24–25. Packer also has a book by the same title (Disley: Orthos, 1990).

8. D. P. Walker, *The Decline of Hell: Seventeenth Century Discussions of Eternal Torment* (London: Routledge & Kegan Paul, 1964).

9. John W. Wenham, "The Case for Conditionalism" in *Universalism and the Doctrine of Hell* (ed. Nigel M. de S. Cameron; Grand Rapids: Baker, 1992), 187.

10. *The Nature of Hell: A Report by the Evangelical Alliance Commission on Unity and Truth Among Evangelicals* (London: Acute, 2000).

11. David Powys takes account of the doctrinal challenge: *Hell: A Hard Look at a Hard Question: The Fate of the Unrighteous in New Testament Thought* (Carlisle: Paternoster Press, 1997).

12. As do Jonathan Kvanvig, *The Problem of Hell* (New York: Oxford University Press, 1993) and Jerry L. Walls, *Hell: The Logic of Damnation* (Notre Dame: University of Notre Dame Press, 1992).

13. Edward W. Fudge has documented the biblical case in *The Fire That Consumes: A Biblical and Historical Study of Final Punishment* (Houston: Providential Press, 1982), chs. 6–14.

14. Christopher D. Marshall, *Beyond Retribution: A New Testament Vision for Justice, Crime, and Punishment* (Grand Rapids: Eerdmans, 2001), 182.

15. Some make an appeal to the story of the rich man and Lazarus to support the view that hell is where sinners live forever in fire (Luke 16:19–31). But the action seems to be set in Hades, not in Gehenna, and may not be about the nature of hell at all. It may refer to what is called the intermediate state. More likely it is a parable about what God expects of us rather than a window into life after death. It is about the kind of piety that will get one to the place of blessing and told in popular terms. See David Powys, *Hell: A Hard Look at a Hard Question*, 218–228.

16. Ladd, *A Commentary on the Revelation of John* (Grand Rapids: Eerdmans, 1972), 270–271.

17. B. B. Warfield finds that the first genuinely annihilationist theory is found in Arnobius in the fourth century. See *The New Schaff-Herzog Encyclopedia of Religious Knowledge*, I.183–186.

18. Jerry L. Walls, *Hell: The Logic of Damnation* (London: University of Notre Dame Press, 1992), 153.

19. C. S. Lewis, *The Problem of Pain* (London: Collins, 1957), 115.

20. Ibid., 100.

21. See Gregory A. Boyd, "Hell, das Nichtige, and the Victory of God" in *Satan and the Problem of Evil* (Downers Grove: InterVarsity Press, 2001), ch. 12.

22. John W. Cooper, *Body, Soul, and Life Everlasting: Biblical Anthropology and the Monism-Dualism Debate* (Grand Rapids: Eerdmans, 1989), 216.

23. Edward White, *Life in Christ: A Study of the Scripture Doctrine on the Nature of Man, the Object of the Divine Incarnation, and the Conditions of Human Immortality* (London: Elliott Stock, 1878).

24. Richard Swinburne, *Responsibility and Atonement* (Oxford: Clarendon Press, 1989), 180–184.

25. Walls, *Hell: The Logic of Damnation*, 136–138.

26. John Stott and David Edwards, *Essentials: A Liberal-Evangelical Dialogue* (London: Hodder and Stoughton, 1988), 314.

27. Hans Küng, *Eternal Life* (New York: Doubleday, 1984), 136–137.

28. Marshall, *Beyond Retribution*, 183.

RESPONSE TO PINNOCK

MICHAEL A. VAN HORN

Professor Pinnock's call to reevaluate the nature of hell is both courageous and potentially consequential for the church's embodiment of the gospel. It is courageous because, as he himself notes, there exists in the church "a resistance to a new model because it is untraditional." I can say from personal experience that this resistance appears to run deep, having personally lost an academic position at an evangelical college over this very topic. For good or for ill, the "traditional" notion of hell is set deeply in the theological imagination of most Christians and has, for a few, become something of a litmus test for orthodoxy. Pinnock's proposal is also potentially consequential, because, as he also implies, the church's idea of hell has a practical outcome. A false view of hell could do serious damage to the way the gospel is proclaimed and embodied. For, the traditional concept of judgment not only justified the burning of heretics many centuries ago, but it still has the potential to encourage a kind of evangelical rage toward our "wicked culture" whenever unfortunate sinners happen to fall into "the hands of an angry church."[1]

If I have read Dr. Pinnock's paper properly, the driving force seems to be this loose syllogism: a) the doctrine of hell is intended to be part of the Christian good news; b) the traditional view of an eternal hell (held almost universally by the historic church) is decidedly *not* good news; c) therefore, the biblical notion of hell deserves a second look. I find myself in wholehearted agreement with the first premise and the conclusion, but still need some convincing of the second premise. First of all, I trust we all agree that the shape of what we would call "good news" must be ultimately determined by God's own revealed speech, and not merely by our own instincts or desires. Much as Queen Mary I and other notorious Inquisitors were savagely misguided about how to execute the judgment of God in this world, we must likewise have the humility to admit that we ourselves can be instinctually wrong about God and God's ways. Some form of cultural blindness affects every generation of the church. Thus, we must maintain a certain humility about our own theological "innovations" while resisting the temptation to be hastily dismissive of the views of the historic church, particularly those ideas which appear to have almost catholic support. For example, the very thought of divine judgment altogether—in any form—will seem distasteful and intuitively wrong to most contemporary people. To our present culture of "tolerance" both the traditional view and Pinnock's view would make God sound tyrannical and bloodthirsty. Yet, we would recognize that this cultural attitude is probably rooted more in sentimentality than in a proper appreciation of the God of Scripture.

So, this is the rub: What precisely does the testimony of Scripture teach about final judgment? Dr. Pinnock's admonition about the hazards of negotiating the "figurative and parabolic" labyrinth of apocalyptic writing is prudent. Such discretion ought to keep us from dogmatism about what R. Niebuhr called "the furniture of heaven and the temperature of hell"—and perhaps even keep us humble about their duration. Sentimentally, I have no vested interest in the everlasting torment of the damned, and I am sadly suspicious that the relish some preachers take in the idea often has less to do with the teaching of the Bible and more to do with a misguided sense of personal worth, coupled with a nasty vindictiveness toward the "undeserving."

Foundationally, I believe Pinnock is correct that a large part of what has fueled the "eternal hellfire" motif is an essentially unbiblical idea, the persistent notion of the soul as a metaphysically indestructible entity. This assumption surely owes more to Greek philosophical idealism than to the writings of the Hebrew prophets and the apostles. This pagan notion of immortality of the soul must be rejected outright as the theological prerequisite for conscious eternal judgment (or reward). If hell is eternal, it is not because of something inherent in the construction of the soul. In the biblical vision, if souls (or bodies!) are eternal, it must be because life comes from God as an ongoing gift (whether conditioned on faith, I am not yet convinced). Pinnock rightly points out that "God *can* destroy both body and soul in hell" (Matt 10:28), but it remains to be seen whether God *will*.

Granting Dr. Pinnock's point that language of hell must be read as "figurative and connotative rather than denotative and literal" and that the proclamation of hell serves as a sober admonishment that "one can exclude oneself from the presence of God and suffer eternal loss," we still must ask, does the use of these figures connote any knowledge about the nature of that judgment? Surely the Bible's rhetoric of judgment is intended to convey something severe, unpleasant, and perhaps naturally unfit for human beings, but can we conclude anything more? Do these concepts of "unquenchable fire," "outer darkness," "prison," "destruction," etc., suggest anything at all from which a coherent theology of hell can be forged?

Pinnock suggests that the heart of the gospel message "is joyful . . . not threatening," and this fact alone insinuates a flaw in the traditional view. But this claim raises a question: Precisely how is a warning of destruction or death any less threatening or any more joyful than the warning of eternal torment? On the surface it may *seem* that annihilation is more "humane" than the possibility of endless suffering, but is that necessarily so? In Tom Stoppard's existentialist play *Rosencrantz and Guildenstern are Dead* one of the ill-fated characters finds himself contemplating—in Hamlet-like fashion—the meaning of life and death. Lying on a funeral slab, Rosencrantz muses about the prospect of being buried in a box alive versus that of being dead and buried. After some reflection he summarily concludes, "[Given the alternatives] life in a box is better than no life at all!"[2] Odd as that may seem to some, it is subjectively possible that the prospect of annihilation may be far more threatening and less joyful to some than the prospect of ongoing punishment. Condemned prisoners with no hope of emancipation may still vigorously seek a commutation of the death penalty, seemingly preferring misery and diminished life to no life at all. Would this principle still be true if the punishment were eternal? I do not know. But, I am simply not convinced that annihilation is necessarily a "happier" prospect than eternal judgment. For my money, if our primary criterion for judging the legitimacy of the traditional view of an eternal hell is the emotion of what seems more humane, then other options win the day. Both C. S. Lewis's view of hell as "eternal autonomy" and Karl Barth's implication of the hopeful triumph of God's grace (cf. Tennyson's "larger hope") seem to meet better Pinnock's criteria of "joyful" and "nonthreatening"—each with their own biblical merit, I think.

So, what do we make of the scriptural language of "death, destruction, ruin, and perishing"? Surely Pinnock is correct when he suggests that such language has gotten very little serious hearing in Christian circles and has all but disappeared in pulpits behind the more familiar Dantean constructs. But, is the prospect of reconciling this language with an eternal hell as troublesome as Pinnock implies? Not necessarily. For example, someone whose world has figuratively collapsed around him or her could easily use the language of "death, destruction, and ruin" to describe such an impossibly bleak situation. A person sentenced to prison could speak of his or her life being over. The end of a marriage is often spoken of as a death. Such uses of death-language for grim life situations seem common enough in our own culture.

Likewise, it does not seem impossible that, as the biblical writers stretched their words around those "realities which lie far outside human experience," the most extreme language available to them was that of death and destruction—even if something decidedly less absolute were actually in view. Isaiah can declare himself "undone" or "ruined"[3] as he encounters the vision of the Lord in the temple (Isa 6:5). Adam can be spoken of in Scripture as "dead" from the day the tree is raided in the garden (Gen 2:17), just as those of us who are "in Adam" can be described as "dead in our trespasses" (Eph 2:1) and still be very much alive.

Therefore, it appears that the common use of language in both culture and Scripture might permit us to say that a person is "destroyed" or "dead" or "ruined," implying something extreme and horrific, yet without demanding total eradication. Lewis suggests that what is cast into hell (or casts itself into hell) "remains." What had once been a human but through persistent rebellion has devolved into something subhuman is now fit for a place prepared (not for humans at all) but for "the devil and his angels." Clearly the Scriptures may use language of destruction as fluidly, which, in my view, reconciles much more naturally with the traditional rhetoric of eternal judgment. The harder case to make, it seems, is Pinnock's. For what reason, other than sentiment, should we read the "destruction" language any less figuratively than the "fire" or "prison" language?[4] Finally, and this is a sincere question veiled as a rhetorical one, I wonder what would be the purpose of a final bodily resurrection of the unrighteous for judgment (Rev 20), if not for eternal punishment? Would not the resurrection of an already dead unrighteous person just to inflict a death sentence be superfluous? If their punishment is death, would not resurrecting them to inflict death again be cruel and unusual? Would it pass the test of being "joyful" and "nonthreatening?" Of course, I confess that God's ways are seldom expeditious by our standards, and so my question may be beside the point.

Professor Pinnock raises important questions about the nature of God and judgment. With much respect for his contribution to the conversation, I am still left with too many "loose ends." For, if our primary concern is to find a doctrine of hell that bespeaks "the victory of redemption" as an "unqualified success," then I would defer to Barth's sensibility that Christ's redemptive suffering is hell enough for everyone. If there still remains the moral problem of free will and the possibility of "rebels who are successful to the end,"[5] then Lewis's option wins my vote. All things being equal, I would be wonderfully surprised and theologically delighted if Barth was correct, intellectually satisfied if Lewis was correct, but not the least bit disgruntled if Pinnock turned out to be right. In the meantime the church needs to have this conversation, and I am grateful for Dr. Pinnock's contribution, while remaining for the moment happily—and, I hope, humbly—agnostic about the final details.

ENDNOTES

1. Dean Merrill's book *Sinners in the Hands of an Angry Church* (Grand Rapids: Zondervan, 1997). The title creatively pilfered from Jonathan Edwards' infamous sermon suggests that the spiritual great-grandchildren of Edwards have become all too happy to take up the role of judgment on behalf of God, due to a series of theological misunderstandings about the nature of church and culture. Merrill documents this attitude of evangelical anger toward culture well, and, while not directly mentioning the doctrine of hell, Merrill speaks to the strong sense of disenfranchisement among conservative Christians which seems to draw deep eschatological

satisfaction from the thought that, in the end, "*we* will be proved right and *they* will get what's coming to them!"

2. Tom Stoppard, *Rosencrantz and Guildenstern are Dead* (Grove Press: Reprint edition, 1991), 73.

3. The Hebrew word is *dāmāh*, "to perish, be destroyed, be ruined, be wiped out," and is used in Isa 6:5 in a figurative way, but it is used elsewhere to describe utter ruin, destruction, and death (cf. Isa 15:1; Hos 4:5, 6; 10:15; Zeph 1:11).

4. Theological language seems to be one key to this puzzle, and among several concerns I have about the treatment of language in Pinnock's paper is the seeming equivocation of terms such as "gehenna" and "hades."

5. C. S. Lewis, *The Great Divorce* (San Francisco: HarperCollins, 1973), 70–75.

REVELATION, EMPIRE, AND THE VIOLENCE OF GOD

JOHN E. PHELAN, JR.

Like many growing up in Fundamentalism in the American South the book of Revelation was a staple of my religious diet. The complex prophecy charts of Clarence Larkin were often hung in the front of our small sanctuary—we called it an auditorium—for long preaching and teaching series on "prophecy."[1] As a small child I knew all about Daniel's seventy weeks, the "ten kingdom confederation," and, especially, the secret rapture of the church. The preachers and teachers I heard scoured the newspaper headlines for signs of the times. Speculating on the identity of the Antichrist was a popular pastime. Russia's latest moves were watched like a hawk and any stirring in the Middle East could cause frenzy among the faithful.

Of course, reading and analyzing the book of Revelation was critical to our "rightly dividing the word of truth." As a child I would shudder in fear of the fate of those "left behind" during the tribulation. I am sure I was not the only child who awoke in a cold sweat convinced the rapture of the church had occurred and that I was fated to face the depredations of the Antichrist and the wrath of God on my own. I could hear the beating wings of the locusts from the bottomless pit who were given authority to torture but not kill the hapless residents of the earth (Rev 9:1–6).

Among some preachers and teachers there was a grim satisfaction about Revelation's carnage. God's enemies would be getting what they deserved. Certainly criminals, crooks, and cheats would experience God's wrath. But perhaps more important, scientists who supported evolution, liberal politicians who opposed school prayer, and skeptical theologians who denied the virgin birth or the miracles of Jesus would feel the scorpions' sting and realize, too late, the error of their ways. When the time for repentance was past, they would recognize in horror that we were right all along.

My studies long ago convinced me of the errors of popular dispensationalism, but my fascination with and even love of the book of Revelation has not diminished. It has continued to be a research and teaching interest. I continue to be moved by the glorious cadences of its worship and the promises of the New Heavens and the New Earth where righteousness dwells. More lately I have been stirred by the powerful cultural critique of imperial violence and the warning to the church to avoid compromise with the empire. For all its difficulty and maddening ambiguity, Revelation's warnings to the hesitating churches of Asia Minor are as fresh and relevant as this morning's newspaper.

THE "DARK SIDE" OF REVELATION

Today any appreciation for Revelation must be tempered by reflections on what some might call the "dark side" of Revelation. The violence of God and the evident relish of the prophet for the fierce judgment of his enemies have troubled many. Luther in the preface to Revelation in his 1522 translation famously wrote, "I miss more than one thing in this book, and this makes me hold it to be neither apostolic nor prophetic. . . . There is one sufficient reason for me not to think highly of it—Christ is not taught or known in it. . . . I stick to the books which give me Christ clearly and purely."[2] Elizabeth Cady Stanton claimed John of Patmos was "evidently the victim of a terrible and extravagant imagination of visions which make the blood curdle." She recommended the book "no longer be read in our churches."[3] D. H. Lawrence called John "a shameless power-worshipping pagan Jew, gnashing his teeth over the postponement of his grand destiny." He called the book "repellent . . . because it resounds with the dangerous snarl of the frustrated, suppressed, collective self, the frustrated power-spirit in man, vengeful." It was the work of a "second-rate mind" that would only appeal to other second-rate minds.[4] George Bernard Shaw dismissed the book as "a curious record of the visions of a drug addict which was absurdly admitted to the canon under the title of Revelation."[5]

It would not be wise to dismiss such critiques too quickly. As Maier comments, "Who, indeed, does not pale at Revelation's two-hundred-mile-long river of human blood, as high as a horse's bridle, pouring out from the winepress of God's wrath (Rev 14:20)? Whose stomach does not turn at that vision of birds gorged on the flesh of the dead (19:17–18)? Who can warm to the damned thrown into lakes of burning fire (19:20; 20:14–15)?" If this and other horrific parts of Revelation's vision are not enough to raise questions, he continues, "Who does not cover their eyes in horror upon witnessing this text's history in culture. . . . Who can estimate the apocalyptic sum of all those gulags and concentration camps designed to usher in a Revelation-inspired millennium?"[6]

Revelation *has* been misused terribly. It has been used to foster a dark and paranoid vision of the world. "We" are the people of God oppressed by "them," and "they" deserve anything and everything God can bring upon them. How many violent, secretive groups have seized on John's visions as a warrant for their hatred and fear? Perhaps an even more disturbing aspect of the misuse of Revelation is its appropriation by comfortable middle and upper class western Christians who long ago compromised with the "empire." There is something obscene about such materially comfortable and relatively secure people gleeful over the judgment of others. Whatever else Revelation is, it is a view from below, from those suffering the effects of imperial violence. Revelation certainly offers no comfort to the complacent and compromised.

Revelation has been manipulated like a wax nose, shaped according to the historical situation, and used to damn a wide variety of real and perceived enemies: Jews and Muslims; the Roman Catholic Church and the Pope in Rome; the Communists and the European Common Market; Hitler and Mussolini; Henry Kissinger and Teddy Kennedy; and, of course, Saddam Hussein. Dislodged from its historical situation the book has functioned as a convenient stick to thrash a variety of cultural, political, or religious opponents. Can its message and vision be recovered? Can Revelation be rehabilitated?

THE VIOLENCE OF GOD

Revelation's violence must be evaluated in the larger context of the violence of God in the Bible. The violence of God in Revelation and elsewhere must also be considered as a potential contributor to a larger crisis afflicting the church and the world. As I was working on this paper, the newspapers reported the bombing of Christian churches in Iraq. Leaflets warned Christians to leave the country, and many are doing just that. The last decade of the twentieth century and the first decade of the twenty-first have been an era of religiously motivated violence. In the 1990s the world witnessed the horror of religious and ethnic violence in Rwanda, reportedly one of the most "Christian" countries in Africa. "Ethnic cleansing" in the former Yugoslavia fostered violence between Muslim and Orthodox Christian Serbs. The endless dreary horror in the Middle East produces teenaged suicide bombers, bulldozed homes, and the rhetoric of holocaust.

Complex issues drive this violence. Competition for limited resources, for land, and for political and cultural power are key elements in these various struggles. The impact of an honor and shame culture also cannot be ignored. Nevertheless, while religion is only a part of the various crises, it is often an important part. In light of all this Jack Nelson-Pallmeyer raises the question "Is Religion Killing Us?"[7] He argues that the problem is a violent God who takes sides in our conflicts, who is claimed as "one of us." Both Osama bin Laden and George W. Bush insist God is on their respective sides of their cultural, religious, and military conflicts. Osama bin Laden asserts:

Our encouragement and call to Muslims to enter Jihad against the American and the Israeli occupiers are actions which we are engaging in as religious obligations. Allah Most High has commanded us in many verses of the Quran to fight in His path and to urge believers to do so.... We have given an oath to Allah to continue in the struggle as long as we have blood pumping in our veins or a seeing eye, and we beg of Allah to accept and to grant a good ending for us and for all the Muslims.

George W. Bush is no less certain:

> The course of this conflict is not known, yet its outcome is certain. Freedom and fear, justice and cruelty, have always been at war, and we know that God is not neutral between them. Fellow citizens, we'll meet violence with patient justice, assured of the rightness of our cause and confident of the victories to come. In all that lies before us, may God grant us wisdom, and may He watch over the United States of America.[8]

According to Mark Noll in lectures given at North Park Theological Seminary in 2004, this is an old problem. Noll argues that the American Civil War created a crisis in biblical interpretation in that both sides claimed biblical warrant for their various positions. Both abolitionists and slaveholders claimed the Bible supported them. Both Unionists and Rebels were sure God was on their side. According to Noll the only person who questioned these confident claims of God's support was President Abraham Lincoln. He averred that he was not so interested in having God on his side as he was on being on God's side. He also wondered if *neither* party in the conflict was on God's side and whether, in fact, the war was a judgment on the nation for the horrors of slavery.[9]

The bloody losses of the Civil War did not dissuade nationalistic Americans from claiming divine support for their wars. At the beginning of the twentieth century American humorist Mark Twain wrote a story entitled "The War Prayer." It spoke of a time when "the country was up in arms, the war was on, [and] in every breast burned the fire of patriotism." In churches pastors preached "devotion to flag and country and invoked the God of Battles, beseeching His aid in our good cause." One pastor prayed a magnificent prayer asking "an ever-merciful and benignant Father of us all" to "watch over our noble young soldiers and aid, comfort, and encourage them in their patriotic work.... His mighty hand, make them strong and confident, invincible in the bloody onset; help them to crush the foe, grant them and to their flag and country imperishable honor and glory." At this point an "aged stranger" stood to complete the prayer with "the many unmentioned results which follow victory":

> O Lord our Father, our young patriots, idols of our hearts, go forth to battle—be Thou near them! With them, in spirit, we also go forth from

> the sweet peace of our beloved firesides to smite the foe. O Lord our God, help us to tear their soldiers to bloody shreds with our shells; help us to cover their smiling fields with the pale forms of their patriot dead; help us to drown the thunder of the guns with the shrieks of their wounded, writhing in pain; help us to wring the hearts of their unoffending widows with unavailing grief; help us to turn them out roofless with their children to wander unfriended the wastes of their desolated land in rags and hunger and thirst, sports of the sun flames of summer and the icy winds of winter, broken in spirit, worn with travail, imploring Thee for the refuge of the grave and denied it—for our sake who adore thee Lord, blast their hopes, blight their lives, protract their bitter pilgrimage, make heavy their steps, water their way with tears, stain the white snow with the blood of their wounded feet! We ask it, in the spirit of love, of Him who is the Source of Love, and Who is the ever-faithful refuge and friend of all that are sore beset and seek His aid with humble and contrite hearts. Amen.[10]

The crowd thought the old man a lunatic. Few had ever or would ever contemplate the outcome of their calling on God to support their heroic violence.

Nelson-Pallmeyer argues that parties in such conflicts call upon God to justify their violence "because the 'sacred' texts to which they turn are filled with images of a violent God/gods and with stories and passages that legitimate human violence against others in service of God's will."[11] The violent rhetoric of the book of Revelation could certainly be seen as a contributor to this. Is this really the intention of John's vision? Does Revelation indeed offer legitimization to those who would "fight for God"? But there is even a larger context for this question.

EVANGELICALS, THE BIBLE, AND VIOLENCE

Evangelicals who affirm the authority and significance of the entire biblical text have long been troubled by violence-of-God passages and often studiously ignored them. God's commands of genocide against the Canaanites and other opponents of Israel are a perennial source of discomfort. In Deut 20:16–18 God commands:

> . . . as for the towns of these peoples that the Lord your God is giving you as an inheritance, you must not let anything that breathes remain alive. You shall annihilate them—the Hittites and the Amorites, the Canaanites and the Perrizites, the Hivites and the Jebusites—just as the Lord your God has commanded, so that they may not teach you to do all the abhorrent things that they do for their gods, and you thus sin against the Lord your God.

One of the beloved verses of the OT is found in 1 Sam 15:22: "To obey is better than sacrifice, and to heed than the fat of rams." The context of these verses is Samuel's rebuke of Saul for his failure fully to carry out the command of God. This command was to "go and attack Amalek, and utterly destroy all that they have; do not spare them, but kill both man and woman, child and infant, ox and sheep, camel and donkey" (1 Sam 15:3). Saul had spared the king Agag and the best of the sheep and cattle and other valuables (1 Sam 15:9). All that was "despised and worthless" was destroyed, including evidently the women and children of Amalek. Saul's disobedience brought down not only the wrath of Samuel but led to the Lord being "sorry that he had made Saul king over Israel" (1 Sam 15:35).

The apparently arbitrary violence of God is seen other places. The Levites are "ordained" through the slaughter of their kinsman. In the wake of the incident of the Golden Calf Moses cried out, "Who is on the Lord's side! Come to me!" When the Levites gathered around him, Moses told them, "Thus says the Lord, the God of Israel, 'Put your sword on your side, each of you! Go back and forth from gate to gate throughout the camp, and each of you kill your brother, your friend, and your neighbor.'" Three thousand people were killed. Moses tells them, "Today you have ordained yourselves for the service of the Lord, each one at the cost of a son or a brother and so have brought blessing on yourselves this day" (Exod 32:25–29). These are only a few of a number of troubling passages.

Various exegetical and hermeneutical approaches are used by evangelical scholars to deal with these difficult texts. In the recent book *Show Them No Mercy* four different approaches are recommended. C. S. Cowles insists these passages must be read through the lenses of the NT and the incarnation of Christ and relativized by God's self-giving love on the cross. Eugene H. Merrill argues that the holy war prescriptions of God in the OT must be accepted as God's will for a particular time and place in Israel's history but "provide no justification in the age of the church except in terms of spiritual conflict."[12] Such explorations are necessary, helpful, and important but do not answer all the questions.

The problem, as suggested, is perennial. How does one bring together the sacrificial love of Jesus who insisted on love for enemies and prayer for persecutors with the fearsome God of violence and judgment? Jesus claimed the love he was recommending was in imitation of his Father who "makes his sun rise on the evil and the good, and sends rain on the righteous and unrighteous" (Matt 5:43–45). Elsewhere we are told that this God is not willing that any should perish but that all would come to repentance (see 2 Pet 3:9; 1 Tim 2:4). Is the God who called the Levites to slaughter their kinsmen and the God who is "not willing that any should perish" really the same God? It is tempting to say no. But in spite of the difficulties, the God of Abraham, Isaac, and Jacob and the God and Father of our Lord Jesus Christ *must* be held together. The solution of Marcion was long ago rightly deemed heretical. And yet, questions remain. Should not the God revealed in Jesus Christ be consistent with the God of Abraham, Isaac, and Jacob as well as the God of John of Patmos—a God of both love and judgment?

However one addresses such perplexing passages, God must not be robbed of the right of judgment. Without judgment can there be a moral order in the universe? Central to the biblical text is the assertion that God will set things right by judging the oppressor and lifting up the oppressed. Those of us in comfortable and secure positions can afford to feel squeamish about God's judgment. We are not threatened by the violence of oppressors, the confiscation of our lands and goods, the death of our children. But those facing such oppression understand the cry of the saints beneath the altar—"How long!" In this case God's justice is rightly seen as a manifestation of God's love.

The challenge of holding God's love and justice together has never been easy. Nevertheless, I will argue that believing in a God of judgment does *not* give his people permission to act violently in support of his judgments. The violence of God in the Bible does not underwrite our own violence. A short paper cannot examine all of the pertinent issues or discuss all of the troubling passages. However, I believe that (perhaps ironically) the oft-despised book of Revelation offers some answers to these vexed questions if we read it aright.

In what follows I will argue that the works of René Girard help us to understand human violence, including the human communities' tendency to create scapegoats and through mob violence destroy those scapegoats in pursuit of a temporary peace. I will suggest that Girard argues correctly that Jesus Christ is the scapegoat to end all scapegoats in that his death on the cross exposed the ways we use God (or the "sacred") to justify violence against those who threaten the peace of our communities. Because of the death of Christ we no longer see scapegoats but innocent victims in need of the love of God. The church resists scapegoating and violence because Jesus as the final scapegoat took the violence to himself.

I will further argue that John of Patmos' analysis of his church's situation is consistent with Girard's observations. John argues that the way of victory over the violence of the empire is ironically through the "slaughtered lamb," a "scapegoat" that parodies the pretensions of the empire. He insists that God's people neither scapegoat God's enemies nor physically fight them but rather win the victory through the sacrifice of the lamb and their witness. The nonviolence of God's people breaks the power of scapegoating and mob violence as they follow the lamb. This does not mean that God is rendered impotent to judge. But it is *God* alone that judges! And in the end God continues to offer an opportunity for all to repent—even the kings of the earth that continue to resist his way.

The ultimate goal of the Scriptures, OT and NT alike, is not to create scapegoats and violence, regardless of the critique of Nelson-Pallmeyer. As Gil Bailie argues in *Violence Unveiled*, "What Scripture is intended to achieve is a conversion of the human heart that will allow humanity to dispense with organized violence without sliding into the abyss of uncontrollable violence."[13] Scripture turns us away from scapegoats and violence to the cross that makes peace, not through one more act of mob violence, but through exposing that violence for what it really is.

THE THEORY OF RENÉ GIRARD

René Girard completed his academic career as the Andrew B. Hammond Professor of Language, Literature, and Civilization at Stanford University. His reputation is built on a series of complex and fascinating works including *Violence and the Sacred, Things Hidden Since the Foundation of the World, The Scapegoat,* and *I See Satan Fall Like Lightning.*[14] Girard's thesis is no less than a theory of the origins of human civilization. As it has developed, its theological implications have been recognized and developed by both Girard himself and various disciples.[15]

Robert G. Hamerton-Kelly argues that for Girard the starting point is a quality of desire he calls "mimesis." "Desire," he argues, "is imitative and acquisitive. It operates by copying someone else's desire for an object."[16] Put a group of two-year-olds in a room with a collection of toys. Have one of them approach a new toy and watch the others all develop an interest in it. Here you have mimesis in action. The children learned what to desire by observing the desire of another. This imitative desire produces a "rivalry" and out of this rivalry violence is born. "Violence is . . . the relationship between desire and the mediator-becoming-an-obstacle in the process of mimetic rivalry."[17] In other words, the two-year-old that first approached the unused toy became a "mediator" of desire and then an obstacle to the desire of the other children. Screeching and hair-pulling are bound to follow!

Girard argues that violence is the "deforming of desire." "Violence describes the deep strategies of deformed desire in the pursuit of its ends in all the modalities of culture."[18] This deformed desire produces what Hamerton-Kelly calls "deviated transcendence" or more simply idolatry. Some object is assigned ultimate transcendence other than God. Rivalry is substituted for love of the neighbor. These desires are not just individual but communal. They become communal because they are infectious. The desires and idolatries spread as the various mediators teach us what to desire. We find ourselves in bondage to one another's desires and in danger of violent conflict because of the limitations of fulfillment. Every two-year-old cannot have the toy.

In the very beginnings of human culture in the midst of the "primal horde," Girard imagines the following process:

1. A crisis point is reached because of the rising tide of violence on account of the mimetic desires of the community.
2. A "scapegoat" is identified and substituted for the object of desire threatening the community.

Revelation, Empire, and the Violence of God

3. All people cooperate in killing the victim, the scapegoat (mob violence).
4. This cooperation enables the group to find unity and reconciliation.
5. This process is eventually ritualized.
6. The victim is divinized as the source of violence and the cause of peace.
7. Ritual sacrifice arises as the controlled transgression of the prohibition of violence as a way to express violence without incurring vengeance.[19]

Bailie argues that "cultures have forever commemorated some form of sacred violence at their origins and considered it a sacred duty to reenact it in times of crisis." This is true, he continues,

> "whether it is the Assyro-Babylonian myth declaring that Marduk created the world by killing the monster Tiamat; or the Teutonic myth telling how Odin formed the world by raising the corpse of Ymir from the sea of Ymir's own blood; or Pope Urban II declaring that God willed the first Crusades; or Thomas Jefferson saying that the tree of liberty must be periodically watered with the blood of patriots and tyrants."[20]

Girard argues that the scapegoating process is obscured in the myths and legends of the various human cultures. In the myths and legends the victimization of the scapegoat is hidden. A key to the "scapegoat mechanism" is that "the scapegoat is an innocent victim who polarizes a universal hatred."[21] In his book *The Scapegoat* Girard illustrates this with reference to Guillaume de Machaut's *Judgment of the King of Navarre*. This fourteenth-century work describes catastrophic events that afflict de Machaut's region of France. These catastrophes are blamed on the perfect scapegoats:

> After that came a false, treacherous and contemptible swine; this was shameful Israel, the wicked and disloyal who hated good and loved everything evil, who gave so much gold and silver and promises to Christians, who then poisoned several rivers and fountains that had been clear and pure so that many lost their lives; for whoever used them died suddenly. Certainly ten times one hundred thousand died from it in country and in city. Then finally this mortal calamity was noticed.
> He who sits on high and sees far, who governs and provides for everything, did not want this treachery to remain hidden; he revealed it and made it so generally known that they lost their lives and possessions. Then every Jew was destroyed, some hanged, others burned; some were drowned, others beheaded with an ax or sword. And many Christians died together with them in shame.[22]

After this slaughter the plague eventually passed and "one day in spring . . . Guillaume heard music in the street and men and women laughing. All was over, and courtly poetry could begin again."[23]

The threat to the social order that the "plague" produced required a victim. Someone had to be at fault, otherwise the whole society would collapse in fear, desire, and violence. Girard argues that "the persecutors always convince themselves that a small number of people, or even a single individual, despite his relative weakness, is extremely harmful to the whole of society."[24] To restore equilibrium the threat must be eliminated. "The crowd's choice of victims may be totally random; but it is not necessarily so. It is even possible that the crimes of which they are accused are real, but that sometimes the persecutors choose their victims because they belong to a class that is particularly susceptible to persecution rather than because of the crimes they have committed."[25] Stereotyping of a group makes this process simpler and more deadly: "All Jews are like this, therefore all Jews must be destroyed." The myths enshrine the violence against the scapegoat in story, and religious traditions enshrine it in ritual. At its most extreme (say in the Aztec religion) the gods require a ritual murder to assure peace and stability. Girard argues that ritualized scapegoating and persecution continues in our cultures to this very day. It does not take long for us to think of examples.

Girard argues that it is the Bible in general and Christianity in particular that undermines scapegoating and sacred violence. "All mythical and biblical dramas," he argues, "including the Passion, represent the same type of collective violence against a single victim. Myth sees this victim as guilty: Oedipus has really killed his father and married his mother. The Bible and the Gospels see these same victims as innocent, unjustly murdered by deluded lynchers and persecutors. Jesus is the unjustifiably sacrificed *lamb of God.*"[26] "The victim," he writes elsewhere, "has the last word in the Bible."[27] Job, for example, is a scapegoat that refuses to act like a scapegoat. He refuses to accept the attacks of his "friends" and their bland interpretations of his fate. He refuses to let them find comfort and unanimity in his suffering![28]

Jesus is also "an unsuccessful scapegoat." His "heroic willingness to die for the truth" will ultimately make the entire cycle of satanic violence visible to all people and therefore inoperative. The "kingdom of Satan" will give way to the "kingdom of God."[29] Jesus' death exposes the violence of the mob and the evil of scapegoating, so it is a small wonder that he calls on his people to love their enemies. One simply cannot love an enemy and participate in their scapegoating and execution at the same time! When the scapegoat becomes an invisible victim, guilty of some vague crime and destroyed through mob violence, the culture's crude method of assuring its survival is once again vindicated. But when the victim is clearly visible and plainly innocent, the very foundations of the culture are rocked.

Jesus, Girard argues, seeks to turn us away from "mimetic rivalries." He does call us to imitate him and his desires. But his desire is to "resemble the Father as much as possible."[30]

> Why does Jesus regard the Father and himself as the best model for all humans? Because neither the Father nor the Son desires greedily, egotistically. God "makes his sun to rise on the evil and on the good, and he sends his rain on the just and on the unjust." God gives to us without counting, without making the least difference between us. He lets weeds grow with the wheat until the time of harvest. If we imitate the detached generosity of God, then the trap of mimetic rivalries will never close over us. This is why Jesus says also, "Ask, and it will be given to you."[31]

Jesus died as an *innocent* to expose the violence and reveal an alternative to the ongoing plague of scapegoating. He did not die as a lawbreaker or blasphemer nor as a way to assuage the Romans and fulfill their need for exemplary victims.

> The victory of Christ has nothing to do with the military triumph of a victorious general: rather than inflicting violence on others, Christ submits to it. What we should retain in the image of triumph is not the military aspect but the idea of an extraordinary event offered to the view of all humankind, a public exhibition of what the enemy had to conceal in order to defend himself. The Cross has stripped away this defense, the reality that exists through deception.[32]

Christ's death is the last violent act—the violent act to end all violent acts. It is the exposure of sin, death, the devil, and the hidden schemes of the principalities and powers: "Christ does not achieve this victory through violence. He obtains it through a renunciation of violence so complete that violence can rage to its heart's content without realize that by so doing, it reveals what it must conceal, without suspecting that its fury will turn back against it this time because it will be recorded and represented with exactness in the Passion narrative."[33] The Passion, then, *was* in a sense a trick played on the devil, but it was a trick played in plain view. An innocent victim exposed the violence, horror, and bloodshed of all human history and the ways the demonic and human forces worked to obscure their work.

The Bible has made it difficult for the violent. This is why it was so hated by the likes of Hitler and Stalin. This is why Nietzsche despised its "slave morality" and support for the victim. He wrote, "Through Christianity, the individual was made so important, so absolute, that he could not longer be sacrificed: but the species endures only through human sacrifice. . . . Genuine charity demands sacrifice, because it needs human sacrifice. And this pseudo-humaneness called Christianity wants it established that no one should be sacrificed."[34] Lenin, Stalin, and Hitler accepted the dictum that human sacrifice was required. "To make an omelet you have to break some eggs." When the "peace and security" of the whole is more important than the sacrifice of the individual, you have a retreat from the gospel toward the myth of sacred violence.

> Because of biblical enlightenment, which in turn gave rise to general enlightenment in the west, we can no longer ritualize or rationalize our violence. We are no longer to produce idols around which to collect and coagulate it. We are thrust into a time of absolute responsibility. Once and for all we know that there is no vengeful god who desires victims, that that god was always only a mask for our own appetite.[35]

When it becomes clear that the victims are really innocent, the mythology becomes difficult to sustain. In his autobiography Whittaker Chambers tells the story of a conversation he had with the daughter of a German diplomat. Her father had been pro-Communist and had become disillusioned with Stalin's regime. Bailie recites the story in *Violence Unveiled.* "She loved her father," Chambers writes, "and the irrationality of his defection embarrassed her. 'He was immensely pro-Soviet,' she said, 'and then—you will laugh at me—but you must not laugh at my father—and then—one night—in Moscow—he heard screams. That's all. Simply one night he heard screams.'"[36]

Because of the cross our culture hears the screams. The imperial ideologies of power would silence them, but the Gospels force us to listen to them and respond to the cries of the victim.

REVELATION AND THE JUDGMENT OF GOD

It is generally agreed that the book of Revelation was written during the reign of Domitian. It is also generally agreed that there was no empire-wide persecution during his reign but rather nagging local oppression and a rising insistence that Christians participate in the emperor cult and other civic/religious activities. John of Patmos addresses his work to seven churches in Asia Minor, not simply or even principally to comfort them in the face of persecution, but to warn them in no uncertain terms about compromise with the empire. His strong words suggest that some Christians were willing to make what they considered minor compromises to preserve their livelihood and their honor. His prophecy minces no words in his condemnation of the empire. John and his community could clearly have been seen as a threat to the vaunted "Pax Romana."

The Pax Romana was a peace purchased through violence and the threat of violence. It was a peace "secured from the centre of power, above all by military means, on orders going out from the metropolis and oriented to it."[37] Peace was for people in Rome—violence and oppression continued at the borders. As Horace said, "who cares about war in wild Spain."[38] Augustus exposed the nature of the Roman peace when he stated with no doubt unintentional irony, "The provinces of the Gauls, the Spains and Germany I reduced to a state of peace."[39] There was "peace" as long as the conquered people did exactly what Rome said and provided exactly what Rome demanded. As one conquered foe put it, "The Romans make a desolation and call it peace."[40] Jesus was crucified, no doubt, as a threat to the Pax Romana.

John of Patmos saw his community locked in a struggle with the empire and its version of "peace." This struggle threatened the integrity of the community through compromise and even the lives of its members through martyrdom. How will he address both his community and the empire? How will he prepare them for the internal and external threats to their communal and individual lives? Revelation is often seen as a grim and humorless book, but Harry O. Maier is convinced there is a good deal of sly humor. With David Aune, Sophie Laws, and others Maier insists Revelation is full of *parody* and *irony*. John of Patmos everywhere seeks to bring the empire down a notch and mock its pretensions to ultimacy and power.

Maier offers the following definition:

> The term *parody* in these studies [those of Aune, Laws, and Eugene Boring] describes the masquerade of an emperor and his minions wanting to play God. The Apocalypse's parody capitalizes on mistaken identities. For John power and might do not belong to the Roman Empire and its henchmen, but to God and the Lamb. God/the Lamb, not the emperor, is the one who goes forth to conquer the nations (19:11–16). John makes fun by representing the emperor and his supporters as dissembling fakes.[41]

How was this done? The primary parody and irony is the prominence of the "slaughtered lamb." Revelation 4 ushers the reader into the divine throne room which itself parodies the Roman imperial court and its ceremonies.[42] All the exclamations of praise and luxury of the throne room "belongs to the drama and ritual of the Roman court. . . . [E]mperors from Julius Caesar onward wrapped themselves in Jupiter's clothing to reinforce the claims of their dynasty to divine sonship and inevitable apotheosis."[43] The throne room scene would be familiar, but "what follows . . . is sharply disjunctive. John sees the 'Lamb . . . standing, as though it had been slain, with seven horns and seven eyes.' This vision of the Lamb, standing in profound tension with the immediately preceding image of the conquering 'lion of the tribe of Judah,' marks an outcome that contradicts, if not mocks, all the high-sounding court language that precedes it."[44] Maier concludes, "John portrays the slain Lamb as the subversive double of imperial power."[45]

Richard Bauckham argues that John uses the themes and language of the "messianic war" and of the "divine warrior" of the OT and Jewish messianic hopes.[46] However:

> John carefully reinterprets the tradition. His Messiah Jesus does not win his victory by military conquests, and those who share his victory and his rule are not national Israel but the international people of God. But still it is a victory over evil, won not only in the spiritual but also in the political sphere against worldly powers in order to establish God's kingdom on earth. Insofar as the hope for the Davidic Messiah was for such a victory of God over evil, Revelation portrays Christ's work in continuity with that traditional Jewish hope.[47]

The followers of the lamb participate in the victory not by acts of violence and bloodshed but by *witness*. "Just as 5:5–6 depicts Jesus Christ as the Messiah who has won a victory, but has done so by his sacrificial death, not by military power, so 7:4–14 depicts his followers as the people of the Messiah who share in his victory, but do so similarly, by sacrificial death rather than by military conquest."[48] In ch. 14 the 144,000 follow the lamb "wherever he goes." For Bauckham this means "imitating both his truthfulness, as 'the faithful witness' and the sacrificial death to which this led. Thus the victory of the Lamb's army is the victory of truthful witness maintained as far as sacrificial death."[49]

The Lamb won the victory through death and witness. His final victory over the forces of evil will be won by a "sharp sword" coming out of his mouth (Rev 19:15). Messiah here wins his victory by his *word*. And so do his followers: "The martyrs conquer not only by their suffering and death as such, but by their faithful *witness* to the point of death (cf. 12:11). Their witness to the truth prevails over the lies and deceit of the devil and the beast. For those who reject this witness, it becomes legal testimony *against* them securing their condemnation. But it entails also a positive possibility: that people may be won from illusion to truth."[50]

The book of Revelation does not offer the slightest support to Christians acting violently toward their "enemies." It offers no encouragement to mob violence and scapegoating. On the contrary, it offers the example of the slaughtered lamb who is victorious through death and witness, who seeks all the way to the end, to the very point of final judgment, to turn his opponents into followers. Even though John of Patmos is clear about the violence and abuse of the empire, he does not permit the churches of Asia Minor to withdraw in disgust, compromise in fear, or attack with violence. He requires and models the much harder task of faithful and risky witness.

A GIRARDIAN ANALYSIS OF REVELATION 17 AND 18

This does not mean there will be no judgment. The empire *is* doomed, but how will it fall? Is the violence suffered by the empire the result of God's direct action or of the empire's own sins and weaknesses—or both? What actually brings the empire down? It could be argued that John viewed the downfall of the empire not so much as a direct act of God as the natural result of its own abuses. Perhaps Girard would see the collapse as a result of uncontrolled mimetic desires, scapegoating, and inevitable violence.

In chs. 17 and 18 John describes the fall of Rome/Babylon, the "great whore." Its fall represents the ongoing "mimetic" crisis of human culture and the violence it entails. The "whore" is obviously an object of desire. The "kings of the earth" have fornicated with her. The merchants of the earth have profited from her desires. The shipmaster and seafarers have grown wealthy from her trade. The political and economic elites have profited from the empire. But, John tells us, "the waters . . . are peoples and multitudes and nations and languages. And the ten horns that you saw, they and the beast will hate the whore" (Rev 17:15–16). These forces under the sway of the whore "will make her desolate and naked; they will devour her flesh and burn her with fire."

Rome's power, wealth, and protection are irresistible. Its "wine of fornication" is intoxicating. All the inhabitants of the earth have become "drunk" on this wine. In addition to these intoxicants Rome drew to it "purple and scarlet, gold and jewels and pearls"—highly desirable luxury goods. Rome also revealed an addiction to violence—it was drunk with the blood of the saints (Rev 18). In a typical mimetic crisis the crowd turns on the whore that has brought it such desirable goods and then destroys her. After participating in destroying her, it mourns! The kings of the earth that participated in her destruction "weep and wail," as do the merchants and seamen. The empire contained all the objects of their desire, but they destroyed it. In one sense, God did not need to lift a finger against the "whore"; the very people that sought her favor sought her destruction.

Here John of Patmos reveals the peril of empire: to be admired, used, and hated all at the same time. No wonder he warns, "Come out of her, my people, so that you do not take part in her sins, and so that you do not share in her plagues" (Rev 18:4). However the empire abused them, the people of God were not involved in her destruction. They were not to destroy but to bear witness. They were not to participate in the "scapegoating" of the empire. In a strange way the empire becomes a victim. Even though it was guilty of many sins, it was only a link in the chain of ongoing violence, and its destruction will not end that violence. A new crisis will arise. A new victim will be identified. A new mob will be formed. And the victim will be destroyed—and then mourned.

The book of Revelation suggests that in the end the empire victimizes itself. With Girard, "Apocalyptic prophecy means no more and no less than a rational anticipation of what men are likely to do to each other and to their environment, if they go on disregarding the [Gospel's] warnings against revenge in a desacralized and sacrificially unprotected world."[51] In spite of the plagues and horrors the empire brought upon itself, John says the people still refused to turn away from their idolatries and violence (see Rev 9:20–21).

On the historical plane the empire generates envy, desire, and finally hatred and violence. Once it is destroyed, the envy and desire simply relocate themselves. A new "empire" seeks to reclaim its place and the cycle starts again. More envy is created along with more victims and more violence. But John tells his people to come out and be separate. Christianity seeks to break the pattern of envy, victimization, and violence. Christianity attacks envy and desire, not because Christians despise desire per se or are seeking a state of "apathy," but because our desires are disordered. Christians differentiate between desire as envy and desire as love. Mimetic desire, envy that produces violence, is what Paul would call lust (see Rom 7). James 4:1–4 powerfully describes this process of envy and desire leading to violence.

John of Patmos acts to break this pattern of desire and violence by insisting that Christians follow the slaughtered lamb in sacrifice and witness. In the end Revelation is *not* about the crowd acting on behalf of God to bring about divine vengeance against the empire. This role, in fact, is specifically denied the crowd; the church is *not* to scapegoat. Rather it bears along with the slaughtered lamb the role of the final scapegoat that ends all scapegoating. It is, as Paul puts it, crucified with Christ. It joins the lamb in nonviolent and compassionate witness.

All this does not rob from God the right to render judgment. God's final judgment is just because it is God *alone* who renders judgment and not the crowd. Those judged are not innocent victims but evil oppressors. There is justice for those crying out from beneath the altar. But as Harry O. Maier points out, even here John has a surprise for us. He accuses John of "destabilizing" his own message. What about "all those once hostile kings and nations whom we thought were slain, deceived by Satan, or cast into the lake of burning fire (Rev 19:17–21, 20:7–10, 15)"? Now they "appear suddenly on the scene again. No longer enemies, they are worshippers, bearing their honor and glory into the city (21:24, 25)."[52] A dramatic reversal? Perhaps. As Bauckham puts it, John longs not so much for the judgment of the nations as their conversion.[53] Miroslav Volf has suggested that in the end perhaps only God can legitimately use violence for the sake of judgment.[54] Perhaps so. But even then, Revelation seems to say that in the end even God's judgment will be the result of a stubborn refusal of God's grace freely offered.

READING AS LAODICEANS

Maier is writing for mainline (or what he calls "sidelined") churches who often turn up their noses at the book of Revelation. He argues that the book's warning about compromise with empire is too important for such heirs of Christendom to ignore. He calls these churches to read as "Laodiceans," ostensibly rich and comfortable communities that because of their compromises with the empire are "wretched, pitiful, poor, blind, and naked" (Rev 3:17). He continues: "At the end of Christendom the Christian church exists to insist on the troubling story of the cross and to form this-worldly believers who contribute to and enrich pluralistic society through lives of spirited public witness to the God incarnate in Jesus of Nazareth, who reveals a way of being human on terms other than the insatiable desire for more, military domination and national security."[55] Yes, and the church exists to expose those and other desires for what they are—envy that leads to victimization that leads to violence. The scapegoats are abundant. Our "deformed desire" continues to lead us to idolatry, lust, and violence.

Maier writes:

> Francis Fukuyama heralds this as the advent of "the end of history," brought to you by the victory of capitalism over communism. Sure, he admits, the sheer boredom of consumerism [organized mimetic desires?], and hence the advent of Nietzsche's "last man"—the modern citizen consumed with triviality, a slave to the mediocrity of creature comforts—threatens the new world order. So there will always be the temptation to return to "the first men" of bloody history, if for no other reason than to interrupt our lives of interminable consumerist boredom.[56]

The group, the mob, always seeks to coalesce its desires. The howling mobs of the "Muslim street" and post 9/11 flag-waving crowds in the United States eager to get revenge are both manifestations of this phenomenon, of mimetic desire that finds "peace" in a common enemy, a victim—but only for a time. Christians who follow the lamb make no scapegoats, seek no victims, and engage in no violence. By this means we bear witness to God's love that seeks the good, the life, and the health of all, even our "enemies."

Evangelical churches need this warning no less than Maier's mainline community. In the United States at least, the prominence and power of Evangelicalism could make of it a new Christendom. Its over-identification with the Republican Party and its political fortunes risk making it simply another tool of the empire, a chaplain for the powerful. Evangelicals are called no less than the mainline to a Laodicean reading of Revelation lest we find ourselves making our offering to the genius of the emperor and participating in the gratuitous violence that preserves imperial power. We are to "come out and be separate" while we bear witness to the "slaughtered lamb" who has already won the victory through suffering and witness. Evangelicals in popular magazines, television shows, and radio broadcasts are these days engaged in a full-scale scapegoating of the culture. Envy and "mimetic desire" are thinly veiled in these attacks on the "empire" by people who are, in fact, fully compromised with the empire and its power. Violence is just beneath the surface. The book of Revelation invites us by our nonviolent witness, by our refusal to join in the popular scapegoating of our culture, and by following the slaughtered lamb to expose the rage and violence at the heart of human culture—including the Evangelical community. It insists that we follow the lamb in suffering and witness and leave ultimate judgment to God, who is still willing that no one should perish but that all would come to repentance.

Neither Girard's theory of scapegoating violence nor John's vision of the slaughtered lamb answers all the questions about the violence of God in the book of Revelation, let alone the violence of God in the rest of the Bible. And yet, together they may "destabilize" our tendency to use violence against attractive scapegoats both in and out of the church. And perhaps the cross itself calls for the reframing of God's violence, if not God's judgment. With Girard in his conclusion to *The Scapegoat*:

> In future, all violence will reveal what Christ's Passion revealed, the foolish Genesis of bloodstained idols and the false gods of religion, politics, and ideologies. The murderers remain convinced of the worthiness of their sacrifices. They too know not what they do and we must forgive them. The time has come for us to forgive one another. If we wait any longer there will not be time enough.[57]

ENDNOTES

1. Clarence Larkin, *Dispensational Truth or God's Plan and Purpose for the Ages* (Philadelphia: Author, 1920).
2. Cited by Harry O. Maier, *Apocalypse Recalled* (Minneapolis: Fortress, 2002), 1.
3. Cited by Maier, 164.
4. Cited by Maier, 47.
5. Cited by Leonard L. Thompson, *The Book of Revelation* (Oxford: Oxford University Press, 1990), 4.
6. Maier, 165.
7. Jack Nelson-Pallmeyer, *Is Religion Killing Us?* (Harrisburg, Pa: Trinity Press International, 2003), 7.
8. Both cited by Nelson-Pallmeyer, 12.
9. Mark Noll, "The Civil War as a Crisis Over the Interpretation of the Bible," and "The Civil War as a Crisis over the Meaning of Providence," The Nyvall Lectures, given at North Park Theological Seminary, March 31, 2004.
10. Cited by Nelson-Pallmeyer, 4.
11. Nelson-Pallmeyer, 10.
12. Stanley N. Gundry, ed., *Show Them No Mercy* (Grand Rapids: Zondervan, 2003), 91.
13. Gil Bailie, *Violence Unveiled* (New York: Crossroad, 1997), 15.
14. René Girard, *Violence and the Sacred* (trans. Patrick Gregory; Baltimore: Johns Hopkins University Press, 1977); *Things Hidden Since the Foundation of the World* (trans. Stephen Bann and Michael Metteer; Stanford: Stanford University Press, 1987); *The Scapegoat* (trans. Yvonne Freccero; Baltimore: Johns Hopkins University Press, 1986); *I See Satan Fall Like Lightning* (trans. James G. Williams; Maryknoll, N.Y.: Orbis, 2001).

15. See the works of Bailie; Anthony W. Bartlett, *Cross Purposes* (Harrisburg, Pa: Trinity International Press, 2001); Robert G. Hamerton-Kelly, *Sacred Violence* (Minneapolis: Fortress, 1992); Raymund Schwager, *Must There Be Scapegoats?* (trans. Maria L. Assad; San Francisco: Harper and Row, 1987); J. Denny Weaver, *The Nonviolent Atonement* (Grand Rapids: Eerdmans, 2001); James G. Williams, *The Bible, Violence, and the Sacred* (SanFrancisco: HarperSanFrancisco, 1991).

16. Hamerton-Kelly, 19.
17. Ibid., 20.
18. Ibid., 21.
19. Ibid., 25–28.
20. Bailie, 6–7.
21. René Girard, *Job: The Victim of His People* (trans. Yvonne Freccero; Stanford: Stanford University Press, 1987), 4–5.
22. Girard, *The Scapegoat*, 2.
23. Ibid., 1.
24. Ibid., 15.
25. Ibid., 17.
26. Girard, *I See Satan Fall Like Lightning,* 1.
27. Girard, *Job: The Victim of His People*, 35.
28. Ibid., 5, 36, 39.
29. Girard, *I See Satan Fall Like Lightning,* 2.
30. Ibid., 13.
31. Ibid., 14.
32. Ibid., 140.
33. Ibid.
34. Ibid., 174.
35. Hamerton-Kelly, 39.
36. Baile, 35.
37. Klaus Wengt, *Pax Romana and the Peace of Jesus Christ* (trans. John Bowden; London: SCM, 1987), 4.
38. Ibid., 12.
39. Ibid., 18.
40. Ibid., 52. Calgaccus' entire speech is well worth reading for the effects of empire on the "frontiers."
41. Maier, 166, 167.
42. David E. Aune, "The Influence of Roman Imperial Court Ceremonial on the Apocalypse of John," *Biblical Research* 28 (1983): 5–26.
43. Maier, 174.
44. Ibid., 175.
45. Ibid., 179.
46. Richard Bauckham, *The Climax of Prophecy* (Edinburgh: T. & T. Clark, 1993), 210–237; and *The Theology of the Book of Revelation* (Cambridge: Cambridge University Press, 1993), 66–108.
47. Bauckham, *The Theology of the Book of Revelation*, 68.
48. Ibid., 77.
49. Ibid., 79.
50. Bauckham, *The Climax of Prophecy*, 237.
51. Bailie, 16.
52. Maier, 168.
53. Bauckham, *The Climax of Prophecy*, 238f.

54. Miroslav Volf, *Exclusion and Embrace* (Nashville: Abingdon, 1996), 301.
55. Maier, 28.
56. Ibid., 23.
57. Girard, *The Scapegoat*, 212.

RESPONSE TO PHELAN

GRANT R. OSBORNE

The main thesis of Phelan's paper provides a very important caution in our day of a rampant patriotism that can turn violent for little reason. In a time of racial profiling, with tribalism a worldwide phenomenon, it is ever so important to make certain that no one misuses the apocalyptic imagery of Revelation to condone violence. It is absolutely critical to realize that the only violence against the ungodly in the book is done by God, and the saints are called to "fight back" only through bold witness, not with fists or guns (contra *Left Behind*!). So let me support Jay's important paper by expanding on two of his points.

Violence and the Saints. In the Middle Ages during the time of the pogroms, so-called Christians would use the book of Revelation as an excuse to persecute and even kill Jewish people in the name of divine judgment. Yet what does Revelation say is the task of the saints in the events portrayed? That is actually quite clear when we look at the details of this work more carefully. The saints are especially addressed in two sections, the letters to the seven churches (chs. 2–3) and the interludes that break up the three judgment septets of chs. 6–16 (7:1–17; 10:1–11:13; 12:1–14:20). The seals, trumpets, and bowls tell of the judgments of God poured down on the earthdwellers (the saints are protected—3:10; 7:4–8; 11:1–2), and one of the major purposes of the interludes is to tell the part the saints will play in those scenes.

It is clear in the letters of chs. 2–3 that the churches are filled with troubles, and the persecution they are enduring (actually directly mentioned in only two—Smyrna and Philadelphia) is not the most serious problem. The major difficulty is a spiritual complacency and lethargy that parallels Heb 5:11–6:3. The biggest need is repentance in the light of a cold orthodoxy (Ephesus), syncretism (Pergamum and Thyatira), secularity (Sardis), and materialism (Laodicea) that is about to bring God's wrath down on them! A major theme in the book is the need for perseverance, seen in the promise of each letter to the "overcomers" (those who are victorious over these serious sins, 2:7, 11, 17, 26; 3:5, 12, 21) as well as in the many passages calling for a renewed faithfulness to God. Jesus provides the model of "faithful witness" in 1:5 and 3:14 and in becoming the "slain lamb" (5:5) who wins the victory over Satan with his death. In addition, other passages call for persevering faithfulness as well (1:9; 2:10, 25–26; 3:3, 10–11; 14:4–5, 12; 16:15; 17:14; 21:7–8; 22:7, 10, 12, 14).

With regard to the issue of violence, a startling passage in the middle of the appearance of the two beasts in ch. 13 is revealing. In 13:9–10 the saints are told, "If any are to go into captivity, into captivity they will go; if any are to be killed with the sword, with the sword they will be killed. This calls for patient endurance and faithfulness on the part of God's people." It is clear that the only human violence in the book is enacted by the evildoers, not the saints. Theirs is on the one hand a passive reaction to the violence enacted against them and on the other a bold witness as seen in the two witnesses (a symbol of the church) in 11:3–6. The saints will neither be cowering in bomb shelters or forests nor fighting back against the forces of evil. Rather, they will be standing up for the Lord in an evil world. Moreover, for them martyrdom is their victory. One of the great ironic passages is 13:7 where God allows the beast ("was given" is a divine passive meaning God has authorized the action of the beast) to "make war against the saints and conquer them." Yet in fact the saints have already "conquered" (same verb) the dragon "by the blood of the Lamb and by the word of their testimony, and they did not love their lives so much as to shrink from death" (12:11). In other words, Satan in taking their lives has participated in his own defeat! This reproduces the death of Christ, when Satan also participated in his own defeat when he entered Judas and led Christ to the cross!

To summarize, this process of passive reaction to violence is the true pattern of the book for the saints. Phelan's use of Rene Girard's principle of "mimesis" is quite informative and helpful in this regard. Not only is Jesus the true "scapegoat" who alone has substituted for our sins on the cross, but the Book of Revelation contains another mimetic element that defines the process. Jesus as the "slain lamb" in 5:5–6 conquers through passive yielding of himself to the hatred of humanity in order to achieve salvation as the atoning sacrifice. His followers are called to follow his model in four stages. They too are: (1) to remain passive to the programmed violence committed against them (13:10); (2) instead of returning violence, leave the vengeance with God (6:9–11); (3) meet the violence with bold witness (11:3–6, the mimesis of Jesus as "faithful witness" in 1:3; 3:14); and (4) accept the violence and even the martyrdom, thereby triumphing over the powers of evil in the process (12:11).

The Violence of God. The ultraviolent nature of the book has caused many (like D. H. Lawrence or George Bernard Shaw) to decry the Book of Revelation as a sub-Christian book not worthy to be in the canon. Yet that is based on a surface reading of the book. In fact, Revelation sums up the theme of the Bible regarding God's violent response to evil. It is clear that God is not an angry teenager getting even with the people he does not like. The problem with many is an inadequate understanding of the nature of sin and God. God is misdefined as purely a loving God who will automatically forgive sin. Love is not the key characteristic of God. In Revelation (and, I think, all of Scripture) God is predominantly a holy God (cf. Isa 6:3 = Rev 4:8), and under his holiness there are two interdependent aspects of his character, his justice and his love. These are not antithetical but work together in his relations with humanity. In Revelation judgment is a primary aspect, but it must be remembered that the book details the final eradication of sin and evil. Many fail to realize that sin is absolutely an abomination to a holy God. The true antithesis is not between God's justice and love but between his holiness and evil in this world. In fact, as in the OT, judgment is an aspect of his love, for it provides an opportunity for repentance. For Israel the cycle of judgment, repentance, forgiveness was an ongoing phenomenon, and the purpose of judgment was to bring the nation back to God.

Perhaps the best way to see this in the book is to study the theological themes of the three judgment septets—the seals, trumpets, and bowls. First, we must begin with the theme of judgment. The "wrath of God/the Lamb" is a critical aspect (6:16–17; 11:18; 14:10, 15:1, 7; 16:1, 19; 19:15), but it must be understood via the major theme—divine justice. The principle of *lex talionis* (the law of retribution) defined the law of the OT, Roman law, and the law of God. Eight times in the book the principle of "judged by your works" is found, used of both believers (2:23; 11:18; 14:13; 22:12) and unbelievers (18:6; 11:18; 20:12, 13). The message is that God's judgment is absolutely just and true (cf. also 15:3; 16:5–7) and was based on the deeds of the people.

In fact, theodicy is a major theme, explaining the necessity of eternal punishment. The absolute depravity of humankind is spelled out again and again. Whenever they are given an opportunity to repent, the earthdwellers refuse to do so (9:20–21; 16:9, 11, 21). Moreover, however one interprets the thousand year reign, in the story form of 20:1–10 the people of the "nations" (20:3, 8) have had one lifetime with Satan and fourteen lifetimes (70 years x 14 = 980 years) with Christ; yet as soon as Satan is released, they desert Christ and flock to him. Those who think a loving God in a billion years will get Hitler and Stalin to repent are wrong. They do not understand the nature of sin. In a billion years Hitler and Stalin will hate God more than they did on the day they died! In other words, Revelation proves that a just God has no choice but to send the nations into eternal punishment, for sin is an eternal force in each of them.

Second, the judgments actually have a redemptive purpose and are part of a mission theme in the book. We have already noted that four times we are told the earthdwellers refuse to repent. This must entail their reaction to a call to get right with God, especially when 14:6–7 tells us an angel flies through the air with the "eternal gospel" proclaiming, "Fear God and give him glory, because his hour of judgment has come." So the judgments are part of this call to repentance. The trumpet and bowl judgments reproduce the ten plagues of Egypt in Exodus, and their purpose was to show that the Egyptian gods were powerless, no more than forces of nature, and that Yahweh alone had power over the natural elements. The judgments have the same purpose here and disprove the earthly gods, showing that God alone is worthy of worship (4:11; 5:12). In other words, they provide a final opportunity to repent.

Third, there is a progressive dismantling of creation as the seal judgments destroy a quarter of the earth, the trumpets a third of the earth, and the bowls affect the whole earth. This prepares for the destruction of all the earth, as seen in 20:11 ("earth and sky fled from his presence, and there was no place for them") and 21:1 ("the first heaven and the first earth had passed away," cf. 2 Pet 3:7, 10). Yet this is not merely an act of judgment but entails the transformation of creation to make way for the "new heaven and new earth" of 21:1. Moreover, this is in keeping with Rom 8:19–22, which tells us that creation itself is "groaning" in "eager expectation" of the day when it will be released and right now is in "frustration," longing to be liberated from its "bondage to decay" caused by the sin and death humanity brought into the world. In short, even in the destruction of this present creation there is a redemptive purpose behind it all.

In conclusion, there is a great deal of violence associated with the judgment of God in this book, but it is at all times just and has a deeper purpose, namely the offer of salvation and the transformation of this sin-impoverished world into the final perfect home for God's people throughout eternity. Moreover, the violence is divine judgment and never employed by the people of God. The saints will be part of the army that accompanies Christ in his second coming as conqueror (17:14; 19:14), but they will not participate in the fighting, as the sword comes out of his mouth and destroys the armies of the beast in a millisecond. There is no battle. As Jay Phelan says in his excellent paper, anyone using Revelation to justify violence "in the name of God" is making a horrible misuse of the book.

JUSTICE AND JUDGMENT IN THE BOOK OF JEREMIAH: DISCERNING THE BOUNDARIES OF GOD'S WRATH

PAMELA J. SCALISE

A God who executes judgments is not an attractive or comfortable figure. Casual observers of the Bible often assign this character to the OT and draw a sharp distinction between the "angry old man" of the old covenant and the compassionate Christ of the new. The purpose of this symposium is to gain a better understanding of biblical teaching on divine judgment in the theological reflection of the church. This paper will attempt to present aspects of the God of justice revealed in the OT, illustrated primarily from the book of Jeremiah.

The "angry old man" picture will not be replaced by a "kindly grandfather," however. Reflection on the judgment of God brings one immediately to the interface between divine goodness and human failings. God would not need to rescue the oppressed, if there were no oppressors. God would not need to decide cases, if there were no disputes. God would not need to put a stop to wickedness, if no one acted wickedly. Most of the OT testimony about God's just judgments has to do with the people Israel. The Lord's passionate attachment to Israel is imaged as that of a husband to his wife, a father or mother to a child, a shepherd to the sheep, and, especially, as a monarch to his subjects. Because of the intensely personal nature of these relationships, human-like emotions—anthropopathisms—are ascribed to God in response to circumstances that call for divine justice. God's wrath and jealousy, on the one hand, and mercy and love, on the other, accompany and motivate the divine judgments. The Lord's power and authority as Creator extend the realm of passionate commitment in other OT texts to include justice for the whole earth. When divine power encounters human rebellion, physical force or verbal violence are factors on both sides.

GOD'S JUST JUDGMENT: A REASON FOR PRAISE AND THANKSGIVING

In the OT God's judgment is first of all a reason for praise and thanksgiving (e.g., Pss 48:12; 67:5; 99:4–5; 111:2, 7–9).[1] Jeremiah 9:23–24 states:

> Thus says the Lord: Let not the wise boast of wisdom, let not the
> strong boast of strength, let not the rich boast of riches; but rather
> let the one who boasts boast[2] of comprehending and knowing me, that I
> am the Lord; I do steadfast love, justice, and righteousness in the earth,
> for in these things I delight—utterance of the Lord.[3]

God's rule is known to be righteous, faithful, loving, compassionate, merciful, and just. Such a reign is beneficial for its subjects, blessing them and doing good for them, creating flourishing families, communities, nations, and a world at peace.

Psalm 72 gives an extended description of the benefits of being ruled by a human king whose reign is an expression of God's sovereignty. It begins with a petition for the foundational gifts of justice and righteousness: "Give to the king your justice, O God, and to the royal heir your righteousness." The blessings of prosperity (Ps 72:3, 6–7) and security (Ps 72:8–11) are made possible by these endowments. The structure and grammar of this psalm indicate a causal connection between the king doing justice and the nation receiving these blessings. The promise of prosperity or well-being, *šālôm*, in v. 3 stands within an envelope formed by two verses about the king's care for the afflicted and poor by means of just judgment. In v. 2 the king judges (*dîn*) the "afflicted ones" with justice (*mišpāṭ*) and in v. 4 he judges (*šāpaṭ*) the afflicted and crushes the oppressor. The king will nourish the people like rain, the righteous will flourish, and the other kings and nations will submit to his enduring rule (Ps 72:5–11) *because* he will deliver, take pity on, save, and rescue the needy and afflicted from oppression and violence (Ps 72:12–14). This ideal description of royal rule does not praise cool, objective legal proceedings in which evidence is examined dispassionately. The psalm bases its hopes for abundant harvests and peace on the king who, by God's grace, helps the oppressed who have no other helper and who values their lives more than gold (Ps 72:12–17).

JUDGMENTS IN COURT

Moses (Deut 1:17), local judges (Deut 16:18–20; Judg 4:5; 2 Chr 19:5–8), and the levitical priests at the sanctuary (Deut 17:8–13) had the authority to decide cases, but the king's authority was the penultimate recourse. Absalom built up a following for his claim to the throne by waylaying people who came to Jerusalem for a decision by the king with complaints about the inefficiency of the royal court system (2 Sam 15:1–6). Solomon made the famous decision regarding the infant who was claimed by two mothers. In this judgment he settled the case by forcing the parties to reveal the truth, yet no one suffered additional loss. His decision rewarded the mother who gave up her claim in order to save her child's life. "When all Israel heard the verdict the king had given, they were in awe before the king, because they saw that the wisdom of God was within him to do justice" (1 Kgs 3:28). This gift of discernment for making just judgments provides the foundation for Solomon's other successes as king. After observing Solomon's reign, the Queen of Sheba concludes that just governance is evidence of God's love: "Because of the Lord's eternal love for Israel, he has made you king to maintain justice and righteousness" (1 Kgs 10:9, NIV).

Other passages affirm that God is the ultimate judge in interpersonal disputes. God is approached as a court of appeal. "Many seek an audience with a ruler, but it is from the Lord that man gets justice" (Prov 29:26, NIV). "You judge not on behalf of human beings but on the Lord's behalf, who is with you when you render a judgment" (2 Chr 19:6). Since there was no higher human authority, David the anointed fugitive lays his case against Saul before the Lord in 1 Sam 24:15: "May the Lord be our judge and decide between us." The prayer of Solomon in 1 Kgs 8 asks for the Lord's help in a series of difficult circumstances. The first of these is the case when an accused person swears an oath at the altar that he is innocent. Solomon's prayer asks God to judge between the parties in each dispute to determine who is guilty and who is innocent (1 Kgs 8:31–32). More than any human judge, the Lord "searches minds and examines hearts" and thus renders true judgments (Jer 17:10). The just resolution of disputes between nations will bring an end to war in the new era promised in Isa 2:4 and Mic 4:4.

The effective operation of judgments in the court is the best hope for justice within communities. Defending the rights of the poor and oppressed is not simply a matter of taking their side in partiality. It is for the good of the whole people when the weakest ones live full and secure lives (e.g., Zech 8:3–4). God's judgments are the final hope for establishing justice and righteousness in the earth (Ps 82).

KINGS DO JUSTICE AND RIGHTEOUSNESS

To do justice and righteousness was God's requirement of every king and government for the sake of the people. Jeremiah 21:12 and 22:2–3 address the Davidic king with a series of commands that should characterize God's realm, with 22:3 being the most specific:

> Do justice and righteousness. Deliver from the hand of the oppressor the one who has been seized. Do not hand over and do not do violence to the sojourner, the orphan, or the widow, and do not shed innocent blood in this place.

Each of these imperatives may apply specifically to judicial procedures or more broadly to interaction with the people.

Second Samuel 8:15 summarizes David's monarchy by saying, "David reigned, doing justice and righteousness." Similarly, Jer 22:15b–16 lifts up Josiah's exemplary reign:

> As for your father, didn't he eat and drink and do justice and righteousness? Then it was well with him. He pled the cause of the poor and needy. Then it was well with him. Is not that what it is to know me?— Utterance of the Lord.

This description appears in the midst of an oracle against Jehoiakim, Josiah's son, that accuses the king himself of being the very kind of oppressor from whom he should have delivered the people. Jehoiakim was using forced labor (corvée) to construct a new palace for himself in spite of imminent international peril.[4] Note Jeremiah's complaint against him:

> Woe to the one who builds his house by unrighteousness, and his upper stories by injustice, by making his countryman serve for nothing, and not paying him his wages. (Jer 22:13)

> But your eyes and your heart are set only on gain made by violence. (Jer 22:17b)

Jeremiah contrasts Jehoiakim's striving for dishonest gain with Josiah's defense of the needy (Jer 22:16–17). The abuse of forced labor for royal construction projects constitutes oppression and extortion that might have extended as far as costing the workers their lives. Jehoiakim was at least robbing his subjects of their strength, time, and the produce of their labor in their own fields. Jeremiah 26:20–23 describes Jehoiakim's murder of Uriah, who had prophesied the same message as Jeremiah. The first part of the chapter recounts the trial of Jeremiah on a capital charge because of this prophecy (Jer 26:1–19). He argues that his accusers would "bring the guilt of innocent blood" on themselves and on Jerusalem if they were to put him to death for speaking God's word (Jer 26:15). The court acquits Jeremiah, but Uriah does not even have a trial. The juxtaposition of the two accounts clearly indicates that Jehoiakim had shed innocent blood when he had Uriah put to death.

The Lord's superiority as ruler and judge is described in a long promise passage in Ezek 34:1–31. This chapter portrays the relationship between the nation and its rulers under the image of the flock and its shepherds. This image of royal rule communicates the caring commitment of the shepherd and the absolute dependence of the sheep. Good shepherds provide abundant pasture and water, they search for and bring back lost sheep, and they tend to the injured and weak members of the flock (Ezek 34:11–16). Israel's human shepherds had failed to care for the flock in this way. They had exposed them to wild animals and even devoured sheep themselves (34:5, 8). God promises to depose the predatory leaders and "shepherd the flock with justice (*mišpāṭ*)" (Ezek 34:16). At this point in the passage the pastoral metaphor begins to break down. One expects a shepherd to make every effort to preserve the lives of sick and injured sheep, but what shepherd would destroy[5] the strongest, fattest members of the flock? Yet that is what the Lord as shepherd promises to do in Ezek 34:16–22. The flock as a whole is safe under God's care, but one aspect of this care is judging between one sheep and another within the flock (Ezek 34:17, 20, 22). The fat and strong sheep deprive the lean and weak sheep of food and water by trampling the pasture, muddying the water, and driving them away. Therefore, but illogically, God will remove the fat sheep from the flock in order to save the weak ones.

JUDGMENT AS VINDICATION

God's judgment is a means of salvation for oppressed people. Decisions in court that vindicate the rights of the weak are acts of deliverance that restore their lives. The just judge defends the rights and the lives of people who have no one else to speak on their behalf. For example, Jeremiah asks God to save his life by judging the men from his hometown who are seeking to kill him (Jer 11:18–20).[6] The archetypical deliverance of Israel from Egypt is also described in terms of judgment. The Lord redeemed Israel "with mighty acts of judgment" (Exod 6:6; 7:4) and "judgment on all the gods of Egypt" (Exod 12:12; cf. Num 33:4). According to 2 Chr 20:12, King Jehoshaphat prayed for God's help against invaders from Ammon, Moab, and Edom by asking for judgment on behalf of the weak: ". . . will you not execute judgment upon them? For we are powerless against this great multitude that is coming against us" (NRSV). A single act of justice as vindication, therefore, may simultaneously punish the guilty and demonstrate faithfulness to the victim (Exod 34:6–7).

Judgment that saves is good news for the powerless. Throughout the OT the covenant people were small, weak, possessed little land, and lacked other material resources in comparison with the great empires that periodically conquered and controlled the region. Israel is the center of attention in God's Word, but it was of little account in the politics of the ancient Near East. All but a tiny fraction of the population survived precariously as farmers. They had so little that any loss was potentially life-threatening.[7] Jeremiah ministered in and to the nation of Judah when it had been reduced by invasion, conquest, and vassalage to Egypt and then Babylon. The final conquest, exile, and loss of king, capital, and temple also happened to Judah during his ministry. Jeremiah 30:13 describes their abandonment: "There is no one to plead your cause, no remedy for your sore, no healing for you." Indeed, the final form of each of the prophetic books or collections is addressed to God's people after they have been reduced to nearly nothing.[8] For such people there is abundant cause to give thanks and praise to a mighty God who loves justice.[9]

WRATH, JEALOUSY, VENGEANCE, AND VIOLENT JUDGMENT

The Lord does justice for the oppressed individual or nation as a response to their cries for help in their misery and distress. This response flows from a passionate attachment characterized by love, faithfulness, mercy, and pity. Metaphors of relationships that create passionate attachment are used in Jeremiah and elsewhere to bind together these attractive characteristics with the terrifying expressions of divine wrath, vengeance, and jealousy in judgment. God as king (or shepherd, husband, parent, potter, farmer) displays the powerful emotions that a human being would feel toward beloved subjects (or flock, wife, child, pottery vessel, crop) that had betrayed or rebelled against God. The Lord also appears in Jeremiah as the Creator with authority to govern creation (Jer 27:5) and even to destroy it (Jer 4:23–26).[10]

The marriage metaphor provides a literary skeleton for the collection of accusations against Israel, Judah, and Jerusalem in Jer 2–4. At the beginning of this collection God recalls the "honeymoon" period following the exodus: "I remember . . . the love of your betrothal time" (Jer 2:2). Against this background some of the coarsest language in the book accuses God's people of flagrant, promiscuous adultery with other deities and allied nations (Jer 2:20–25, 32–33; 3:1–4, 6–10, 20[11]). Accusations of betrayal, ingratitude, and appalling foolishness pile up within this framework (e.g., Jer 2:11–13). First person speech by God ("I") addressed to the people ("you") dominates this section, making the heated rhetoric intensely personal. Questions directed by God to Israel express frustration and anger—"How can you say, 'I have not defiled myself . . .'?" (Jer 2:23); "Where are your gods, which you made for yourselves?" (Jer 2:28); "Why do you bring charges against me? All of you have rebelled against me" (Jer 2:29). The tone is one of bitter jealousy and anger.[12]

The indictments in these chapters are overwhelmingly focused on infidelity to the exclusive relationship with Yahweh. The accusation in Jer 2:34 shows concern for the oppressed: "On your skirts is found the lifeblood of the innocent poor . . . " By extending the search to Jer 5 and 6 one finds charges against priests and prophets for false leadership (Jer 5:30–31; 6:13–14) and a fruitless search for a person who deals honestly and seeks the truth (Jer 5:1). The search turns up "wicked men" whose "wicked deeds have no limit; they do not do justice in the case of the orphan . . . they do not defend the cause of the poor" (Jer 5:26–28). Oppression, violence, and destruction inhabit Jerusalem (Jer 6:6–7).

The oracles collected in these chapters, however, are much more concerned with apostasy than with oppression. Readers of Jeremiah may acknowledge, perhaps reluctantly, that sometimes oppressors had to be overthrown by violent means or that oppression must be stopped by force. But why does God use violence against apostasy? Whom, other than God, does apostasy hurt? Posed in this way, these questions separate God's will from God's person. The OT does not. "Israel does not first know God, and then later discover what God wants. Knowledge of his person and will are identical, and both are grounded in his self-revelation."[13] Apostasy is the root of oppression. To rebel against the Lord is to rebel against the One who abounds in steadfast love and mercy, who loves justice and righteousness, and who is the source of all life.

What benefit was the destruction of political Judah for the little ones who died in the process? Rachel, weeping in Jer 31:15, mourns for these lost children. In the book of Jeremiah the question is answered in the long view. The children's hope depends on the survival of the people Israel. God was present in the judgment that brought about the end of Judah as an autonomous kingdom in order to make way for the recreation of Israel as a people whose identity is determined by their relationship with God.[14]

The human emotion of jealousy is implied in the Lord's accusations against God's people for going after other gods.[15] Jealousy is consistent with the marriage metaphor in Jer 2–4, but it actually derives from the fact that Yahweh claims sovereignty over and exclusive worship from Israel (Exod 20:5).[16] Jealousy can be an unattractive and illegitimate passion among human beings. When one person claims exclusive rights to the devotion of another, he or she may seek to control the other and demand that the other person's life be shaped to serve the jealous one's needs. A jealous person may become angry and violent when this selfish desire is not satisfied. What is illegitimate in interpersonal relationships is suitable to the relationship between human beings and God. Since the Lord alone is Creator, sovereign and holy, the Lord has the right to be jealous of Israel's worship and obedience. When enemies threaten, however, Yahweh may be jealous *for* Israel (Ezek 36:5–6) or Zion (Isa 42:13).

A prayer in Jer 10:24 asks, "O Lord, correct me, but in just measure; not in your anger, lest you diminish me to nothing." God's wrath and jealousy are fearsome, spilling over onto the innocent (e.g., Jer 6:11, 21; 9:21 [Heb. v. 20]; 13:14). Like the Babylonians the Lord became Judah's enemy: "I am about to make war on you with an outstretched hand and a mighty arm, with anger, with fury, and with great wrath" (Jer 21:5; cf. Jer 21:7). God had chosen to bring the kingdom of Judah to an end "by his [Nebuchadnezzar's] hand" (Jer 27:8). As a result, God and the Babylonians often do the same things in the book of Jeremiah (e.g., Jer 13:22 and 13:26; 13:14 and 21:7).[17] In the end, however, God's wrath will turn on Babylon, because "she has sinned against" (Jer 50:14) and "arrogantly defied the Lord" (Jer 50:29). The Lord promises to repay Babylon and her inhabitants for the wrong they did in Zion (Jer 51:24, 49) and to take vengeance on them for the temple (Jer 50:11, 34–37).

The severity of this rhetoric of indictment and judgment corresponds to three crucial features of the book of Jeremiah. First, the people's sin and rebellion are profound and permanent, and they permeate the whole society (Jer 17:1–4). Second, the judgment inflicted on Judah and Jerusalem by means of the Babylonian conquest is commensurate with their sin. The demise of political autonomy, and the loss of king, temple, and land constitute a measure-for-measure judgment.[18] Third, the people must acknowledge their sin and accept the judgment in order to benefit from the promised restoration.[19] Shocking, relentless indictments and judgments attempt to break down the people's resistance to making this confession (Jer 2:35; 3:4–5). One of the most vulgar portrayals of Israel's apostasy (Jer 2:21b–25) is addressed to people who have said, "I have not defiled myself, I have not gone after the Baals" (Jer 2:23a).

BOUNDARIES ON WRATHFUL JUDGMENT

The book of Jeremiah portrays God's jealousy and wrath in judgment within a context that also indicates boundaries and ameliorating factors.[20]

Historical Circumstances of Jeremiah. The book of Jeremiah looks back on the catastrophic judgment in the sixth century B.C. in which the Babylonian empire under Nebuchadnezzar brought the southern kingdom of Judah to an end. Babylon eventually subjugated all the small neighboring states. They destroyed temples and cities. They took large numbers of the inhabitants captive and resettled them in the vicinity of their capital city, Babylon.[21] The book of Jeremiah performs the theological task of making known the will of God with regard to these cataclysmic world events.[22] The first boundary on violent judgment in Jeremiah is the historical particularity of this judgment on Judah. The only comparable crisis in Israel's history had been the Assyrian destruction of the northern kingdom 135 years earlier. Conquests by Assyria in the eighth century B.C. and Babylon in the sixth century B.C. were phases one and two in the death of the Israelite kingdoms, but the Babylonian conquest dealt the final blow. Nebuchadnezzar's forces demolished the temple in Jerusalem and removed the last descendant of David from the throne. Such a severe judgment is unique, not typical.[23]

The book of Jeremiah looks back to God's judgment on Israel and forward to the judgment on Babylon, when the devourers would be devoured in turn by a third party. This judgment against Babylon would mean deliverance for Israel (Jer 30:16; 51:1–10).

Prevention. In the OT God seeks to promote justice by revealing in the Torah the principles and practices of the just and righteous life for the nations, its communities, its families, and their individual members. Deuteronomy 4:8 praises God's law revealed to Israel: "And what other great nation has statutes and ordinances (*mišpāṭîm*) as just as this entire law that I am setting before you today?" (NRSV). Obedience to these statutes and ordinances would demonstrate Israel's "wisdom and discernment" to other nations (Deut 4:5–6). Deuteronomy repeatedly exhorts God's people to walk in God's way and thus choose life, bounty, and blessing (e.g., Deut 30:15–16; cf. Jer 5:4–5), rather than the judgment of death. Similarly, the Lord's invitation in Jer 6:16 is, "Stand at the crossroads, and look, and ask for the enduring paths, which is the good way, and walk in it, and find rest for yourselves."

In various ways the prophetic books in the OT call the people to adhere to God's instructions and law. One way is by means of short lists of imperatives that epitomize torah.[24] The list in Jer 7:5–6 addressed to all the people resembles Jer 21:12 and 22:3, which are addressed to kings, and says, ". . . act justly one with another . . . do not oppress a sojourner, an orphan, or a widow, do not shed innocent blood in this place . . . do not go after other gods to your own hurt." Habakkuk's complaint links the ineffectiveness of torah directly to the impotence of justice: "So the law becomes slack and justice never prevails" (Hab 1:4a, NRSV).[25] Mere possession of the law is not enough to produce wisdom and obedience (Jer 8:8).

In the book of Jeremiah a frequent motif claims that God had persistently sent prophets to warn the people, but they would not listen (e.g., Jer 7:25). Jeremiah 6:17 expresses the same motif in non-stereotyped terminology: "I raised up sentinels for you: 'Pay attention to the sound of the trumpet!' But they said, 'We will not pay attention.'" The people's persistent resistance provides another justification for the judgment: "Hear, O land, I am about to bring disaster on this people, the fruit of their plots, because they have not paid attention to my words; and as for my teaching (*tôrâ*), they have rejected it" (Jer 6:19; cf. Jer 7:26, the typical prose formula). Like Jeremiah the former prophets had "prophesied of war, calamity, and pestilence to many nations and against great kingdoms" (Jer 28:8). God had tried to forestall the necessity of judgment by sending prophets since ancient times.

The teaching of the Torah and exhortations by the prophets function nationally in a way similar to God's counseling with Cain in Gen 4:7: "Sin is crouching at the door . . . and you must master it." Jeremiah and the other prophetic collections claim that Israel had not followed the Lord's counsel any more than Cain had.

Act-Consequence and Measure-for-Measure Retribution. Although the wrath of God cannot be quenched by human power and threatens to overflow all limits, the book of Jeremiah offers justifications for the extent of the judgment in terms of retribution. Two ways of understanding judgment are suggested in God's announcement of judgment in Jer 6:19.[26] The disaster that God will bring is "the fruit of their plots." The image of harvest pictures the natural results of their sin, consequences that are part of the way that God has created the world:[27] "I will pour out their wickedness upon them" (Jer 14:16). God is the agent, but there is an organic connection between actions and the punishment or reward that they bring.

The judicial type of retribution appears in the second half of Jer 6:19: "because you have not paid attention to my words." The words are exemplified earlier in this passage, "walk in [the good way]" (Jer 6:16) and "pay attention to the sound of the trumpet" (Jer 6:17). The seconding line specifically accuses the people of rejecting the Lord's Torah, "and as for my Torah, they have rejected it." The book of Jeremiah uses the Sinai/Horeb covenant to ground the judicial type of retribution. The people Israel had broken the covenant that they had sworn in Yahweh's name to uphold (Jer 11:10). Their punishment was specified in "all the words of this covenant" (Jer 11:8) that also provides boundaries for God's wrath.

In the larger OT context Deut 28 gives a thorough list of curses that will be applied when the covenant is broken. The judgments on Israel and Judah in the book of Jeremiah correspond in several ways to the list of curses. The ultimate consequence of violating the covenant would be for Israel to lose its land and be sent into exile. Jeremiah 34 also reports covenant breaking in Jerusalem in the last months before Nebuchadnezzar's army took the city. The Sinai/Horeb covenant put limits on the period of service of debt slaves. Slave-holders in Jerusalem had violated the terms of the covenant, but under King Zedekiah's leadership they made a sworn covenant to keep the commandment and release their debt slaves. When Babylon reestablished the final siege of the city, they forced their slaves back into service. This oppressive and cynical act violated the original covenant and also the oath they had just taken to observe it.

The promise in Jer 30:11 is addressed to people living in exile under the ongoing effects of judgment: ". . . I will not make an end of you. I will discipline you justly, and I will certainly not withhold punishment from you" (cf. Jer 46:28). "You" is singular in this promise. It addresses the nation as a single entity. Measured judgment will not make an end of Israel (also Jer 4:27; 5:10, 18), but it does not guarantee that every individual will experience suffering that is strictly proportionate to their sins. The innocent and the relatively less guilty may die alongside the wickedest oppressors. The innocent dead may hope to be remembered when Israel survives as God's people.[28]

Divine Reluctance. God's reluctance to execute judgment places boundaries around violence and wrath. In Jer 5:1 God initiates a search for one person in Jerusalem "who acts justly and seeks the truth so that I may pardon Jerusalem." This reluctance to judge is evident in several ways in the book of Jeremiah.

God's *anguish* is the first evidence of his reluctance to judge. The most memorable expressions of God's compassion and love for Israel articulate anguish over the way the people will suffer when the threatened judgments fall upon them. In the poems in Jer 4:19–22 and 8:18–9:1 God's voice emerges from the prophet's voice. The affectionate title "daughter, my people" is God's special name for Israel. These poems describe physical and emotional distress, grief, and pain.

> My anguish, my anguish! I writhe in pain! Oh, the walls of my heart! My heart is beating wildly; I cannot keep silent; for I hear the sound of the trumpet, the alarm of war. (Jer 4:19, NRSV)

> O cheerfulness, go away! Grief is upon me, my heart is faint. . . . Over the fracture of my poor people I am broken, I mourn, and dismay has taken hold of me. (Jer 8:18, 21)

> I have put the beloved of my life in the hands of her enemies. (Jer 12:7b)

In Hos 11:8–9 God's pathos is the explicit reason for withholding judgment against Ephraim. Ephraim also appears in Jer 31:20: "Is Ephraim my precious son, my darling child? For as often as I speak of him, I surely remember him again. Therefore my inmost being stirs for him; I surely have compassion for him— utterance of the Lord." God in mercy will hear Ephraim's repentance and his request "bring me back" and will bring the judgment to an end. The metaphor of parent and child communicates the kind of relationship in which God must discipline Israel but longs to avoid doing it.

The second evidence of God's reluctance to judge is the fact that God is *willing to relent*, to "change his mind" about the punishment that has been announced. The way the potter reworks a vessel that has been spoiled on the wheel illustrates in Jer 18 God's willingness to withdraw punishment: "But if that nation will turn from its wickedness . . . then I will change my mind about the calamity that I planned to do to it" (Jer 18:8). At some point during Jeremiah's ministry God decided, "I am weary of relenting" (Jer 15:6) and, "I have spoken, I have purposed; I have not relented nor will I turn back" (Jer 4:28). These statements imply that relenting had previously been God's regular practice. This boundary for divine wrath had been removed before Judah and Jerusalem were finally destroyed. This change is another indication that the sixth century judgment is unique.

The third evidence of God's reluctance is the focus on *repentance*. Although there is considerable disagreement about whether or not Jeremiah the prophet ever preached repentance to Judah and Jerusalem, the canonical form of the book certainly does.[29] In Jer 2–4 one finds several invitations to return (Jer 3:12–14, 22; 4:1–4). The literary effect of these invitations and the accompanying prophecies of hope (Jer 3:15–18) is to break up the relentless march of harsh indictments and judgment prophecies. There is an alternative to the terrible cost of sin. The prose narratives in Jer 26 and 36, dated in the early years of Jehoiakim's reign, indicate that a collection of judgment oracles could have the purpose of turning Judah and Jerusalem to the Lord: "Perhaps the house of Judah will hear all the calamity that I am planning to do to them, and all of them will turn from their evil ways, so that I will forgive their iniquity and their sin" (Jer 36:3; cf. Jer 26:3). Turning God's people from their sin is the purpose of prophetic ministry according to Jer 23:22.

A fourth evidence is seen in Jeremiah's *intercession*. Intercession by a prophet is often a factor when God relents. For example, Amos 7:1–9 recounts a series of visions of judgment on the northern kingdom. At the end of each of the first two visions Amos asks God to "forgive" or "stop." He asks God to view the people of the kingdom as small Jacob: "How can Jacob stand? He is so small." God relents and promises to withhold the punishment. Following the third vision Amos does not intercede, and the announced judgment proceeds. Jeremiah also ministered at the end of a kingdom. In those unique circumstances God announces that Jeremiah's intercession is forbidden (Jer 11:14–17; 14:11). Even if the famous prophets and intercessors, Moses and Samuel, were to stand before God on behalf of Judah, God would not respond to them (Jer 15:1). In the book of Jeremiah, intercession enters by other routes. In six prayers of personal lament, called Jeremiah's "Confessions," Jeremiah asks for God's help. When he is preserved alive through Nebuchadnezzar's onslaught, Jeremiah becomes a sign for the survival of God's people. In Jer 30:12–17 God's promise mirrors a prayer for Israel with its incurable wounds and promises healing.[30] In this passage God sees Judah as needy, persecuted, and despised as the result of the Babylonian conquest. Like Jacob in Amos 7, the people who are under judgment are seen as small and helpless. Then God will intervene to save them.[31]

The limits of time are a major boundary for violent judgment in the book of Jeremiah. God's willingness to delay judgment is a reason for concern. Jeremiah prays in 15:15 for retribution on the people who are persecuting him. He complains that he might be killed if God waits too long to judge them. The Babylonian conquest finally took care of Jeremiah's persecutors and initiated an extended period of devastation and exile for Judah and Jerusalem. Although other prophets encouraged the people to believe that the exile would be short (Jer 28:1–4), the distinctive motif of the book of Jeremiah is that God had granted Nebuchadnezzar and his successors the right to rule over the region for a long but limited time, seventy years (Jer 25:12; 29:10; cf. 27:7). Adults in Jeremiah's audience would not see the end of the exile, but their grandchildren might. The collection of salvation oracles in Jer 30–31 addresses the people who are still suffering the effects of conquest and exile. They are wounded, plundered, and outcast (e.g., Jer 30:15–17), but after they have been "disciplined justly" (Jer 30:11), their enemies will be taken captive and their plunderers will be plundered (Jer 30:16). Judah's exile and Babylon's hegemony will end when Babylon itself is judged (Jer 25:12; 30:16). The removal of Babylon will mean salvation for Judah (e.g., Jer 50:1–4). The Lord had become the exiles' enemy (Jer 30:14), but the motifs of the seventy-year Babylonian rule, of punishment in just measure, and of eventual judgment on Babylon all serve to distinguish God's purpose in this judgment on Judah from Babylon's imperial ambitions.

The final boundary on wrathful judgment is its purpose as instruction or *discipline*.

> Behold, the storm of the Lord!
>   Wrath has gone forth, a sweeping tempest.
>   It will burst on the head of the wicked.
> But the blazing anger of the Lord will not turn back
>   until he has executed and accomplished the purposes of his heart.
> In the latter days you will understand this. (Jer 30:23–24 [=23:19–20])

The people had not accepted earlier divine words and actions as correction (Jer 2:30; 5:3; 7:23; 17:23; 32:33). Their refusal to respond to God's discipline is a reason for the judgment on Judah. The representative figure of repentant Ephraim in Jer 31:18 acknowledges a corrective purpose for the Babylonian conquest and exile: "You disciplined me and I have been disciplined." The severe and widespread suffering was not meant to destroy Israel completely; it was meant to restore and reform them as God's holy people. This understanding of the judgment on Judah is gained in retrospect. It is an insight for survivors and a source of hope. God had not abandoned them to death.

IMPLICATIONS FOR THEOLOGY

The imagery of passionate attachment, especially the marriage and parental metaphors for God's relationship to Israel, have long provided a way to unify the contradictory biblical reports of divine wrath in judgment and claims of compassion that is slow to anger and ready to forgive.[32] God has many children, we think, and sometimes God must use force to prevent some of them from hurting the others. Some say that wrath is the obverse of love. God as the loving husband, father, or king can be trusted to use his wisdom, knowledge, and power to do what is best for his beloved wife, child, or subject in the long run, even if it entails suffering and loss. This resolution is more attractive and less frightening than a system of blind justice operating strictly according to the rule of law or natural determinism inexorably working out the consequences of our actions. God is over the law, not subject to it. In God's freedom there is room for forgiveness and mercy.

These images of personal relationship are true to the revealed character of God in the OT, but they do not reveal everything about God. They succeed provisionally at describing an integrated divine personality that is comprehensible, although not entirely predictable.

Patrick Miller describes how God makes a decision to judge:

> . . . the Lord resists the judgment as long or as much as possible. The signs of such resistance are varied and indicative of the fact that judgment is not simply a matter of divine decree but the outcome of a complex process of divine wrestling, anguish, attempted overtures to the people, calls for repentance, warnings that keep the door open, and the like.[33]

This description fits most of what has been said in this paper about God's judgment in the book of Jeremiah. If we omitted the term "divine," it could also describe ourselves or someone we know, struggling to achieve reconciliation with another person. This description has rationalized the unresolved tension between violent judgment and love by expanding and expounding the anthropomorphisms inherent in the family metaphors. God's human-like thoughts and emotions are complex like human thought processes and feelings.

Recent critiques of the family metaphors also deserve notice. Renita Weems, for example, acknowledges that the marriage metaphor absorbed the contradictory sides of Israel's experience with God, namely, compassionate advocacy and jealous, unpredictable abuse.[34] She argues that the marriage metaphor was able to deflect God's "abuse and unpredictability" from being construed as "defects in God's character" by implying that they were part of "the messiness of intimacy" in marriage.[35] Weems also maintains that violence against wives was accepted and expected by the ancient audience.[36] In other words, the metaphor only works to integrate the tensions within God's character when one accepts that husbands may physically punish their wives.[37] Weems reads the marital image as the ruling metaphor in Jer 2–4, so that all violent judgment in these chapters is carried out by God as husband.[38] Weems's conclusions are very different from Miller's, but her method is similar. By expanding the anthropomorphic portrayal of God in line with what she imagines Israelite husbands were like, Weems strengthens the metaphor's ability to embrace the contradiction between judgment and love. She strengthens the metaphor in order to reject it, however.

> There is nothing compelling about the prophetic vision. Why should I as reader leave the world where I presently live, where violence against wives is unjustifiable, to inhabit a world where violence against wives is taken for granted? The marriage metaphor is useless therefore for shedding light on the theological question of punishment and judgment.[39]

The marriage metaphor does not accomplish its intended purpose unless one accepts that husbands have the right to beat their wives as punishment or discipline within a relationship of loving care. The parent-child metaphor would fall short for the same reason.

In the book of Jeremiah *the* judgment of God is the devastation, conquest, and exile of Judah in the sixth century B.C. Decades ago attention to covenant helped to rationalize the severity of this punishment within the ongoing relationship of God to Israel. Recently, eloquent descriptions of the pathos of God in judgment have attempted to justify the violence of the sixth century experience. Where might OT theology go from here? Perhaps reflection on the purposes of God in judgment in the particular sixth century setting will be fruitful for understanding the judgment of God in Christian theology.

With regard to ethical implications, a final comment will merely state the obvious limits on applying the OT understanding of God's judgment to contemporary life. First, one may not conclude that a person who is suffering is being punished by God. Jeremiah suffered because he was obedient to God's call and commission. Second, one may not reverse a metaphor. God is revealed as husband, father, king, judge, potter, and shepherd in the book of Jeremiah. God also threatens and enacts violent judgment against Judah, other nations, and Babylon. These two facts do not lead to the conclusion that human husbands, parents, and other leaders have the responsibility or right to use violent force. Finally, one cannot move directly from the book of Jeremiah or even from the OT as a whole to Christian theological or ethical conclusions. Nevertheless, we ought to affirm that God who was with the exiles from Judah to save them (Jer 30:11), and who loved them with an everlasting love (Jer 31:3), is the same God who "so loved the world, that he gave his only Son, so that everyone who believes in him may not perish but may have eternal life" (John 3:16, NRSV).

ENDNOTES

1. These verses from the Psalms use the terms "judgments, justice, rule justly, work justice, just works, done what is just" to exalt divine governance. All of them translate forms of the same Hebrew root word, *šāpaṭ*, including the noun, *mišpāṭ*. God's judgments (*mišpāṭîm*) are aspects of divine rule or government (*šāpaṭ*) over Israel and all of creation, as their Creator and sovereign.

2. The Hebrew word is *hll*, which also means "praise."

3. All translations are the author's, unless noted otherwise.

4. Compare 1 Kgs 4:5 which lists "Adoniram son of Abda, in charge of forced labor" among Solomon's chief officials.

5. The Septuagint, Syriac, and Vulgate versions have read *šmr*, "guard, protect," rather than *šmd*, "destroy."

6. Compare the similar prayers in Pss 7; 10; 35; 43.

7. Carol Meyers, *Discovering Eve* (Oxford: Oxford University Press, 1988), and Philip King and Lawrence Stager, *Life in Ancient Israel* (Louisville: Westminster John Knox, 2001).

8. Walter Brueggemann says, "This rhetoric of violence is characteristically on the lips of those who otherwise have no effective weapons . . . [and] on the side of the reestablishment of justice and the redress of abuse." See his *Theology of the Old Testament* (Minneapolis: Fortress, 1997), 245. Renita Weems reminds readers to "hear these metaphors with the ears of a tiny kingdom . . . a vulnerable, powerless, imperiled nation." See her *Battered Love* (Minneapolis: Fortress, 1985), 20.

9. William Bellinger cites a comment that is characteristic of members of oppressed groups in our society: "Talk all you want about 'God is love,' but give us the powerful God of the Hebrew Scriptures who can get us out of all the suffering, trouble, and woe of our life." See "The Hebrew Scriptures and Theology: Resources and Problems," *PRSt* 31 (2004): 130.

10. Jer 4:23–24 describes the reversal of creation (cf. Gen 1) reminiscent of the effects of the flood (Gen 7:20–23). This passage serves as a reminder near the beginning of the book of the potential extent of the destruction "before his fierce anger."

11. NIV and NRSV both translate the verb *bgd* in Jer 3:20 as "[be] unfaithful." "Be treacherous" may carry more of the connotations of the Hebrew verb.

12. The invitations to repent and the promises of restoration that also appear in these chapters will be discussed below.

13. Brevard S. Childs, *Old Testament Theology in a Canonical Context* (Philadelphia: Fortress, 1985), 51.

14. Samuel Terrien argues that the birth of Judaism after 587 B.C. did not result from faith in Yahweh who delivered Israel from Egypt, but on the prophetic vision of Jeremiah and Ezekiel who "'saw' in the catastrophe, not the sign of Yahweh's absence, but, on the contrary, the manifestation of his presence in judgment." See *The Elusive Presence* (San Francisco: Harper and Row, 1978), 262. See also P. Miller, "'Slow to Anger': The God of the Prophets," in *The Forgotten God, Perspectives in Biblical Theology* (eds. A. A. Das and Frank J. Matera; Louisville: Westminster John Knox, 2002), 39–55.

15. The Hebrew word *qin'ah* that is translated "jealousy" or "zeal" does not occur in the book of Jeremiah.

16. Walter Brueggemann refers to Yahweh's "self-regard," including glory, holiness, and jealousy. One could substitute the term "pride." ". . . Yahweh's self-regard is massive in its claim, strident in its expectation, and ominous in its potential." See his *Theology of the Old Testament*, 296.

17. See the discussions in P. Scalise, "Jeremiah," in *The IVP Women's Bible Commentary* (eds. C. Clark Kroeger and M. J. Evans; Downers Grove, Ill.: InterVarsity, 2002), 380; and T. Fretheim, "'I Was Only a Little Angry,' Divine Violence in the Prophets," *Interp* 58 (2004): 368–372.

18. The claim is not made that individuals other than the kings suffered precisely according to the measure of their sins.

19. J. G. McConville, *Judgment and Promise* (Winona Lake, Ind.: Eisenbrauns, 1993), 112. P. Scalise, "The Way of Weeping," *WW* 2 (2002): 415–422.

20. The description that follows here results from my openness to be persuaded, and my effort to discern answers within the book of Jeremiah to the question of how to deal with the violence of God's words and actions. Many biblical critics would work in the opposite direction, to deconstruct the boundaries that the text seems to offer (e.g., Robert Carroll). To such critics, this discussion will seem overly optimistic. On the other hand, one must also recognize that a fully Christian response to the violence of God's judgment cannot be derived from the book of Jeremiah alone. It will require considering the full revelation of Scripture and the historical and

contemporary insights of exegetes and theologians and using the methods of systematic theology and Christian philosophy.

21. Daniel L. Smith-Christopher (*A Biblical Theology of Exile*, Minneapolis: Fortress, 2002, 27–73) gives a sociological, historical, and theological description of the exile.

22. R. Clements, *Jeremiah* (Atlanta: John Knox, 1988), 152.

23. Patrick Miller describes judgment in the OT as "momentary, transient, occasional, and situational" ("Slow to Anger, The God of the Prophets," 41). The judgment on Judah in the sixth century B.C. was longer than "momentary," enduring rather than "transitory" in its effects, and having to do with a unique, potentially final "occasion." Miller's point remains valid, however. Judgment is only one way in which the justice of God is experienced.

24. E.g., Mic 6:8; Ezek 18:5–8; Zech 7:9–10; 8:16–17. In Jer 7:9; Hos 4:2; and Mal 3:5 the lists appear in indictments.

25. NIV gives a more extreme translation of this rare verb, *pwg*—"the law is paralyzed."

26. Stephen B. Chapman effectively illustrates how these two types of retribution are juxtaposed and layered in 2 Sam 12. "Reading the Bible as Witness: Divine Retribution in the Old Testament," *PRSt* 31 (2004): 171–190. See also Fretheim, "'I Was Only a Little Angry'," 370–371.

27. Terence Fretheim offers a sustained theological exposition of the book of Jeremiah in which the relationship between sin and judgment is seen to be intrinsic. God "mediates" or "sees to" the movement from act to consequence (*Jeremiah*, Macon, Ga.: Smyth and Helwys, 2002, 34–35 and *passim*).

28. Hope for a resurrection for judgment in which the righteous dead will be vindicated does not appear in Jeremiah.

29. Donald Gowan (*The Death and Resurrection of Israel, Theology of the Prophetic Books*, Louisville: Westminster John Knox, 105) holds the position that Jeremiah did not preach a pre-exilic offer of redemption. G. McConville (*Judgment and Promise*, Winona Lake, Ind.: Eisenbrauns, 1993, 27–41) argues on the basis of his exegesis of Jer 3 that Jeremiah had indeed presented God's invitation to repent and avert the announced judgment. The present form of the book holds out to its audience in the exile and beyond an invitation to repent and accept the Lord's offer of restoration. See P. Scalise, "Scrolling through Jeremiah: Written Documents as a Reader's Guide to the Book of Jeremiah," *Review and Expositor* 101 (2004): 201–225.

30. P. Scalise, *Jeremiah 26-52* (WBC 27; Dallas: Word, 1995), 95–101.

31. "YHWH will act for Judah, it seems, precisely because of her incapacity to escape from the consequences of her guilt" (McConville, *Judgment and Promise*, 95).

32. Abraham J. Heschel's *The Prophets* (New York: Harper, 1962) is a classic text.

33. Miller, "Slow to Anger," 46.

34. Weems, *Battered Love*, 75.

35. Ibid., 78.

36. Ibid., 106.

37. Ibid., 124, n. 9.

38. The image of God and Israel as husband and wife is scattered in Jer 2–4. Much of the material in these and subsequent chapters is not related to the marriage metaphor. God judges as king or Creator, not always as husband. On the intersection of the marriage metaphor with descriptions of the treatment of conquered peoples see P. Scalise, "Jeremiah," 379.

39. Weems, *Battered Love,* 106.

JUDGMENT: BY WHOSE AUTHORITY? WHO WILL COME TO JUDGE THE QUICK AND THE DEAD?

D. STEPHEN LONG

How shall we hear well the scriptural witness concerning judgment? This is a particularly vexing question because, as the theologian Hans Urs von Balthasar reminded us, Holy Scripture sets forth two series of statements which could potentially be read as contradictory.[1] One series speaks of the threat of judgment and the possibility of a loss for all eternity: Matt 5:22, 29f.; 10:28; 23:33; 8:12; 22:11f.; 25:30; Mark 9:43; 19:20; 20:10; 21:18. The other series speaks of God's will and ability to save all: 1 Tim 2:1–6, especially v. 4; John 12:32; 17:2; Rom 5:12–21; 11:32. Can these two sets be reconciled? Should they be? Perhaps the tension between them should be left unreconciled, for they may very well point to the eschatological reserve that ought always to frame any theology of judgment, which all of us who venture to teach and preach on this subject should bear in mind. It seems to be Jesus' counsel as well, for when the risen Lord was asked by his apostles about these matters, "Lord, is this the time when you will restore the kingdom of Israel?" his response was, "It is not for you to know the times or periods that the Father has set by his own authority" (Acts 1:6–7, NRSV). Our response to Christ's judgment is not to speculate but to witness. But to what do we witness when it comes to judgment? Which brings us back to our initial question, how shall we hear well the Scriptures on judgment?

In reading Scripture I find it always most helpful to begin in two places: first, the Apostles' Creed and second, the witness of the saints. The church's creed and its traditional doctrines are, as David Yeago pointed out, "guides to a faithful and attentive reading of the [biblical] texts." Yeago persuasively argues that the West's fascination, even obsession, with the historical critical methodology has blinded us to the reality that doctrine and dogma are the proper starting places for hearing Scripture well. He writes:

> . . . one has only to look at the sermons, commentaries and treatises of the Fathers, Aquinas, or Luther to see how seriously they took, for example, the Trinitarian and Christological doctrines as analyses of the logic of the scriptural discourse, formal descriptions of the apprehension of God *in* the texts, which then serve as guides to a faithful and attentive reading *of* the texts. Where this conviction is no longer intelligible, the classical doctrines come to seem, in one way and another, superfluous to the life of faith and of the believing community, venerable baggage perhaps invoked from time to time for respect for the ancients (a commodity in short supply just lately!) but scarcely objects of zealous and painstaking study. No theory of the development of doctrine which attempts to save the classical doctrines without accounting for the unanimous conviction of the Christian tradition that they *are the teaching of scripture* can overcome the marginalization of the doctrines which is so evident in the contemporary Western Church and theology.[2]

How are the Apostles' Creed and Christian doctrine the teaching of Scripture on judgment? They secure the proper place for any such teaching; it must be rendered intelligible only in terms of Christology and Trinity, which includes the doctrine of God's perfections. Every doctrine of judgment which appeals to Scripture outside of these doctrines will miss something significant and conclude in saying way too much (as Hal Lindsey did in his *Late Great Planet Earth*[3]) or way too little (as Gulley and Mullholand appear to do in their *If Grace is True*[4]).

In one sense, the creed teaches us all that can safely be said about the scriptural witness concerning judgment: "He will come to judge the quick and the dead." This is orthodox teaching, and it is beautiful in its simplicity. Much like the church's traditional teaching on the atonement, it does not authorize any particular theologian's teaching as normative but first and foremost insists on who will be the judge—Jesus Christ. That he is judge, of course, only makes sense from the biblical witness. Christ receives his authority to judge from his obedience to the Father. It leads to his ascension where he is, as the creed states so eloquently, "seated on the right hand of God." It is "from thence that he will come in glory to judge the living and the dead." To offer a theological interpretation of the scriptural witness on judgment that neglects the creed and Christian doctrine is to place upon ourselves that unbearable modern burden where everything must be rebuilt, everything must be "new and improved" in every generation.

The creed and Christian doctrine are starting points that let us know what we can safely say about the scriptural witness to the judgment, but they do not exhaust all that can be said. They offer us the appropriate hermeneutical boundaries within which we can rightly hear the Scriptures. It helps us stand within the context of the communion of saints where Scripture alone makes sense. As Stanley Hauerwas has argued, "Scripture can be rightly interpreted only within the practices of a body of people constituted by the unity found in the Eucharist."[5]

This unity is never merely synchronic but always exists diachronically as well, which should cause us to resist the modern burden of always making things new. Christianity is (as Chesterton is reputed to have said) a democracy of the dead. But a people constituted by the unity found in the Eucharist must also be a people who know how to repent, and this is necessary for a right theological interpretation of Scripture. St. Athanasius reminds us:

> . . . for the searching of the Scriptures and true knowledge of them an honorable life is needed, and a pure soul, and that virtue which is according to Christ. . . . For just as, if a man wished to see the light of the sun, he would at any rate, wipe and brighten his eye, purifying himself in some sort like what he desires, so that the eye, thus becoming light, may see the light of the sun . . . —thus he that would comprehend the mind of those who speak of God must needs begin by washing and cleansing his soul, by his manner of living and approach the saints themselves by imitating their works.[6]

Playing on this image of repenting, wiping our eyes or purifying ourselves in order to search the Scriptures well, I shall argue that unless we first rid ourselves of some very bad cultural and philosophical habits we will not be able to hear well the scriptural witness concerning judgment. Those bad habits are a modern moralism where Christ's authority as judge is usurped by a more rigid form of judgmentalism. Beginning with Enlightenment philosophers, a creedal and theological doctrine of judgment is replaced by a moral one. This (modern) moral judgmentalism is a vague semblance of the Christian doctrine of judgment, which makes it dangerous and prevents us from hearing the full scriptural witness. This modern judgmentalism is grounded in an arbitrary willfulness that loses the christological and Trinitarian context for the doctrine of judgment and thus loses God's perfections. It is no coincidence that the loss of God's immutability, impassibility, eternity, and perfections occurs when modern judgmentalism usurps Christ's authority as judge. I fear that unless we first rid ourselves of the bad habits of this modern, moralistic judgmentalism we will not be able to hear the biblical witness, for it will too readily be received within the modern context, and the only purpose of judgment will be to establish moralism.

The first step toward a theological interpretation of the scriptural witness concerning judgment is to purify our intellects of the dangerous, vague semblance of that witness in modern morality, which makes judgment merely a function of will and power. The second step is to make judgment reasonable by understanding its role within God's economy.

Before elaborating these two steps I must begin with a confession. I am a United Methodist, and as such I think I occupy a very different context from many others presenting here. I have been a United Methodist for thirty plus years, and in all that time I do not recall hearing a sermon on judgment, hell, or damnation. They are no longer part of our Methodist vocabulary. This is ironic in that Mr. Wesley began the Methodist movement in order to help people "flee from the wrath to come." We Methodists originated from a palpable sense of Christ's final judgment. But this initial reason for Methodism's existence is as far from contemporary Methodism as riding horses is from flying airplanes. We no longer exist to help people flee from the wrath to come; on the whole we do not anticipate Christ's final judgment. We do not await any final judgment because we have no need of it. I believe that most of the churches in North America, even though they may be fundamentalist or evangelical where hell and damnation seem to be live possibilities, are more likely to become similar to the United Methodist Church than we are likely to become similar to them. Once the christological doctrine of judgment disappears, the change seems to be irrecoverable. In fact, most of the preaching on hell and damnation in those churches may already be more a species of modern moralism than Christic judgment, which puts them well on the way toward a loss of Christ's proper role in the doctrine of judgment.

What we Methodists now teach explicitly is also present in most other mainline churches and has been for some time. In 1937 H. Richard Niebuhr penned his memorable indictment of Christianity in the United States where "a God without wrath brought men without sin into a kingdom without judgment through the ministrations of a Christ without a cross."[7] Fifty years later Martin Marty wrote an essay entitled, "Hell Disappeared. No one Noticed. A Civic Argument."[8] A loss of any final christological judgment characterizes much of mainline Protestant Christianity. And given the popularity of Gulley and Mullholand's recent work, *If Grace is True*,[9] it may increasingly characterize evangelical Christianity as well. But has judgment disappeared?

That we no longer find it necessary to proclaim "the Great Assize" and anticipate Christ's final judgment may have less to do with a loss of judgment per se and more to do with the fact that we live in a time of such harsh and unyielding judgment that we simply cannot imagine any other form of judgment could usurp the thoroughly regimented and regulated world we have made ourselves. We moderns may have no need of Christ's judgment because our moralistic culture offers us all the judgment we can tolerate. The loss of Christ's final judgment in much of contemporary Christianity results less from a permissive society that eschews judgment altogether than from a shift in authority as to who judges, a shift that constitutes a usurpation of Christ's role as judge. Judgment has not disappeared; it is ever present with us. It is so present that Christ himself has been squeezed out of his role. Christ's judiciary powers (his "kingly" function as both Aquinas and Calvin put it), won by the merits of his obedience to the Father through his life and crucifixion and entrusted to the saints, have now been leveled, democratized, and attributed to each individual to exercise against him or herself. The dominion that was once Christ's has now become the individual's to exercise against her or himself, whose power to exercise is protected by the state. I do not think hell disappeared because we live in a more permissive society. Hell disappeared because the modern age is so thoroughly defined by rigid regulations that some other final judgment appears implausible.

WIPING OUR EYES: USURPING CHRIST'S AUTHORITY BY THE AUTHORITY OF THE INDIVIDUAL WILL

That what we moderns experienced was less a loss of judgment and more a shift in authority as to who judges finds supporting evidence in three characteristics of the modern era: its unparalleled ability to enforce law; its commitment to God's final judgment as the only reasonable Christian doctrine that survived Enlightenment critique; and its emphasis on the bare power to will as the sole basis for harmonious social exchanges.

Modern Judgmentalism. No people living on earth ever held greater and more effective means at their disposal to render final judgments than we now possess. We moderns developed and rationalized the arts of surveillance, policing, and military and judicial power to such perfection that they work almost imperceptibly. We produced the greatest carcereal society that ever existed. As Michel Foucault argued, we produced a society whose foundation is "to discipline and punish."[10] One wrongly assumes we live in a more "permissive" society than previous generations. Slajov Zizek argues that this is a worn-out cliché that avoids the obvious: "It is today's apparently hedonistic and permissive postmodern reflexive society which is paradoxically more and more saturated by rules and regulations that allegedly promote our well-being."[11] Whether it is something as potentially ominous as the Patriot Act, the narrow dogmatism of the politically correct ideology that now defines much of academic culture, or something silly such as the recent ban on smoking in all bars by the local city council of Skokie, Illinois (where I live), we live in a much more regulated society than ever before. This is due to the very moral foundation of modern society.

We are commanded to pursue happiness, where happiness has been defined as increased utility. To do so we must be free individuals bound by the command to "be happy." The result is a moral burden that takes on a regiment of its own. We are now forced to make our lives secure and happy through our own resources, to live by the command "be morally well," which functions to micromanage our lives in an increasingly regulated way: don't smoke, wear your seatbelt, take Viagra for erectile dysfunction, make over your body, never cook with lard, save your money to travel in retirement, lose weight, be pleasant to others, if not see the therapist or take Prozac, etc. As Carl Elliott put it in his wonderful book, *Better than Well*, this is the only spiritual pilgrimage moderns affirm. We are the "inheritors of a cultural tradition" where "the significance of life has become deeply bound up with self-fulfillment."[12] In fact, as he persuasively argues, "finding yourself has replaced finding God."[13] But this is no easy quest; to find one's self is a demanding and rigorous vocation that may be more arduous than the quest for the Holy Grail. It may require hours in the gym, under the surgical knife, or on the therapist's couch. It requires a rigorous commitment to discipline. Perhaps hell disappears in such a society, not because it is overly permissive but because hell becomes unnecessary. We live in an age of moral rigorism where anyone who does not internalize its judgmentalism is pathologized. After all, as has been said, "Hell is where God gives you what you want."

Enlightenment Dogmas: God and the Will as Judge. That philosophers such as Foucault and Zizek are correct in characterizing the culture of modernity as producing an ever-increasing regulatory apparatus makes sense of what might otherwise be viewed as an oddity. A modern culture where hell disappears emerged out of a philosophical commitment by two of its greatest founders (Kant and Locke) to the doctrine of God's final judgment. The shift in authority in judgment is not the consequence of some secular rejection of God but results from the one remaining proof for God's existence that survived reason's critique—"the moral proof." For while the doctrine of the Trinity and orthodox Christology was quickly dismantled in early modernity—try to find a doctrine of Christ's ascension in Kant or Locke, the doctrine of the deity's final judgment was tenaciously affirmed.

The modern era birthed a new proof for the existence of God, the moral proof. This proof argued that although God's existence—and especially God's essence as Triune—could not be rationally defended or rejected, "God" was defensible based on morality. The moral proof assumes that we all know what it means to be moral. It is to exercise one's freedom to follow universal laws. These laws are not mediated by any particular people; they are known through nature alone. Every traditional or conventional account of morality points in the direction of this final universal moral obligation. They are only understood as anticipations of the latter. But the ability to fulfill such obligation presupposes the freedom necessary to attend to what nature itself demands. This freedom could not be found in nature; thus if morality is grounded in freedom, it needed something beyond nature as its foundation. The very necessity of the freedom to fulfill the moral law suggests the need to postulate the existence of God. If we are to have morality, then we must have God. Now God becomes defined primarily as the universal lawgiver who gives us the freedom to will obedience to universal moral laws naturally known by all right thinking people. This entails that the relationship between God and creation is mediated primarily through morality rather than Christology. God does not need to be Triune in order to provide the conditions for the possibility of morality. God simply must insure a basic structure to human existence that secures will, freedom, and obligation.

Kant and Locke, who differ on so many other points, both assume this basic structure. It makes God useful, but not necessary, for morality. Kant stated this explicitly in his preface to the first edition of *Religion within the Limits of Reason Alone*. He writes, "So far as morality is based upon the conception of man as a free agent who, just because he is free, binds himself through his reason to unconditioned laws, it stands in need neither of the idea of another Being over him, for him to apprehend his duty, nor of an incentive other than the law itself, for him to do his duty."[14] Morality does not need God for its intelligibility, but God needs morality; for Kant continues, "Morality thus leads ineluctably to religion, through which it extends itself to the idea of a powerful moral Lawgiver, outside of mankind, for Whose will that is the final end (of creation) which at the same time can and ought to be man's final end."[15] The idea of "God" provides the human agent the freedom to will the moral law, and this same idea helps solidify the binding character of the moral law. Despite all Kant's unorthodox theology, he preserves the one dogma that God will judge the quick and the dead based on their obedience or disobedience to the moral law. Notice, however, that he never refers to Christ as judge. Moral agents should do their duty irrespective of hope for reward or pain of punishment, but a final judgment is necessary if "well-doing" and "well-being" are not to be divorced; for otherwise the freedom to be moral and our nature as moral human beings would contradict each other.[16]

Like Kant, the only quasi-orthodox Christian dogma Locke practically uses is God's final judgment. But for Locke the hope for reward or fear of punishment plays a much more significant moral role. We are not simply to do our duty for duty's sake, but also with regard to our own self-interest. Other than this, Locke assumed the basic moral structure Kant assumed. Like Kant, he thought it was possible for educated, enlightened men to be moral solely based on reason alone. However, the authority of God's will, with the possibility of future judgment, offered moral incentives to the vulgar masses.

> It should seem, by the little that has hitherto been done in it, that 'tis too hard a task for unassisted reason, to establish morality, in all its parts, upon its true foundations, with a clear and convincing light. And 'tis at least a surer and shorter way, to the apprehensions of the vulgar, and mass of mankind, that one manifestly sent from God, and coming with visible authority from him, should, as a King and law-maker, tell them their duties, and require their obedience, than leave it to the long, and sometimes intricate deductions of reason, to be made out to them.[17]

God gives the moral law to the wise through reason alone, but for the vulgar masses the notion of a lawgiver who comes down from heaven is necessary. This same lawgiver will judge and distribute rewards and punishments accordingly, which is a moral incentive for those unable to find their way to morality through reason alone.

Given this beginning to modernity, how did it occur that judgment disappeared? This disappearance has less to do with a rejection of Kant and Locke's "moral proof" for the existence of God than its logical consequence. I would suggest that this emphasis on God's final judgment as the ground for morality bears responsibility for the shift in the authority of judgment in the modern era from Christ to the human will for the following reasons. God is understood primarily in terms of a moral relation between a divine lawgiver and the created receiver. Knowledge of God is mediated through this moral relationship. In a sense, we only know God inasmuch as we know that God is that which makes *our* moral freedom possible. This means that our freedom to be moral agents and God's freedom to be for us as moral agents is greater than God alone. The ancient principle: *Deus non est genere* (God is not in a genus, or God's essence is equal to God's existence, or God is that than which nothing greater can be conceived) is undone. A bare freedom to will is now a category greater than God to which even God must be held accountable. As Feuerbach rightly noted, in the modern era theology is anthropology, for to argue that we need God for the sake of our freedom to be moral has the logical correlate that God needs our freedom to be moral for God's own intelligibility.[18] We become God's judge because of our own morality.

A particular egregious example of this is found in the work of the thoroughly modern Methodist theologian A. C. Knudsen where the bare freedom to choose between good and evil is projected even onto God. As Knudson puts it, "God himself as a moral being must distinguish between good and evil and must be metaphysically capable of choosing either."[19] Once this basic moral structure is in place the fact that we judge God is a logical correlate. Knudsen continues, "The only way in which the idea of a moral universe can be maintained is by ascribing moral responsibility to God and a limited independence to man. As Creator of the world, God is a responsible Being, and we his creatures have rights over against him as well as duties to him."[20] The freedom to will has displaced God as the true Sovereign of the Universe. This egregious example of theology gone bad, with its culmination of humanity itself functioning as the one who comes to judge the quick, the dead, and the deity, may be limited to the United Methodist tradition. But I think (unfortunately) it is broader than that. I believe that Process Theology, Openness Theology, and all those theologies that lose God's impassibility or seek to make a real relation between God and creation—theologies that may be the logical consequence of Luther himself—inevitably lead to a usurpation of Christ's authority to judge humanity by humanity's putative authority to judge God. This occurs when goodness and truth are rendered asunder.

When only the will is good, the true disappears. Modern philosophy sacrificed the concept of the will as rational appetite in favor of the will as a brute freedom to choose irrespective of what was true. As Immanuel Kant put it, only a good will is good, and because the will is primarily a disposition not available to human scrutiny, no one is able to judge the true goodness of another.[21] This was a rejection of the medieval theology that the will is "rational appetite." Here the will was not just an internal disposition immune from public scrutiny, but it was related to truth. In fact, will and intellect were knit together. It was thought one could only love what one knows and one can only know what one loves. But this notion of the will was rejected in modern philosophy. Hobbes stated it succinctly, "The Definition of the *Will*, given commonly by the Schooles, that it is a *Rationall Appetite*, is not good. For if it were, then could there be no voluntary act against reason. For a voluntary act is that which proceedeth from the will, and no other."[22] The will and its pursuit of goodness are now separated from the intellect and its pursuit of truth. Ethics and doctrine are decisively separate. This has become modern dogma.[23] Who today would believe, as both Thomas Aquinas and Mr. Wesley believed, that true morality was found in the vision of the Triune God? We are convinced that moral goodness is a more universal category than the truth of the Triune God. But with this move, the will takes on a titanic power of its own that eventually seeks to subordinate God to itself.

God's Perfections: Truth as Counter to Power. The will took on titanic proportions in late medieval scholastic theology, especially in nominalism. This can be seen in the development of a new theological doctrine that so distinguished revelation and reason that it made God's will alone the basis for good and refused even the suggestion that God was bound by previous moral judgments. This led to questions such as the question of the hatred of God. Is it possible for God to will one person to hate him and another to love him so that someone could actually love God and be disobedient, where another's disobedience was hatred of God?[24] This question arose as an effort to secure God's sovereignty. God is not bound by anything outside God. It also helps make sense of biblical claims such as that God hardens Pharaoh's heart. What would have happened had Pharaoh's heart not been hardened? What would have happened if Pharaoh finally gave into Moses? Thankfully, Pharaoh was obedient and thus God redeemed Israel. Pharaoh's obedience in persecuting God's chosen is the cause for our redemption. Could not the same be said of Judas? This late medieval emphasis on God's sovereign will led to an inability to discriminate between Pharaoh and Moses or Jesus and Judas. Who is the true cause of redemption? If we cannot distinguish between Pharaoh or Moses, Jesus or Judas, then goodness and truth become unrecognizable; they are purely arbitrary. Likewise, any doctrine of judgment can only be viewed as an arbitrary exercise of will.

According to Michael Gillespie, Descartes' efforts to found knowledge on the *Cogito* is his response to this capricious nominalistic God.[25] If God's will is "transrational" then everything is uncertain. We could potentially be deceived by everything. In response to this, Descartes constructed his basis for secure knowledge, not in the ability to know, but in our ability to suspend judgment and say, "I doubt it."

> I shall suppose, therefore, that there is, not a true God, who is the sovereign source of truth, but some evil demon, no less cunning and deceiving than powerful, who has used all his artifice to deceive me. I will suppose that the heavens, the air, the earth, colours, shapes, sounds and all external things that we see, are only illusions and deceptions which he uses to take me in. I will consider myself as having no hands, eyes, flesh, blood or senses, but as believing wrongly that I have all these things. I shall cling obstinately to this notion; and if, by this means, it is not in my power to arrive at the knowledge of any truth, at the very least it is in my power to suspend my judgement.[26]

Descartes creates modern epistemology as a response to the nominalistic transrational God. He does so not by grounding true knowledge in reason but in the power of the will to suspend judgment. As Gillespie puts it, "This emphasis on will is an intrinsic part of Descartes' attempt to find a secure basis for human freedom and reason in the face of the omnipotent God. . . . In his attempt to construct a bastion against the transrational God of will, Descartes attempts to refound reason upon an inherent human will that is invulnerable to divine deception."[27] When all that matters is the God of will whose judgments bear no consistency or relation to the true, then the most reasonable response to God is to use our own will to refuse to be taken in, to stand in judgment of God and say "I doubt it." But notice what happens. Judgment does not disappear. The will's ability to judge and suspend belief even in the face of God becomes the sole basis for our knowledge. Judgment is not lost; it merely finds a new and more rigorous authoritative basis—the brute ability for humans to will. Unless we clear our eyes of this moralistic dogma, any doctrine of judgment will only be used to serve its titanic power.

APPROACHING THE SAINTS:
CHRISTIAN DOCTRINE AS BIBLICAL HERMENEUTIC

Although the modern era maintains the dogma that God will judge, and this gets transformed into the dogma "will judges God," it did not maintain the orthodox Christian dogma where the final judgment is Christ's. The final judgment is not a moral but a christological claim. It is based solely on Christ's ascension. "He will come to judge the quick and the dead" because "worthy is the Lamb that was slaughtered to receive power and wealth and wisdom and might and honor and glory and blessing" (Rev 5:12). This christological reading of the final judgment should be what keeps it from becoming moralistic. Christic judgment is not for the sake of our morality; it is for the sake of revealing to the world God's perfections. It shows us what it means to have our lives taken up into a Triune God whose processions are knowledge and love. We cannot participate in the Triune God without at the same time willing this judgment, celebrating and rejoicing in it. Only because God is holy and perfect and we are called to be perfect as God is, does the judgment make sense. In fact, to do away with the doctrines of hell and judgment is to require God to be less than holy, less than perfect. It makes God mutable like us, incapable of distinguishing between good and evil, for to do away with hell and judgment is to ask God to make evil good by fiat. This would make God's economy ruled by arbitrary will. If this were so, Christ's passion, the resurrection, (where Christ's permanent wounds are revealed to his disciples), and the ascension would not be necessary. Yet if God is Triune and characterized not by arbitrary will but by perfection, then not only do Christ's passion, resurrection, and ascension make sense, but also his kingly role as judge. We see precisely this trinitarian and christological emphasis on the final judgment in theologians like Wesley and Aquinas.

In his sermon "The Great Assize," Wesley takes as his text Rom 14:10: "We shall all stand before the judgment seat of Christ." I do not think Wesley would be troubled that the textual variant "of God" has replaced "of Christ" in modern translations of this passage. The context supports the fact that Paul is speaking of Christ even if he uses *theou* instead of *christou*. In fact, if Paul used *theou*, it would only strengthen Wesley's first point, for he begins his sermon emphasizing that Christ alone is the judge because he is "the express image of the Father" (a reference to Heb 1:3).[28] Because he is "of God," Jesus receives the authority to judge. Since all of Wesley's theology, like that of Irenaeus and Aquinas, is based on our return into the image of God, this is not simply a pious throwaway line. As the only true image of the Father, Jesus is the one who both reveals all that the Father is and makes possible our return to him. He is the full and definitive manifestation of God such that no other is needed. As the Second Person of the Trinity, the Son is not simply some act of will that God chooses, which could be other. He is the very truth and wisdom of God who discloses God's perfections. God's "freedom" is not to choose to be or not be Triune; God is Triune. This is God's omnipotence. It is also God's truth and goodness. Thus it must manifest itself, not out of a capricious act of will, but because of the truth itself. It cannot be other. This requires judgment. As Wesley says,

> . . . it is apparently and absolutely necessary, for the full display of the glory of God, for the clear and perfect manifestation of his wisdom, justice, power and mercy toward the heirs of salvation, that all circumstances of their life should be placed in open view, together with all their tempers, and all the desires, thoughts and intents of their hearts. Otherwise how would it appear out of what a depth of sin and misery the grace of God had delivered them? And, indeed, if the whole lives of all

> the children of men were not manifestly discovered, the whole amazing contexture of divine providence could not be manifested. . . . And then only when God hath brought to light all the hidden things of darkness, whosoever were the actors therein, will it be seen that wise and good were all his ways; that he "saw through the thick cloud" and governed all things by the wise "counsel of his own will"; that nothing was left to chance or the caprice of men, but God disposed all "strongly and sweetly," and wrought all into one connected chain of justice, mercy and truth.[29]

Note several important claims Wesley makes here. First, judgment is a manifestation of God's glory. Unlike Locke and Kant it is not an incentive for us to be moral. Instead, it brings to light what God has already done, who God always is. Second, by bringing to light our wickedness God does not damn us but shows forth his own wisdom. We discover that even though it appeared life was simply capricious, in fact, God knit the world together through justice, mercy, and truth and not arbitrary will. What is the result of the judgment? Wesley tells us it is "the discovery of the divine perfections." Our sins are the lack of what God possesses in full. This is grace, for our perfection does not depend upon us securing our own perfection by our own resources; rather we participate in God's perfections. This is why the righteous "rejoice" in the revelation of God's perfections. Wesley writes, "And in the discovery of the divine perfections the righteous will rejoice with joy unspeakable; far from feeling any painful sorrow or shame for any of those past transgressions which were long since blotted out as a cloud washed away by the blood of the Lamb."[30] In the light of God's glory, that perfect splendor of luminosity which blinds from its brilliance, human creation cannot but be judged. This must occur because we cannot see God unless we are made like God—perfect. Note how Wesley assumes that human sin is subordinate to God's perfections: ". . . only when God hath brought to light all the hidden things of darkness, whosoever were the actors therein, will it be seen that wise and good were all his ways." God's perfections are the true ground of our being. They lack nothing and thus God needs nothing from us. Sin then is a mere lack that poses no threat to God and is not necessary for moral existence. It must and can be judged precisely because God's perfections are the true norm.

Neither pagan nor modern ethics can make sense of this. They are both reactive; they need the evil against which the good only makes sense. In so doing, ethics always justifies evil and gives it substance. Christian theology should never justify evil; it always remains unintelligible, unknowable—a surd that is surprising and ultimately not to be made into a thing because it is nothing. St. Augustine put it this way: "The movement away from God does not come from God, so where does it come from? If you put the question like that, I must reply that I do not know. That may sadden you, but my answer is still right. There can be no knowledge of what is nothing."[31]

Such a statement makes an ethics predicated on the knowledge of good and evil a theological impossibility. Unfortunately, the Christian tradition, and Augustine himself, did not always adhere to the nonknowability of evil. Hans Urs von Balthasar noted both the "ethical nonnecessity of sin" in Augustine as well as its "aesthetic necessity." By finding in sin and evil an aesthetic harmony Augustine put forward a nonbiblical account of evil that, as von Balthasar put it, "opens up the abyss."[32] That is to say, it makes possible evil as an intelligible event in God's own life and in God's good creation. Evil becomes a necessary part of an aesthetic order, part of the inscrutable wisdom of God. Scarcity, lack, and sin become the basis for the possibility of the good. The ancient pagan religion of Manichaeism (where evil and good are competing things constituting our world) and the variations on Manichaeism in much of western morality remain.[33] When this occurs, judgment becomes resentment; it secretly desires the very thing it condemns.

Perhaps we should go so far as to say, contra Augustine and Aquinas, God does not and cannot *know* evil because it is unintelligible.[34] There is nothing substantive to it that can be known. Perhaps this can help us make sense of something both process and openness theology point toward, but without jettisoning orthodox Christianity. It helps us make sense of those biblical passages where God seems not to know what occurs, those passages that perplexed theologians and rabbis. The first such instance of God's apparent lack of knowledge occurs after Adam and Eve sinned. God asks them, "Where are you?" But this is puzzling. How would the God who created the universe not know where his creatures were? The second such lack of knowledge on God's part is found after Cain killed Abel and God says to him, "What have you done?" But if we think of evil as privation, then these passages make sense. That God does not know evil implies no limitations on God's knowledge. It implies no challenge to God's omniscience; it only means that evil itself is nothing. It cannot be known. And if it cannot be known, it cannot stand before God. As C. S. Lewis depicted so wonderfully in *The Great Divorce*,[35] it brings its own judgment upon itself. Evil cannot provide social bonds. It is always already judged.

But Christ's judgment of sin is never a moralistic exercise. Its purpose is not (contra Locke and Kant) to establish the moral law and make people more compliant within an ethics of obligation. To the contrary, as nearly every Christian theologian recognized, what Christ accomplishes is the fulfillment of not only the moral but also the ceremonial and judicial precepts. In so doing, his work constitutes a new political community, one based not upon power but holiness. As Matthew Levering has noted, this is the point of the gift of torah and temple within Israel: "God wishes Israel to become, through the gift of the law, a uniquely virtuous community."[36] Christ is the fulfillment of torah and temple, not because he negates the law, but because he is its perfect performance. If we do not see

Christ as the fulfillment of the law, we will not read Scripture well. And Christ's authority as judge is inextricably linked with his fulfillment of the law.

Thomas Aquinas understood this quite well precisely because he was such a careful reader of Scripture. He divided biblical law into three categories: the moral law, which could be known universally by natural reason and was unchangeable; the ceremonial law, which was changeable only by God and the basis for "the life of his covenant people"; and the "juridical precepts" upon which were based God's judgments. Christ fulfills all three kinds of law, which is the basis for his threefold role as prophet, priest, and king.[37] It is in his kingly role as judge that Christ establishes, not the moral law per se, but the political reality of a new community whose bonds are founded upon what is noble, true, good, and charitable rather than upon mere power and will. And this is the sole reason for the judgment. It makes possible a city founded solely upon holiness, upon God's glory.

Aquinas (or the Thomists who wrote the supplement to the *Summa*), following Augustine, makes this explicit in his doctrine of hell and damnation. He writes, "Sin renders a person worthy to be altogether cut off from the fellowship of God's city, and this is the effect of every sin committed against charity, which is the bond uniting this same city together."[38] This appears to be a reference to the expulsion from the garden. Because hatred and arbitrariness cannot be the true basis for social life, hell is a possibility. It is expulsion from God's holy city. Hell is the judgment against our unwillingness to forge substantive bonds of our life together through charity. Because our evil actions have social consequences that outlast us and our intentions, a final judgment is necessary to restore the bonds of charity that alone make creation possible and alone can be eternal. In his discussion of the "final judgment" Aquinas says that we must have a final judgment and not just a judgment at our deaths, because our sin, like our faithfulness, bears social consequences that must be redeemed if we are to live in God's city.[39] Christ's kingly and priestly roles do not come to an end; they are eternal. This is not because expiation for sin will be necessary in God's city, but because that city is "consummated" by Christ's glory. Aquinas makes this point by appealing to Rev 21 and the New Jerusalem: "The saints who will be in heaven will not need any further expiation by the priesthood of Christ, but having been expiated, they will need consummation through Christ Himself, on Whom their glory depends, as is written (Apoc. xxi.23). The glory of God hath enlightened it—that is, the city of the Saints—and the Lamb is the lamp thereof."[40] This is the purpose of the judgment. It is not to establish the moral law but to constitute what we cannot constitute on our own, a city based on the glory of God rather than the violence of Cain and Abel.

CONCLUDING REFLECTIONS

Perhaps Dante was more correct than Nietzsche presumed when he placed the inscription above the entrance into hell: "This too was made by love."[41] If we assume that this inscription only makes sense when we recognize that true freedom can only be had when the bonds of charity and not arbitrary will unite God's creation, then hell is that place within God's economy where those who refuse such bonds still have a place. But this doctrine of a final judgment drove Nietzsche mad. "There would be more justification," wrote Nietzsche, "for placing above the gateway to the Christian Paradise and its 'eternal bliss' the inscription 'I too was created by eternal hate'—provided a truth may be placed above the gateway to a lie! For what is it that constitutes the bliss of this Paradise?"[42] For Nietzsche the answer was simple—resentment. This is why Christians were obliged to take delight in the punishment of the damned. Tertullian, Augustine, Aquinas, and nearly every other premodern theologian did teach that Christians should rejoice in the punishment of the damned. Nietzsche points it out to us and argues it shows the weakness and vengeance present in our doctrines. How can such a teaching be defended? We need not necessarily do so; it is not orthodox dogma. Neither the Apostles' Creed nor Scripture demands it.

Following Hans Urs von Balthasar and many other theologians we can distance ourselves from some of the harsh Augustinian elements of the doctrine of damnation. We do not know it is eternal. We do not know it must be populated. We do not know that the mass of humanity belongs there. We do not know that we have an obligation to delight in the punishment of the damned. However, we should at least be cautious about siding so easily with Nietzsche and the modern/postmoderns against the ancients like Tertullian, Augustine, and Aquinas. Why did they tell us to rejoice in the plight of the damned? Was it a sadistic desire for revenge? Or was there something more charitable to it than Nietzsche's psychologized reading of it? Could it be an indirect effect of a desire for that other city, the city brought together by the glory of God, who is Christ, and not through the violence of Romulus and Remus or Cain and Abel? Could they rejoice in the damnation of evil for the same reason we cheer at movie theatres when the tyrant finally gets his just deserts and is run out of town? Perhaps this is a noble inclination (even though a dangerous one), for cities cannot be well-established by tyrants and bullies, by those who would use violence, fear, and intimidation. As Augustine taught us, peace is ontologically prior to violence. The violent have no place in God's perfect economy, although God graciously still provides a place for them in hell.

Nevertheless, I find wisdom in the "issue" and "charge" present in Hans Urs von Balthasar's *Dare We Hope 'That all Men Be Saved'?*[43] The issue is that we all stand under judgment and must if God's perfections are to be the ground and end of our existence. The charge is to raise the question whether it is legitimate and faithful, given that hell is within God's economy, to hope that all persons are saved? Augustine and Aquinas thought no. Perhaps Calvinists must still do so today. We Methodists continue to sing, "Come sinners to the Gospel feast, let every soul be Jesus' guest; ye need not one be left behind for God hath bid all humankind."[44] While this can quickly lead to the liberal, bourgeois Christianity H. Richard Niebuhr rightly pilloried, it also recognizes the biblical truth with which this paper began. Scripture contains two series of statements about judgment. As indicated at the beginning of this article, one speaks of the threat of judgment and the possibility of a loss for all eternity, while the other series speaks of God's will and ability to save all. Interestingly, as von Balthasar noted, "The threatening remarks are made predominantly by the pre-Easter Jesus, and the universalist statements (above all in Paul and John) with a view to the redemption that has occurred on the Cross."[45] One cannot make too much of this except to be reassured that once Christ receives his proper dominion, a day which we must pray to come quickly, hell will receive its proper place. Until that day, both sets of Scripture must be proclaimed within the gracious context of the creed where we are reminded that it is Christ, the same one who died for us, who will judge us.

ENDNOTES

1. Hans Urs von Balthasar, *Dare We Hope 'That all Men Be Saved'?* (San Francisco: Ignatius, 1988), 29–39.

2. David Yeago, "The New Testament and the Nicene Dogma," in *The Theological Interpretation of Scripture* (ed. Stephen E. Fowl; Oxford: Blackwell, 1991), 87–88.

3. Grand Rapids, Michigan: Zondervan, 1970.

4. Phillip Gulley and James Mulholland, *If Grace is True: Why God Will Save Every Person* (San Francisco: HarperCollins, 2003).

5. Stanley Hauerwas, *Unleashing the Scriptures* (Nashville: Abingdon, 1993), 23.

6. Athanasius, "On the Incarnation," *Christology of the Later Fathers* (ed. Edward R. Hardy; Philadelphia: Westminster, 1954), 110.

7. *The Kingdom of God in America* (New York: Harper and Row, 1937), 193.

8. Quoted in George Hunsinger's wonderful essay on hell and damnation, "Hellfire and Damnation: Four Ancient and Modern Views," *SJT* 51 (1998): 409. Marty's article appeared in *Harvard Theological Review* 78 (1985): 381–398.

9. See n. 4.

10. See Michel Foucault, *Discipline and Punish: The Birth of the Prison* (New York: Vintage, 1995).

11. Slavoj Zizek, *The Fragile Absolute—Or Why the Christian Legacy is Worth Fighting For?* (London: Verso, 2000), 132.

12. Carl Elliott, *Better than Well* (New York: W. W. Norton, 2003), xx.

13. Ibid., 35.

14. Immanuel Kant, *Religion within the Limits of Reason Alone* (trans. Theodore M. Greene and Hoyt H. Hudson; New York: Harper, 1960), 3.

15. Ibid., 5.

16. For a fuller explanation of this see my *The Goodness of God* (Grand Rapids: Brazos, 2001), esp. p. 64.

17. John Locke *The Reasonableness of Christianity* (ed. I. T. Ramsey; Stanford, Calif.: Stanford University Press, 1958), 60–61.

18. Feuerbach said, "The task of the modern era was the realization and humanization of God—the transformation and dissolution of theology into anthropology." See his *Principles of the Philosophy of the Future* (Indianapolis: Hackett, 1986), 5.

19. Albert C. Knudson, *The Principles of Christian Ethics* (New York: Abingdon, 1943), 82.

20. Ibid., 283.

21. Kant said, "Nothing in the world—indeed nothing even beyond the world—can possibly be conceived which could be called good without qualification except a *good will*" (*Foundations of the Metaphysics of Morals*, New York: Macmillan, 1987), 9.

22. Thomas Hobbes, *Leviathan* (Glasgow: William Collins, 1983), 127.

23. I try to explain how this occurs in my forthcoming *John Wesley's Moral Theology: The Quest for God and Goodness* (Nashville: Abingdon, 2005).

24. I have put this more baldly than it probably should have been put. The question as asked was more nuanced. In his Third Quodlibet, William of Ockham does suggest that to love God requires "to love God and to love whatever God wills to be loved." William of Ockham, *Quodlibetal Questions*, vols. 1 & 2 (trans. by Alfred J. Fredosso and Francis E. Kelly; New Haven & London: Yale University Press, 1991), 214.

25. Michael Gillespie, *Nihilism before Nietzsche* (Chicago: University of Chicago Press, 1995), 14–28.

26. Descartes, *Discourse on Method and the Meditations* (London: Penguin Classics, 1986), 100.

27. Gillespie, *Nihilism before Nietzsche*, 41.

28. *Wesley Works, I* (ed. Albert Outler; Nashville: Abingdon, 1984), 359.

29. Ibid., 364–365.

30. Ibid., 365.

31. Quoted in Hans Urs von Balthasar's *The Glory of the Lord: A Theological Aesthetics, II: Studies in Theological Style: Clerical Styles* (San Francisco: Ignatius, Crossroad, 1984), 105.

32. Ibid., 127–129.

33. Ibid.

34. See St. Thomas Aquinas, *On Evil* (trans. by Jean Oesterle; Notre Dame: University of Notre Dame Press, 1993), Question 1, article 2.

35. C. S. Lewis, "The Great Divorce," in *The Best of C. S. Lewis* (Grand Rapids: Baker, 1969).

36. *Christ's Fulfillment of Torah and Temple: Salvation According to Thomas Aquinas* (Notre Dame, Ind.: University of Notre Dame Press, 2002), 20.

37. Ibid., 25.

38. Ibid., 203.

39. Aquinas writes, "Just as from the deceit of Arius and other false leaders unbelief continues to follow us down to the close of the world; and even until then faith will continue to derive its progress from the preaching of the apostles" *(Summa Theologiae* III. 59 art. 5).

40. *Summa Theologiae* III. 5 art. 5 ad. 1. See also Levering, p. 139.

41. Nietzsche, *On The Genealogy of Morals* (ed. and trans. by Walter Kaufman; New York: Vintage, 1989), 49.

42. Ibid.

43. *Dare We Hope 'That all Men Be Saved'?* 29–39.

44. First line of a hymn by Charles Wesley, "Come, Sinners to the Gospel Feast," *United Methodist Hymnal* (Nashville: The United Methodist Publishing House, 1989), 616.

45. Von Balthasar, 29–39.

RESPONSE TO LONG

D. LYLE DABNEY

Let me begin by saying unambiguously that Stephen Long has written a fine paper. It lays out a case not only for a method of interpreting divine judgment but also for understanding why this doctrine has become so obscure in much of modern Christianity. He raises in a powerful and compelling way the question of where we are to turn for judgment, the very question of modernity itself—and the question of Christian theology. I for one appreciate what he has done. Now having said that, my assignment in the following is to explore the weaknesses in the paper's argument and to offer a critical response. I do find issues in the paper that seem puzzling. While my questions are many, I have time for only two, and both concern method.

The first question I want to ask Dr. Long is what you mean by "tradition." What I understand you to be arguing in essence is that the ancient and medieval church got it right, while the modern church, having listened to the siren song of the Enlightenment, gets it wrong. Thus, with David Yeago you would return to "the unanimous conviction of the Christian tradition" as seen in the creeds and dogma of the patristic and medieval periods in order to find there a guide to recognizing God *in* Scripture and thus to attaining a faithful reading *of* Scripture and its witness concerning judgment. Well and good! I applaud the fact that you, unlike so many of our contemporaries, religious and otherwise, would take the past seriously. I seek to do so myself. But a whole cluster of questions about your treatment of this issue immediately arise that I cannot ignore.

On the one hand I must ask to what extent can we say that there is a body of doctrine and practice that is the "unanimous conviction of the Christian tradition"? The question is unavoidable today, and to disregard or dismiss it is not the same as answering it. Is the Christian tradition really the monolith this paper seems to assume, or is it a much more pluriform entity? Historically it is unquestionably pluriform; indeed, there is virtually nothing upon which the tradition has agreed "unanimously." For, in the history of Christianity even your examples of the christological and Trinitarian dogmas have been matters of debate—and for some on both the left and the right still are. Notice that we have not even touched upon the questions that have divided and still divide the major ecclesiastical bodies in the West, the questions of soteriology and authority. Which one belongs to "the" tradition, and why does the other not? Moreover, remember that at one point, even a figure like Calvin thought the doctrine of the Trinity to be problematic. Are we to conclude that Calvin, at that point at least, is not a part of "the" tradition? On what grounds could we say he is or is not? It is incumbent upon your paper to specify what you take to be the authoritative tradition, and why you do so. Failing that, it appears that the notion of "tradition" is for your argument the infamous "wax nose" that can be bent in any direction and take any form that you desire. Or, to change the metaphor, it seems that the invocation of "tradition" functions in this paper as a kind of blank check that allows you to draw from the historical account whatever suits your purposes at the moment, conveniently ignoring what does not support your argument. Could you help me understand your notion of tradition more clearly?

On the other hand, a further question about your invocation of tradition that I cannot ignore is this: What of the possibility that the tradition you would see as our guide gets something wrong, or, perhaps better said, does not finally get it right? One example that immediately comes to mind is a doctrine you invoke both as a criticism of process and openness-of-God theologians and as the (apparent) presupposition of your notion of God's perfections, the doctrine of divine impassibility. When Christianity emerged out of the Jewish subculture into the dominant Hellenistic culture of the Roman empire in the second century, it immediately faced a profound problem in communicating and defending the gospel of Jesus Christ. Their claim—as evidenced by baptismal formulas, creeds, hymns, prayers, and sermons of the period—was that Jesus Christ is God. When that claim had been made in a Jewish context, the response was often what we see in the NT depiction of many of Israel's leaders: blasphemy! But in the context of a culture defined by Hellenistic dualism the response was not pious outrage but confused incomprehension, or worse, intellectual dismissal. For in Hellenism the divine belonged to the realm of the timeless and changeless and was thus *impassible*. When Christians said that God was incarnate in a man who lived in time and space, who was born and grew to manhood in the ordinary way, suffered a disgraceful death on a cross, and was then supposedly raised from the dead, all the Hellenists heard were literally meaningless sounds, vacuous words. Those Christians might as well have been speaking in tongues! In terms of substance, it was as if they were claiming that circles were squares. Thus the Hellenists did not hear blasphemy; what they heard was nonsense. The theological task of the patristic period, therefore, became explicating what Christians meant when they called Jesus Christ God. That is as unmistakable in the apologetic of Justin Martyr in the second century as it is in the creeds and councils of the fourth and fifth centuries. The outcome for dogma was the identification of the being of the Son with that of the impassible Father and the doctrine of the two natures of Christ that separated the Son's impassible divinity from the change and suffering of Jesus' humanity. In this way Christianity made its message about Christ comprehensible and compelling in a Hellenistic world.

As long as those philosophical presuppositions held sway in western culture, those dogmatic formulas were necessary and effective tools in Christian theologizing. But the modern period saw those presuppositions challenged, first through philosophical critique and then through social change that made such dualism itself incomprehensible. In that context the doctrine of divine impassibility has been challenged by Christian theologians, not on secularist or naturalist grounds, but on the basis of the biblical witness itself—the "bad conscience" whose murmuring has always been heard throughout the tradition. Therefore, this is not "Luther's fault," as you would have it; it is Scripture's "fault." For if the NT does indeed depict Jesus Christ, God's Son, as divine—and I for one believe it does—then it does so in depicting him as utterly human. And that means as utterly passible. The God of Abraham, Isaac, and Jacob, the God of Jesus Christ, is depicted in the Bible as faithful, and God's perfections are to be understood as an expression of that concrete faithfulness to God's own self and to God's own creation, not as abstract aseity, complete unto itself, unaffected by all that is not God. Out of such faithfulness the God of the scriptural witness enters into creation's suffering and thus is not impassible but is rather passible precisely in that faithfulness. If the early church had to turn a blind eye to that aspect of Scripture in order to make what it took to be the essential aspect of Scripture comprehensible and compelling in their social world there and then, then we must reclaim that biblical witness today to achieve the same thing in our social world here and now. And that means that in the judgment of many of our contemporary theologians—and I count myself among them—the creeds and dogmas of the early church did not get this one finally right. This, it seems to me, bodes ill for any claim that traditional dogma and creed is the unerring guide to our contemporary theologizing. Can you help me understand how you would see this otherwise?

The second question I want to ask is related to the first, at once more specific and more general. I want to ask you about what seems to me to be a false dichotomy that undergirds your paper and its argument, a dichotomy that appears to be yet another reflection of the methodology you espouse that causes me such puzzlement. Once again, I understand your construal of the theological situation to be summed up as follows. The dogmatic and creedal tradition is the guide to true understanding, but, having been abandoned by modernity, that tradition must be reclaimed to rightly interpret Scripture's witness to judgment. The modern is in this sense the problem, to which the past is the solution. What I want to point out now is that you seem then to extend that into a kind of absolute difference between now and then, present and past, as if the theological task faced by those who formulated those creeds and dogmas operated on a totally different plane from the task we face today. I see this when you write: "To offer a theological interpretation of the scriptural witness on judgment that neglects the creed and Christian doctrine is to place upon ourselves that unbearable modern burden that everything must be rebuilt, everything must be 'new and improved' in every generation." I have a hard time understanding you here. Was the creed of 325 not "new" in its day, as was the ecumenical council out of which it grew? Was the creed of 381 not "new" in its day? Was the dogma of the two natures of Christ not "new" in its day? And in the same sense, and even earlier, were not the so-called Apostolic Fathers doing something "new" when they struggled with their fledgling theological formulations? What of Irenaeus, of Justin, of Tertullian, of Origen, or later of Augustine and Aquinas? Were not each of these involved in something "new" in response to the new challenges they found themselves facing? According to many of their contemporaries, what each of them was doing was indeed new, and they often complained about the legitimacy of that novelty.

Now your real point, I think, is to repudiate the arrogance of the modern assumption that today we are the enlightened, and thus for the first time in human history we at last employ reason aright and, therefore, can and must measure the past by the present. This is an attitude that is notable both in much of the theological and most of the nontheological discourse of modernity. Against this privileging of the now over the then, you seek to reverse the categories: theology must instead hew to the past and reject the modern. In doing so you are in good company, for as surely as modernity was marked by the elevation of the present over the past, so it was also marked by a counter movement—theological and otherwise—that protested in favor of the earlier over the later. This was and is the voice of Romanticism in all its many forms, and it has been represented by figures as diverse as Goethe in the seventeenth century; Wesley, Coleridge, and Delacroix in the eighteenth century; Schleiermacher and Wagner in the nineteenth; and Catholic and Protestant conservatisms of the twentieth. In each case the notion is that the alternative to modern arrogance is a return to an imagined united and pure state of an earlier time, be it cultural or ecclesiastical. Note carefully, that claim is just as characteristically modern as that against which it protests. The question that must be asked is this: Does this claim get us anywhere, or is it just the idealization of the past as an alternative to an overweening present? Is this anything more than the second verse of the same song we have sung since the Enlightenment?

Where then do we turn for judgment? That is the question posed and answered by this paper in two very different ways. On one level—the level of theological substance in the paper—it declares that judgment belongs to God and has been illegitimately claimed by modern humanity. With that I am in complete agreement, and I applaud the clarity with which Dr. Long elucidates that claim.

But on another level—the level of its methodological discussion—the paper asks this question not in terms of "who," i.e., the risen Christ, but in terms of "when." And there I must part company with Dr. Long. We cannot escape our time, and as those who follow the one who was incarnate in time, we should not try to. We do not live in the patristic period, and we do not face the challenge of giving account of faith in Christ in the midst of a culture defined by Hellenistic dualism. Nor do we live in the medieval period, called to speak as to how God mediates grace to human nature across the divide between eternity and time. Again, we do not find ourselves in the Reformation period, having to attack the very theological and intellectual structures of the medieval world in order to protest the corruption of the church and the gospel that they had engendered and defended. We live in another kind of time and place, and we face a different kind of challenge. Christendom, that synthesis between church and culture that has defined much of western civilization for most of two millennia, is no more. And the cultural project, modernity, that was both a chief agent of Christendom's demise and the period of time in which it passed away, is itself in crisis. The theological question that now faces us is what it means to be Christian in a world post-Christendom, a world in which the intellectual and social presuppositions that we have traded on for millennia have disappeared. In answering that question it simply misses the point entirely if we think we can declare for the present against the past or for the tradition against the arrogance of the present. It is time for Christianity to quit playing in the orchestra of modernity as our cultural Titanic sinks beneath the waves. Certainly we can and must hear the witness of our sisters and brothers who have gone before, saints indeed; they have much to teach us. But we cannot simply say what they said, for what they said is often little more than a non-sequitur in the subsequent moments of the conversation between Christian witness and cultural context that is Christian theology. Yet while we cannot simply say now what they said then, we can and must do now what they did then. They gave account of the proclamation of Christ in the social worlds in which they found themselves, and we must do the same in our own. That is to say, we must not only *study* theology, we must *do* theology. Thus I affirm the question that pervades this paper: Where do we turn for judgment? And I ask a question in turn: How does the method you champion help us to answer the challenge we now face? I would remind you that Karl Barth famously exhorted his students to theologize with a Bible in one hand and the newspaper in the other. Maybe it is time for all of us to think about renewing our subscription.

THE IMPLICIT "JUDGMENT OF GOD" IN THE NARRATIVE THEOLOGY OF MARK: SOME POSTCOLONIAL RESERVATIONS

EMERSON B. POWERY

I must confess. This topic frightens me. Discussion of the topic in some Christian circles is analogous to the shifting of the warning signals by the Department of Homeland Security from a blue ("guarded") to an orange ("high") to a yellow ("elevated") to a red ("severe") alert. If you grew up in a religious setting in which a literalistic reading of these difficult texts occurred *and*, perhaps more importantly, such texts were dominant forms of discourse to determine an exclusive community, oftentimes even to the exclusion of other biblical themes, then you may understand my dilemma. Yet, there may be another way to understand these texts without jettisoning them whole.

What is needed is a broadening of the "theological" lens through which many interpret. A "political" interpretation could and should function as a corrective to a theological one. Richard Hays notes the connection: *"The church needs apocalyptic eschatology for the gospel's political critique of pagan culture."*[1] I appreciate this assessment, although I would not suggest as great a divide between church and culture. Also, in a published lecture, N. T. Wright highlights this point, using Richard Horsley's work on Paul.[2] Horsley's recent work on Mark will inform us as well, as he challenges the conclusions of some recent interpreters:

> Recent liberal interpreters of Jesus are clearly uncomfortable with the judgmental side of Jesus' mission.... This is a dramatic departure from the earlier view made popular mainly by Albert Schweitzer of Jesus as an "apocalyptic" prophet who preached the end of the world. To modern Western sensitivities, however, the apocalyptic Jesus seems perilously close to being a deluded fanatic, since his predictions of a presumed "cosmic catastrophe" proved false. Some recent American interpreters have avoided this embarrassing conclusion by rejecting as secondary any

of Jesus' sayings that might seem "apocalyptic" in tone or motif. This makes Jesus into an utterly unique historical figure—a historical impossibility, of course—different from both his Jewish contemporaries before him and his own followers after him.[3]

Of course, Horsley is correct, as was Albert Schweitzer: Jesus was an apocalyptic, eschatological prophet whose keen sense of the end of time penetrated his present understanding of his actions and words.[4] Moving beyond this analysis, Horsley then recognizes the political ramifications of this type of figure, one who "pronounc[ed] and demonstrat[ed] God's condemnation of intolerable rulers so that renewal of the society was possible."[5] Yet, to some extent, the idea of future judgment is downplayed, at least for the earliest written Gospel (which is my primary focus), and—when mentioned—implicit rather than an "in your face" Tim LaHayian method of future-oriented scare tactics for manipulating present crisis moments. The sophistication of this earliest theological narrative of the story of Jesus should be read on its own merit as one in which the judgment of God is not ignored but is primarily implicit.

So, how would the theme of "God's judgment" as depicted in the narrative theology of the Second Gospel look if read through a socio-political theological lens? Addressing this question is the intent of this paper.

In 1906, as Schweitzer was publishing his *magnum opus* in the European world, another event—American in origins—occurred which would affect discussions on eschatological ideas and the biblical text more among the populace. This event was the Azusa street revival, which was led by a one-eyed African American preacher (one generation removed from enslavement), who (arguably) initiated the origins of the worldwide Pentecostal movement. The movement grounded its mission in an eschatological fervor not unlike the narrative depictions of the book of Acts. During this same year sixty-two African Americans were reportedly lynched.[6] This juxtaposition is an important reminder that each person has particular lenses (claimed and unclaimed) that shape our discourse and arguments. Other voices linger at the surface of this presentation as well, ancestral voices for me, necessary reminders that looking at such categories like vindication and destruction have implications beyond what we may discuss in this conference and *always* have greater ramifications for those on the margins.[7] So, I attempt to recover a few perspectives on judgment from the formerly enslaved, as they thought through the tensions of the biblical narrative, surrounding the idea of God's justice with the complexities of their own inhuman situation. Turning to the slave narrative is a natural move because nineteenth-century antebellum African slave life is as precise an analogy to first-century Christianity as one may find. According to Cornel West, "Christianity also is first and foremost a theodicy, a triumphant account of good over evil. The intellectual life of the African slaves in the United States—like that of all oppressed peoples—consisted primarily of reckoning with the dominant form of evil in their lives. The Christian emphasis on against-the-evidence hope for triumph over evil struck deep among many of them."[8]

JUDGMENT OF GOD IN THE GOSPEL OF MARK[9]

The language of judgment is rare in the Gospel of Mark. Neither the phrase "judgment of God" (*krisis tou theou*) nor the word "judgment" (*krisis*) occurs. A form of the term *krima* ("condemnation") occurs once in the entire narrative at 12:40. This occurrence in a statement of Jesus does not clearly stipulate whether God is the agent of condemnation, although a future orientation is implied with *lēmpsontai* ("they will receive").[10]

Reading in canonical order, this omission from Mark is striking. At the "head" of the canon Matthew's Gospel exploits the theme of God as judge, and eschatological parables of judgment abound (cf. chs. 24–25). As Vicki Balabanski recently argued, "Matthew heightens the expectation to fan an imminent End *vis-à-vis* the Markan *Vorlage*, seeing this reiteration of imminence as the appropriate message for the Matthean community."[11] But Mark's strategy appears radically different when read alongside of Matthew.

With regard to the narrative of Mark, with the primary exception of the phrase the "reign (or kingdom) of God" (cf. 1:14–15; 4:11, 26, 30; 9:1, 43–49; 10:15–16, 23–25, 37; 11:10; 12:34; 14:25; 15:43), the heart of Mark's judgment motif occurs in chapters 12 and 13 after Jesus enters Jerusalem. Additional concepts occur earlier, but each is used sparingly (e.g., "heaven" only in 10:21; "eternal life" only in 10:17, 31).[12] Our attention, then, will focus on these two chapters.

God as "Judge" of the Vineyard/Tenants (Mark 12:1–12). In Mark 12 Jesus provides a story about God the judge. In fact, this parable is the most apparent indication in the narrative that God, "the owner of the vineyard," would finally lose patience with God's "tenants" (i.e., Jerusalem temple leadership) and eventually perform three acts, which Jesus keeps in the future tense. First, the land owner will "come" (*eleusetai*). Then, God will "destroy" (*apolesei*) the tenants. Finally, God will "turn over" (*dōsei*) the vineyard to others. What concerns this presentation is God's destruction of the tenants. Before we turn to the main verb, *apollumi* ("to destroy"), it will help to situate this parable in its narrative and intertextual context.

Following Jesus' temple action the temple leadership rightfully questions Jesus' authority. Jesus offers two replies, the first more ambiguous than the second. First, he associates his mission with John's by questioning the leaders about the origins (and, thereby, authority) of John's baptism. Second, Jesus recounts the parable of the vineyard. Then following this parable, God's authority (and Jesus' own, as God's agent) is challenged again by posing the question whether Caesar should receive taxes.

The "vineyard" in Isa 5, the intertext for Jesus' parable, was a metaphor for the "house of Israel" and "the people of Judah," the northern and southern kingdoms of ancient Israel. In Isaiah's account the *vineyard* was destroyed (Isa 5:5). In Jesus' account the patient "lord" would destroy the unfaithful tenants and preserve (i.e., deliver over) the vineyard to others. In other words, as the temple leaders grasp (12:12) and a comparison to Isaiah clarifies, Jesus condemns their care of the people of Israel, and concurrently, their custody of the temple.

In the Gospel of Mark the verb *apollumi* ("to destroy") indicates a level of vindication not specifically defined in ch. 12, but it is used elsewhere of humans (3:6; 4:38; 9:22; 11:18), of spirits (1:24; 8:38), and of things (2:22 and 9:41) with a clear indication of finality.

If we push the allegorical interpretation further, as many interpreters (including myself) are rightfully reluctant to do, other characteristics of this future judge appear:

1. Care of the vineyard opens and ends the parable (vv. 1, 9), which involves an expectation of production;[13]
2. There is a kind of stubbornness, as he sends "slave" (*doulos*) after "slave"; perhaps it expresses the cultural bias against and lack of care for the *douloi* or a naiveté about the tenants' desires;
3. Should we call it vulnerability or patience? From the owner's thought process we learn "they will heed my son," for which there has been no evidence except for a general cultural awareness that such respect should occur;[14]
4. Finally, while there is an apparent hesitancy to provide punishment, it will come, as the story goes, and it will come completely (*apolesei*).

Within the Gospel of Mark this parable provides Jesus' theological conception of God's coming judgment upon the Jewish leaders. As Klyne Snodgrass concluded more than twenty years ago, "this parable is of the utmost significance for understanding Jesus and his mission. . . . Rejection of him is disastrous in that one loses participation in God's Kingdom and faces judgment."[15]

The Markan narrative continues this judgment motif through the agencies of the Spirit and the expected Son of Man in a genre more conducive for the discussion. Chapter 13 has generally been described as Mark's "little apocalypse."

Spirit as "Judge" of Rulers and Kings: The Political Dissent of Jesus' Followers (Mark 13). Standard dictionaries generally depict apocalyptic discourse as literature of resistance against the major political forces of the day. They may not all use the term, "resistance," but other synonyms are appropriated. Even in the more conservative and now dated *International Standard Bible Encyclopedia* J. E. H. Thomson wrote, "Apocalypse could only have been possible under the domination of the great empires."[16] One of the primary gurus of the genre, John Collins, suggests, "It [apocalyptic] entails a challenge to view the world in a way that is radically different from the common perception. . . . The legacy of the apocalypses includes a powerful rhetoric for denouncing the deficiencies of this world."[17] The "little apocalypse" of Mark 13 is no exception. Numerous scholars compare it understandably to Revelation, *4 Ezra* (11:1–12:39), and *2 Baruch* (36:1–46:7), other major apocalyptic discourses of the day.

While in a narrative sensitive reading generic features in the story are leveled out and may not be seen as significant, it is still interesting to recall Leander Keck's question, "Why does Mark suddenly give us an apocalyptic Jesus in contrast with the rest of the Gospel?" Of course, how one defines "apocalyptic" may cause one to consider Keck's question misguided.[18] References to the "Son of Man" and the "Spirit" elsewhere in the narrative are certainly not nonapocalyptic features. However one might define apocalypticism, it is the nature of apocalyptic literature to indicate, frequently in coded language, that things are misguided politically or religiously (an unnecessary distinction in the first century), so that (1) God will/must intervene soon (and judge), and (2) followers of God must be alert, patient, and on guard. What role humans should play in this apocalyptic drama differs from one text to the next. As Collins notes, "The visionaries were rarely revolutionaries." Yet, Mark advocates a human response in 13:11, a response instigated by the Spirit of God.

"Witness against them." What the disciples may say—as granted by the Spirit—is a mystery, but why they are in this predicament seems attainable from the passage. They are to stand as a witness against them (*eis marturion autois*). The NRSV's ambiguous "as a testimony to them" does not quite provide any direction for this discourse, whether it is an affirming or critiquing gesture from the disciples. Many scholars have interpreted this expression as the extension of the message of salvation in a modern evangelical sense of proclaiming the gospel, but it is not the only available reading.[19] Much depends on the interpretation of the dative *autois*.

The entire expression occurs two other times in Mark's narrative (1:44; 6:11). In the first chapter Jesus tells the healed leper to show himself to the priests, *eis marturion autois*. Although the editors of NRSV maintain their consistent but ambiguous "as a testimony to them," many commentators sense antagonism in Jesus' reaction to a priestly system that would distance the leper from regular religious practices.[20]

The other occurrence, Mark 6:11, is a clear instance of the antagonistic use of this phrase. Jesus tells the disciples to shake the dust off of their feet *eis marturion autois*, as a sign of the audience's rejection of their message. Even the NRSV breaks its pattern by translating the phrase "as a testimony *against* them" (my italics).[21]

If we conclude, as I think we should, that this phrase should be read in a hostile way in 13:11, connecting it to other occurrences in Mark, then this may redefine what the Spirit is saying to the *hegemonic* elite of the day. These are words "against" the abuses of the authorities, analogous to John before Herod. It is a word of prophetic judgment. It would also force us to view the disciples' political opposition as good news as well, but it may not be simply a proclamation of the kind that many contemporaries expect. Rather, it appears that their response, that is, their gospel message, included words of resistance to the practices of the rulers. Their "evangelical" message included dissent from the political order. In many ways, it is a form of judgment originating with the Spirit, although the Spirit's activity of judgment, unlike God's or the Son of Man's, is reserved for foreign rulers.

Son of Man as Judge in Mark? It may be true that an apocalyptic "Son of Man" figure would arrive as judge (cf. Dan 7:13), but such is not clear in the Markan text. In fact, *how* the Son of Man comes is much more explicit than *why* he comes. He comes (1) "in his father's glory with the holy angels" (8:38); (2) "with much power and glory" (13:26); (3) "seated on the right hand of power and coming with the clouds of heaven" (14:62). Only three clues suggest *why* the Son of Man comes, a coming which might convene an occasion to assess a final verdict: (1) "to be ashamed of" (to bring shame to?) those ashamed of his words (8:38); (2) "to gather the elect from the four winds" (13:27); (3) simply "coming with the clouds of heaven" (14:62).

The narrative of Mark is more explicit about Jesus' earthly authoritative role as the Son of Man who forgives sins (2:10), rules the Sabbath (2:28), and suffers (8:31–32; 9:31; 10:33–34; cf. 10:45) than about any future action.[22] Of course, the references to a suffering Son of Man also include an eventual resurrected Son of Man. But none of these repeated predictions of Jesus include any unambiguous notion of vindication following the resurrection.[23]

The Son of Man's action of "being ashamed" (*epaischunthēsetai*) of those ashamed of Jesus and his words is fitting culturally in an honor/shame society.[24] But what are the eschatological implications from this shame? Many contemporary scholars claim that clear images of judgment are present as the Son of Man arrives "with the holy angels" (8:38) and offer suggestions about his explicit role as "judge,"[25] "accuser,"[26] or even "prosecutor."[27] But the nature of this coming shame is not so clear, and no other action is suggested in this first statement about the Son of Man's future activity.

In ch. 13 the action is more positive than in ch. 8: "He will send out his angels and gather together the elect" (13:27). In fact, any hint of a condemnation of the nonelect is completely absent at this point, which is more striking in light of its immediate literary context following on the heels of "false messiahs" and "false prophets" (cf. 13:21–29).[28] The "goal," as E. Schweizer succinctly notes, "is not the annihilation of his enemies or their condemnation to everlasting punishment. It is the power and glory of the Son of Man, which involves the homecoming of the dispersed to ultimate fellowship with their God."[29]

Finally, what is suggested in the Son of Man's location "seated on the right hand of power" and "coming with the clouds" (14:62)? Observing that these words are spoken to Jesus' accusers,[30] Hooker concludes that it is an unmistakable expression of "the exaltation and vindication of the Son of Man himself," comparing it to Acts 7:56 where the Son of Man stands.[31] For Hooker, this passage—more so than 13:27—"implies a future judgement scene, in which the Son of Man's position is recognized by everyone."[32] She is not alone in this assessment of the passage, and it is understandable how scholars have come to this conclusion. The allusions to Dan 7 and Ps 110 are explored in most commentaries, in which, as Craig Evans fills in the gaps, "As 'the son of man' Jesus will take his seat next to God himself (Ps 110:1); he will 'come with the clouds' (Dan 7:13); the court will sit 'in judgment' (Dan 7:9); and his 'enemies' will become his 'footstool' (Ps 110:1)."[33] I do not deny that the theme is present in Mark. What is curious is that even here judgment is only implicit. It is not clear that "court" is yet in session.[34] What is clearer is that Jesus will receive a dignified, exalted position.

The expanded traditions in the Gospels of Matthew and Luke, however, exploit Mark's implicit judgment motif and may be responsible for the overemphasis in commentaries on the Second Gospel. Within the first two of Jesus' three predictions of the future activity of the Son of Man, Matthew often includes additional features that clarify ambiguous images or ideas.[35] For example, in the first prediction of the Son of Man's return, Matthew omits the more indefinite action of the Son of Man's "being ashamed," *yet* includes the explicit statement of recompense: "and then he will repay everyone for what has been done" (Matt 16:27).[36] In the second prediction of this future action, in addition to the "loud trumpet call," Matthew includes the mourning of all tribes (24:30).

The other Gospels offer additional stories portraying the judging activity of the Son of Man. Matthew's parables of eschatological judgment are well known (e.g., chs. 13, 24, and 25). In Jesus' interpretation for the "parable of the tares" (cf. 13:24–30) we find: "The Son of Man will send *his* angels, and they will gather out of his kingdom all causes of sin and all evildoers, and throw them into the furnace of fire; there men will weep and gnash their teeth. Then the righteous will shine like the sun in the kingdom of their Father" (13:41–43). The parable of the net has similar words: "The angels will come out and separate the evil from the righteous, and throw them into the furnace of fire; there men will weep and gnash their teeth" (13:49–50). One final example from Matthew should suffice. At the end of the series of parables in chs. 24 and 25 comes Matthew's clearest statement on the last judgment: "When the Son of Man comes . . . he will separate them one from another as a shepherd separates the sheep from the goats" (25:31–32). "And they will go away into eternal punishment, but the righteous into eternal life" (21:46). Such ideas are not reserved only for these parables, as Matthew includes statements about the judging activity of the Son of Man elsewhere as well (cf. 19:28).[37]

The Gospel of Luke contains its own distinctive traditions on this theme. There is nothing comparable to Luke 17:22–37 (entitled "The Day of the Son of Man" in Aland's Synopsis) in the other Gospels, although a few of the verses are scattered in Matthew and Mark. Only in Luke do we find, "The days are coming when you will desire to see one of the days of the Son of Man, and you will not see it" (17:22). This "day" is clearly a day of judgment, during which "one will be taken and the other left" (//Matt 24:20). Perhaps less clear but obviously pertinent in light of its literary connection following 17:22–37 is the parable of the unjust judge, to whom God is compared in the final two verses (18:7–8): "Will not God vindicate his elect, who cry to him day and night? Will he delay long over them? I tell you, he will vindicate (*ekdikēsin*) them speedily. Nevertheless, when the Son of Man comes, will he find faith on earth?"[38] Finally, while all three Gospels share the idea of watchfulness, only Luke includes the need to "watch at all times, praying that you may have strength to escape all these things that will take place, and *to stand before the Son of Man*" (21:36).

The Gospel of Mark shares *none* of these sentiments explicitly with its parallels. Perhaps such are implied in a Son of Man figure who "comes," "is ashamed," "gathers the elect," and "sits on the right hand." But perhaps not. It is possible that the theology of the Markan narrative supports N. T. Wright's thesis that the emphasis is more on *coming* "enthronement" than "judgment." It may be time to give Wright's thesis its due.[39]

TWO "POSTCOLONIAL" RESERVATIONS: STEPHEN MOORE AND BLACK THEOLOGY[40]

In a recent SBL presentation Stephen Moore recognized the ambivalence of issues of power within the Markan narrative. Judgment language, of course, falls under this category as well, since only one with legitimate power and authority can function as judge. In a narrative that has maintained a level of ambiguity about the ruling political power of the day, Rome, such dissent (as in 13:9–13) seems odd. Although Mark has not hidden the tension between Jesus and the Jewish authorities, opposition to Rome is less obvious in the overall narrative. In fact, in ch. 13 Rome may even be seen as the agent of God, albeit indirectly, in the destruction of the temple (13:1–2).[41] Even Jesus' trial before Pilate leaves readers with an uncertain sense about this political figure, who appears to carry out the wishes of the Jewish populace (cf. 15:2–15). Furthermore, as is well known, the final confession and the first *human* acknowledgement of Jesus as "son of

God" derives from a Roman centurion (15:39). In many ways, Mark's depiction of Rome is not the critique of the empire of the book of Revelation.[42] Nor is it, however, the apparent acquiescence of a Rom 13 or 1 Pet 2.[43] Is judgment of God upon Rome apparent in this story of Jesus?

Yet, Moore concludes that unambiguous instructions about the power struggle are present in Mark's portrayal of Jesus' discussion of the parousia: "What the parousia will signify," argues Moore, "is the unceremonious cessation of the Roman empire, as of every other human *basileia*. Jesus will bump Caesar off the throne."[44] All political readings of the Gospel of Mark affirm this interpretation.[45] For them the Gospel of Mark is a political manifesto of liberation, "unambivalently anti-imperial" (in Moore's words).[46]

But, in his postmodern and now postcolonial phase, Moore also shows how Mark's "ideology falls prey to ambivalence . . . where its message of emancipation subtly mutates into oppression."[47] A series of questions from Moore provides an indication of the direction of his argument:

> By insisting on returning "with great power and glory" (13:26), does Mark's Jesus betray Mark's own latent desire for a top-heavy, authoritarian, universal Christian empire, an über-Roman empire, so to speak—the kind that will arrive all too soon, anyway, unbeknown to Mark, long before Jesus himself does? By insisting on returning in imperial splendor . . . does Mark's Jesus relativize and undercut the radical social values that he had died to exemplify and implement? . . . Can radical apocalypticism only mirror imperial or colonial ideologies . . . or can it instead be consonant with a counter-imperial or counter-colonial ethic?"[48]

Before we attempt to defend Mark too quickly and find in Jesus' language of the parousia a "peaceful" resolution to the wars and destructions of the world's empires, careful attention must be paid to the theologies and ideologies that shape the interpretations of this narrative *and* continue to shape our (i.e., Western, Christian) own contemporary thoughts, words, and actions and its imperialistic thrust.

I hesitate to support wholeheartedly Moore's reading of Mark, especially when the Second Gospel is read in light of its canonical partners. Rather it appears that Mark's returning Son of Man, as God's agent, arrives in the eschaton primarily to carry out a mission of regathering those elected.[49] Of course, we can only surmise about the nonelect. Tensions with the imperial order of the day certainly provide a tense and confrontational atmosphere (e.g., 13:9–13), but Mark's narrative is cautious about the intent of the Son of Man's return.

From the opening of the Gospel, the idea of a "new order" has permeated the mission of Jesus and the rhetoric of the narrative: *the "coming rule" of God as a prophetic, political stance.* There is a short leap from "the reign of God is at hand" (1:14) and the judgment that is ensuing in the mission of Jesus (most evident in the "binding the strong man" in exorcism activity) to the prophetic and apocalyptic actions and messages of chs. 12–13.

Jesus' arrival as God's agent involves "insiders" and "outsiders." Outsiders should beware. Except for the narrative of chs. 12–13, specific details about the future of "outsiders" are less clear. That God will judge (12:1–9) is clear. What this might mean for those excluded from the elect is less specific. Details of the final verdict are not part of the rhetoric of Mark's narrative, which itself then may serve as a counterbalance to the thrust of harsher judgment language of the other narratives.

"ESCHATOLOGY IN BLACK":[50]
THE POLITICAL NATURE OF JUDGMENT LANGUAGE

My findings of a deemphasized theme of judgment in Mark allows for some critical distance from the eschatological fervor of my religious heritage. Yet, to listen only to Mark's "solo" in the canonical choir would be detrimental to a full understanding of the diversity of opinion among early Christian communities, so a brief glance at Matthew and Luke and their exploitation of this motif was also presented. Mark's voice, however, provides a bridge between the eschatological expectancy of the Gospel of Matthew and the book of Revelation and the realized eschatology of the Fourth Gospel.

In like manner, it would be inappropriate to ignore particular voices in Christian tradition which infrequently receive a hearing on this topic. There is a growing body of literature analyzing the "texts" of the formerly enslaved as a primary source informing Black Theology.[51] Before I turn to a brief discussion of the theme of God's judgment within a few select "slave narratives,"[52] let me attempt to set up this discussion.

In 1982, Gayraud Wilmore published a general introduction to eschatology, a work informed partly by views from the "underside."[53] In his analysis of the spirituals (among other sources), he concludes that there were three basic responses among the enslaved to the concept of the end of the world. Some turned away completely from Christianity.[54] Others internalized "the excitement about the immediate return of Christ by the intensification of charismatic phenomena and spirit possession."[55] This second type of response "produced" William Seymour, the modern father of Pentecostalism. Such a response, as Wilmore rightly notes, was not reclamation of a futurist idea to the exclusion of the immediate one but "the adoption of an 'immediatist' orientation" in which "Christ came back to the black Christian community in the ecstasy of worship."[56] Finally, some reacted, similar to the second response, in a way that brought the future and the present into closer contact, allowing for the potential interaction of ancestors in the lives of

Christians. For Africans and African Americans the reign of God is "the criterion of the present world, a model of perfection which stands in judgment upon it."[57] In other words, as Wilmore continues, "the general direction of black spirituality has been toward stubborn resistance by subterfuge and non-conformity in the interest of survival. It more frequently sought to transform existing reality by demanding a materialization of eschatological hope. . . ."[58]

There was an additional response as well, which Wilmore does not discuss, but it may fit as a subset under his third category. The formerly enslaved believed in the necessity of judgment or else considered God's justice trivial. The "future" judgment could/should be actualized now.

Nat Turner (1831). In 1829 David Walker, one of the leading African Americans in Boston, wrote a treatise entitled *Appeal,* which was famous in his day and still is in ours.[59] The *Appeal* was a condemnation of American Christianity, which Walker viewed as complicit with American slavery. Such a sentiment was shared by many, so opposing political forces attempted to keep this document isolated to northern cities. There is no evidence that Nat (the "prophet") Turner read or even heard about this *Appeal*; yet, more than likely he "felt the same frustrations that Walker did and was swept up in similar religious and revolutionary fervor."[60]

In one of the bloodiest insurrections among the enslaved in the antebellum South, Nat Turner led a couple of dozen slaves for almost two days killing fifty-seven whites. In reprisal, more than two hundred African Americans were killed, many of whom were not involved or even aware of Turner's plans. Part of what drove the actions of this group was Turner's religious sentiments. In his *Confessions* dictated to Thomas Gray (a white court-appointed attorney) he reveals his mindset leading up to this revolt.[61] As a person who had become accustomed to hearing revelations from the Spirit, he did not fully understand the revelation of 1825, at which point he heard "to seek the kingdom of Heaven and all things shall be added unto you."[62] Other visions followed over the next few years which affirmed his belief that he was to plan and stage a revolt in an effort to throw off the bondage of slavery.

Finally in 1828 he received a revelation that "judgment day" was near: "the Spirit instantly appeared to me and said the Serpent was loosened, and Christ had laid down the yoke he had borne for the sins of men, and that I should take it on and fight against the Serpent, for the time was fast approaching when the first should be last and the last should be first."[63] His response to Gray's next question was most revealing. Gray asked, "Do you not find yourself mistaken now?" "Was not Christ crucified?" he responded. "I should arise and prepare myself, and slay my enemies with their own weapons."[64] At this point he began to communicate his plans with his deepest confidants. His theological conception of God's impending judgment combined with his openness to the Spirit's revelation and religious fervor. Furthermore, an active piety encouraged his political decisions to do what was necessary to alter the prevailing status quo of life in Southampton, Virginia.

While African Americans debated the role of physical revolt to overthrow the condition of the enslaved, Nat Turner's action became legend: "Nat's rebellion [w]as the 'First War' against slavery and the Civil War [w]as the second."[65] The discussion continues, as contemporary African American ethicist Garth Baker-Fletcher emphasizes:

> As heretical as it may seem, those who experience the boot of fierce power on their throats do not envision Jesus as anything but full of righteous indignation for the injustices visited on them in the name of Jesus. So, the historical Nat Turner and all of his psycho-symbolic ancestors still living inside of black men look to Jesus as the Eschatological One, coming to set things aright. Since Martin Luther King and Malcolm X could not change the destructive, oppressive ways of the United States, Jesus will.[66]

Frederick Douglass (1845, 1855). The most widely read "slave narrative" of the nineteenth century came from the pen of Frederick Douglass, the former slave turned abolitionist, whose words on God's judgment were more reserved. In 1843 at a national convention of African Americans, Douglass opposed publicly Henry Highland Garnet's advocacy for slave insurrection, whether violent or not. He published his first edition of his *Narrative* in 1845. By 1849, however, he reversed his position,[67] a few years before publishing his "second edition" in 1855. The theme of God's judgment became more prominent.

In his appendix to the first edition (1845) he distinguished between "slaveholding religion of this land" and "Christianity proper": "for, between the Christianity of this land, and the Christianity of Christ, I recognize the widest possible difference—so wide, that to receive the one as good, pure, and holy, is of necessity to reject the other as bad, corrupt, and wicked." Douglass compared "slaveholding religion" to the scribes and Pharisees of Jesus' day.[68] In his paraphrasing of Matt 23 and Luke 11, Douglass included the idea that to them will come "the greater damnation."[69] More importantly, just before his final "parody" of the hymn "Heavenly Union" with which he closed his *Narrative*, Douglass ended with a citation from Jer 5:29: "'Shall I not visit for these things?' saith the Lord. 'Shall not my soul be avenged on such a nation as this?'"[70] Concluding his story with the motif of judgment demonstrates, according to David Blight, "a deeply political and unconventional ending for a slave narrative."[71]

In the second narrative of his former life (1855), a "quiet and thorough revision,"[72] he included a letter he wrote to his former slaveholder (Thomas Auld), to whom he writes, "It is an outrage upon the soul—a war upon the immortal spirit, and one for which you must give account at the bar of our common Father and Creator."[73] In addition to including a positive reference to Nat Turner in the second edition,[74] Douglass exchanged the appendix of the 1845 edition with this letter and other letters and speeches condemning the evil institution of slavery.

James Pennington (1849). James W. C. Pennington was one of the leading abolitionist African American preachers of his day. He was a close acquaintance of Douglass and presided at Douglass's wedding to Anna Murray shortly after Douglass's escape from slavery.

In his 1849 narrative, also in an appendix, he includes two letters that he had written in 1844:[75] one to his parents, who were still enslaved, and one to his former slave owner. What is striking for our purposes is the use of the theological language of judgment in each.

In his letter to his family Pennington makes a passionate appeal that his family would accept the gospel message so that as they "approach another world, how desirable it is that [they] should have the prospect of a different destiny from what [they] have been called to endure in this world during a long life."[76] He goes to great lengths to distance God from the great sin of slavery: "There is not a solitary decree of the immaculate God that has been concerned in the ordination of slavery, nor does any possible development of his holy will sanctify it."[77] While his appeal is direct, no pressure of facing a vengeful God is appropriated in this discourse.

Yet, as Pennington turns his attention to the former slave owner, the shift in rhetoric is blatant. His image is similar to Douglass's:

> You should, at this stage, review your life without political bias, or adherence to long cherished prejudices, and remember that you are soon to meet those whom you have held, and do hold in slavery, at the awful bar of the impartial Judge of all who doeth right. Then what will become of your own doubtful claims? What will be done with those doubts that agitated your mind years ago; will you answer for threatening, swearing, and using the cowhide among your slaves?"[78]

Then, he continues: "Sir, I will meet you there. The account between us for the first twenty years of my life will have a definite character upon which one or the other will be able to make out a case." In fact, Pennington imagined an opportunity for himself "with a complaint in my mouth."[79] But Pennington not only has the future in view with this theological rhetoric and belief, but he also wanted to effect change in the present: "Can the pride of leaving your children possessed of long slave states, or the policy of sustaining in the state the institution of slavery, justify you in overlooking a point of moment to your future happiness?" Finally, in this vein, the letter ended with an appeal: "In yonder world you can have no slaves—you can be no man's master—you can neither sell, buy, or whip, or drive. Are you then, by sustaining the relation of a slaveholder, forming a character to dwell with God in peace? With kind regards. . . ."[80]

Of course, the African American theological tradition, as Wilmore shows, was not uniform in its appropriation of this theme. But throughout its history issues of justice were often at the center of its theological reflection. Such is no less the case in these early political and theological treatises on freedom.

CONCLUSION

The primary observation of this paper was *not* to suggest that no judgment theology exists within the Second Gospel. But, in the scheme of the whole story, it is rare. God will eventually come to judge those "tenants" who desired to appropriate the goods from the vineyard for themselves. Also, the Spirit, through human agency, is actively involved standing against foreign rulers who abuse their own authoritative regimes. But such judgment in Mark's theology is reserved for the elite, that is, human powers that determine and dictate the ideologies, economic policies, and societal constraints for their respective communities. It is here then that the critique of the formerly enslaved should still be heard. As for those who are the "elect," the Son of Man will so come from his elevated position of rightful authority to gather those change agents operating in the spirit of God's reign.

As Collins states, "The apocalyptic revolution is a revolution in the imagination."[81] As Mark attempts to imagine the faithful role of Jesus' followers in his own day, so are we called to imagine the relationship between our theologies about God's judgment and politics in a post 9/11 environment. One of the many challenges that will require intense spiritual imagination is when the "magistrates" become Christian.[82] The formerly enslaved utilized their theological imaginations to deal with such scenarios. What will the Spirit's word about judgment be in the present? What will the Son of Man do?

The judgment of God, as Mark portrays it, is ironically inclusive in its reluctance and seeks to retain the "common good" for the human race.[83] Its end time story has implications for the present order. It too is political. As James Cone concluded in his studies on the spirituals, "God's eschatological presence arouses discontentment and makes the present subject to radical change."[84]

ENDNOTES

1. "'Why Do You Stand Looking Up Toward Heaven?' New Testament Eschatology at the Turn of the Millennium," in *Theology and Eschatology at the Turn of the Millennium* (eds. James Buckley and L. Gregory Jones; Blackwell, 2001), 125; his italics.

2. "Paul's Gospel and Caesar's Empire," *Center for Theological Inquiry Reflections* 2 (Spring 1999): 42–65.

3. N. T. Wright, *Jesus and Empire: The Kingdom of God and the New World Disorder* (Minneapolis: Fortress, 2003), 80; also see his *Hearing the Whole Story: The Politics of Plot in Mark's Gospel* (Louisville: Westminster John Knox, 2001).

4. Horsley is apparently reacting to scholars from the Jesus Seminar whose collected project *The Five Gospels: The Search for the Authentic Words of Jesus* included conclusions like the following: "The Jesus Seminar awarded a pink designation to all the sayings and parables in which the kingdom is represented as present; the remaining sayings, in which the rule of God is depicted as future, were voted black" (New York: Macmillan, 1993), 137.

5. Wright, *Jesus and Empire*, 103.

6. This number was up from 57 reported lynchings in the previous year (1905) and less than the 89 reported in 1908 (Lerone Bennett, *Before the Mayflower: A History of Black America*, sixth revised edition; New York: Penguin, 1987, 514–515). As far as other world events in 1906, China and Britain agreed to a reduction of the opium production, women were forbidden internationally to work night-shift, and, for baseball fans, Chicago (AL) beat Chicago (NL) 4–2 to win the World Series (*The Timetables of History*, new third revised edition, ed. Bernard Grun, based on Werner Stein's *Kulturfahrplan*, New York: Simon & Schuster, 1975, 459).

7. The Iraqis, even those predisposed towards a positive view of the U.S. military's intentions, certainly view the presence of foreign occupation differently from North Americans.

8. *Prophesy Deliverance: An Afro-American Revolutionary Christianity* (Philadelphia: Westminster, 1982), 35.

9. For recent research on the judgment theme with sensitivity towards the Gospel of Mark, see Vicky Balabanski, *Eschatology in the Making: Mark, Matthew and the Didache* (Cambridge: Cambridge University Press, 1997), 55–134. Other scholarship tends to deal more directly with the judgment motif and the "historical Jesus." See Marius Reiser, *Jesus and Judgment: The Eschatological Proclamation in its Jewish Context* (trans. Linda Mahoney; Minneapolis: Fortress, 1997; German orig., 1990); Steven M. Bryan, *Jesus and Israel's Traditions of Judgement and Restoration* (Cambridge: Cambridge University Press, 2002).

10. Other related terms also occur rarely (*hypokrisis* only in Mark 12:15; *hypokritēs* only in Mark 7:6) or *not at all* (*krineō*; *kritēs*).

11. Balabanski, *Eschatology in the Making*, 207–208.

12. Other terms that imply "judgment" in Mark are also rare: gehenna (9:43, 45, 47), future rewards/punishments (10:31).

13. Cf. Isa 5.

14. The decision to send the son may also express, as Mary Ann Tolbert suggests, "the graciousness and slowness to anger of the owner" (*Sowing the Gospel: Mark's World in Literary-Historical Perspective,* Philadelphia: Fortress, 1989, 236). Although such an assessment is part of the general "Christian" interpretive history, it is the stark ramifications (i.e., the loss of slave after slave) of such "slowness" that is disturbing.

15. Klyne Snodgrass, *The Parable of the Wicked Tenants: An Inquiry into Parable Interpretation* (WUNT 27; Tübingen: Mohr-Siebeck, 1983), 112. For a survey of literature on this parable from 1983 until 1998, see Snodgrass, "Recent Research on the Parable of the Wicked Tenants: An Assessment," *Bulletin for Biblical Research* 8 (1998): 187–216.

16. J. E. H. Thompson "Apocalyptic Literature," in *The International Standard Bible Dictionary* (ed. James Orr; Grand Rapids: Eerdmans, 1947), I.162.

17. John Collins, *The Apocalyptic Imagination: An Introduction to the Jewish Matrix of Christianity* (New York: Crossroad, 1984), 215. Furthermore, he writes, apocalyptic literature "is far more congenial to the pragmatic tendency of liberation theology (than to systematic theology), which is not engaged in the pursuit of objective truth but in the dynamics of motivation and the exercise of political power." Yet, Collins recognizes the difference from contemporary liberationist agendas as well: "The apocalypses often address the issues of political and social liberation, but they conspicuously lack a program for effective action. . . . The visionaries [citing *4 Ezra* and *3 Baruch*] were rarely revolutionaries. Their strong sense that human affairs are

controlled by higher powers usually limited the scope of human initiative. The apocalyptic revolution is a revolution in the imagination. It entails a challenge to view the world in a way that is radically different from the common perception. . . . The legacy of the apocalypses includes a powerful rhetoric for denouncing the deficiencies of this world. It also includes the conviction that the world as now constituted is not the end."

18. Leander Keck, "The Introduction to Mark's Gospel," *NTS* 12 (1966): 365.

19. Even Horsley asks, "What are the disciples preaching about?" (*Hearing the Whole Story*, 86). Also Herman C. Waetjen, *A Reordering of Power: A Sociopolitical Reading of Mark's Gospel* (Minneapolis: Fortress, 1989), 198.

20. E.g., Horsley, *Hearing the Whole Gospel*, 100. Cf. Morna Hooker, *The Gospel According to Saint Mark* (Peabody, Mass.: Hendrickson, 1991), 82; Ben Witherington, *The Gospel of Mark: A Socio-Rhetorical Commentary* (Grand Rapids: Eerdmans, 2001), 104. Note the NEB's benign "that will certify the cure."

21. Cf. Jas 5:3.

22. The link between the three sets of Son of Man sayings, as Morna Hooker observed almost 40 years ago, is the theme of authority "whether it is an authority which is exercised now, which is denied and so leads to suffering, or which will be acknowledged and vindicated in the future" (*The Son of Man in Mark: A Study of the Background of the Term 'Son of Man' and its Use in St Mark's Gospel*, Montreal: McGill University Press, 1967, 180). For recent scholarship on understanding the Son of Man in its Jewish milieu, see John J. Collins, "The Son of Man in First Century Judaism," *NTS* 38 (1992): 448–466; and Thomas B. Slater, "One Like a Son of Man in First Century CE Judaism," *NTS* 41 (1995): 183–198.

23. Hooker finds vindication explicit in the concept of the resurrection itself: "But the belief in the ultimate vindication of the Son of Man is contained in every one of the Marcan passion predictions, expressed in terms of the resurrection" (*The Son of Man in Mark*, 181).

24. The use of this verb in the LXX is never an action of the Son of Man. Rather, God is often the subject of the term (cf. Isa 1:29).

25. Hooker, *Mark*, 210.

26. Horsley, *Hearing the Whole Story*, 128.

27. Ched Myers, *Binding the Strong Man: A Political Reading of Mark's Story of Jesus* (Maryknoll, N.Y.: Orbis, 1989), 249.

28. Contra Francis J. Moloney, who cites Hooker approvingly (*The Gospel of Mark: A Commentary*, Peabody, Mass.: Hendrickson, 2002, 267).

29. E. Schweizer, *The Good News According to Mark* (trans. Donald H. Madvig; Atlanta: John Knox, 1970), 277.

30. Hooker, *Mark*, 361; Craig A. Evans, *Mark 8:27–16:20* (WBC; Nashville: Thomas Nelson, 2001), 451.

31. Hooker, *Son of Man in Mark*, 197.

32. Hooker, *Mark*, 362; Hooker, *Hearing the Whole Story*, 128.

33. Evans, *Mark 8:27–16:20*, 451; see also the fine intertextual work of Joel Marcus, *The Way of the Lord: Christological Exegesis of the Old Testament in the Gospel of Mark* (Louisville: Westminster/John Knox, 1992), 164–171.

34. Also Waetjen, *Reordering of Power*, 223-224.

35. Luke tends to follow the second Gospel closely in these three sections.

36. Cf. Blaine Charette, *The Theme of Recompense in Matthew's Gospel* (JSNTSup 79; Sheffield: JSOT, 1992).

37. Matt 19:28 is missing from the parallel stories in Mark and Luke, although Luke includes the idea of the disciples as future judges *without* mentioning the Son of Man later in the narrative (22:28–30). In a careful study Balabanski concludes the following: "In the study of

Matthew's eschatology, I found that this evangelist gave particular prominence to the eschatological horizon of judgement. I argued that Matthew reinterpreted the Markan discourse for the Matthean community by using a two-sequence technique, which was a remarkable scribal achievement, at once conservative and flexible. . . . Matthew heightens the expectation to fan an imminent End vis-à-vis the Markan *Vorlage*, seeing this reiteration of imminence as the appropriate message for the Matthean community, which presumably did not universally share this outlook" (*Eschatology in the Making*, 207–208). Also Charette, *The Theme of Recompense*, 12.

38. The term "vindication" occurs only in Luke (noun: 18:7, 8; 21:22; verb 18:3, 5).

39. N. T. Wright, *Jesus and the Victory of God* (Minneapolis: Fortress, 1996), 642–644. Even more succinctly, he states, "It would be a serious misreading of the Daniel reference and a serious misjudging of its first century meaning, to see this as a reference to Jesus flying downwards towards the earth" (p. 643). While Wright makes this claim for the entire tradition in an attempt to understand the historical Jesus, I am less ambitious utilizing his claim solely for the Gospel of Mark's theological portrayal. Among recent commentators on Mark, Waetjen (*Reordering of Power*, 223–224) comes closest to this idea that for Mark the Son of Man's judgment is reserved for only a few, that is, the leaders of Israel. Most others (i.e., "sinners") are forgiven.

40. Postcolonialism is not a method, but a sensitivity towards alternative voices that have only recently appeared in the discipline of biblical studies. This "sensitivity" is particularly attentive to the relationship between interpretation ("knowledge") and power structures, both in the ancient world and texts *and* in contemporary ones. For its relationship to biblical studies, see *Postcolonialism and Scriptural Reading*, Semeia 75 (1996); R. S. Sugirtharajah, *Postcolonial Criticism and Biblical Interpretation* (Oxford: Oxford University Press, 2002); *idem*, *Postcolonial Reconfigurations: An Alternative Way of Reading the Bible and Doing Theology* (St. Louis: Chalice, 2003).

41. As Stephen Moore recently argued, "Mark thereby obliquely signals his conviction that the Roman annihilation of the temple and city that brought the Jewish rebellion of 66 C.E. to a catastrophic close was an act of divine retribution"; "Mark and Empire: 'Zealot' and 'Postcolonial' Readings" (paper presented at the 2003 SBL meeting, Atlanta, Ga.), 1. I am grateful to Prof. Moore for sharing a draft of his presentation with me.

42. Also Myers, *Binding the Strong Man*, 352; Moore, "Mark and Empire," 9–12.

43. Moore concentrates his observation from Romans on Rom 13, but one should consider the groaning language of ch. 8 as potential cries for the incomplete socio-political order as a balance to the acquiescence of Rom 13:2. See my "The Groans of 'Brother Saul': An Exploratory Reading of Romans 8 for 'Survival'," *WW* 24 (2004): 315–322. Joel Green suggested to me in private conversation that 1 Pet 2:17 should be recognized as an attempt to provide a more balanced statement on the relationship between Christians and the state in 1 Peter in that honor is given to *all* persons, including the king.

44. Moore, "Mark and Empire," 8, also see 11–12.

45. Myers; Waetjen; Horsley; and Brian K. Blount, *Go Preach! Mark's Kingdom Message and the Black Church Today* (Maryknoll, N.Y.: Orbis, 1998).

46. Moore, "Mark and Empire," 9, n. 17. Joanna Dewey calls it "perhaps the most liberating Gospel in the Christian Testament for any oppressed or marginalized group," because it "presents a nonhierarchical, nonauthoritarian, egalitarian view of community" ("The Gospel of Mark," *Searching the Scriptures: Volume Two: A Feminist Commentary*, ed. E. Schüssler Fiorenza; New York: Crossroad, 1994, 470–471).

47. Moore, 9.

48. Ibid., 16.

49. Myers also concludes that "Mark is not attempting to solve the paradox of power he has just articulated by promising eschatological retribution. Such a view is merely a last-ditch attempt to resolve the scandal of the cross by an appeal to a hermeneutics of triumphalism: 'Bear the cross and wear the crown!'" (*Binding the Strong Man*, 248). Horsley *(Hearing the Whole Story*, 262, n. 19) offers a similar response specifically to Tat-siong Benny Liew's work *Politics of Parousia: Reading Mark Inter(con)textually* (Leiden: Brill, 1999).

50. The section title is borrowed from chapter six of Gayraud Wilmore, *Last Things First* (Louisville: Westminster/John Knox, 1982).

51. In biblical studies, see, for example, Brian K. Blount's *Then the Whisper Put on Flesh: New Testament Ethics in an African American Context* (Nashville: Abingdon, 2001), 23-44.

52. Some scholars prefer the designation African American autobiography for this body of literature (e.g., William Andrews, *To Tell a Free Story: The First Century of Afro-American Autobiography*, Urbana, Ill.: University of Illinois Press, 1986).

53. Wilmore, *Last Things First*, 77.

54. Ibid., 79–80.

55. Ibid., 81–82. An excellent representative of this response was Sojourner Truth, whose chief contemporary biographer described her as an early "Pentecostal" (Nell Irvin Painter, *Sojourner Truth: A Life, A Symbol*, New York/London: W. W. Norton, 1996, 293, n. 4).

56. Wilmore, *Last Things First*, 82.

57. Ibid., 83.

58. Ibid., 87. Wilmore does not fail to recognize that some "escapism" and "otherworldliness" exists, but in response to James Cone he does not view it as the "whole story" (87). Also, there is no apparent connection between these three "responses" and (black) existential interpretations of eschatological discourse as in Howard Thurman's and Martin Luther King, Jr.'s, sermons and writings.

59. "Walker's Appeal, in Four Articles," in *Afro-American Religious History: A Documentary Witness* (ed. Milton C. Sernett; Durham, N.C.: Duke University Press, 1985), 188–195.

60. Stephen B. Oates, *The Fires of Jubilee: Nat Turner's Fierce Rebellion* (New York: Harper & Row, 1975), 51.

61. "The Confessions of Nat Turner," in *Afro-American Religious History: A Documentary Witness*, 88.

62. Ibid., 90.

63. Cf. Mark 10:31.

64. "The Confessions of Nat Turner," 92.

65. Oates, *The Fires of Jubilee*, 145.

66. "Xodus Musings: Reflections on Womanist Tar Baby Theology," *Theology Today* 50 (1993): 38–43. The first section of the quotation bears repeating: "It is Nat Turner, and not Jack, who is empowered by the Spirit to go forth slaying and killing slave owners in the name of the wrathful judgment of God. Such imagery of spiritual empowerment by violent overthrow is terrifying for whites. It is 'un-Christian' and 'against all of the teachings of Jesus.' Doesn't this understanding of Jesus and the Holy Spirit fly in the face of many centuries of 'solid' nonviolent Christian social ethics? Perhaps, but it does so based on Nat Turner's apocalyptic visions, which conceived of a wrathful, second coming Jesus, rather than the meek and mild Jesus so precious to European and American Christian tradition. As heretical as it may seem . . . ."

67. Benjamin Quarles, *Black Abolitionists* (Oxford: Oxford University Press, 1969), 228; also James Brewer Stewart, *Holy Warriors: The Abolitionists and American Slavery* (rev. ed.; New York: Hill & Wang, 1997), 143.

68. *Narrative of the Life of Frederick Douglass, An American Slave, Written by Himself* (ed. David W. Blight; Boston: Bedford, 1993; orig. 1845).

69. Ibid., 106.

70. Ibid., 107.

71. Ibid., 115, n. 73.

72. Andrews, *To Tell a Free Story*, 217.

73. Published Sept. 1848 in two separate newspapers; see the Blight edition, 140.

74. Frederick Douglass, *My Bondage and My Freedom* (New York: Dover, 1969; orig. 1855), 200. Douglass relates a story about a slaveholder telling him that if he did not cease his Sabbath school activities (i.e., teaching other slaves to read) then he would suffer the fate of Nat Turner. In light of this analogy literacy was viewed as "insurrection."

75. James Pennington, "The Fugitive Blacksmith; or, Events in the History of James W. C. Pennington, Pastor of a Presbyterian Church, New York, Formerly a Slave in the State of Maryland, United States," in *I Was Born a Slave: An Anthology of Classic Slave Narratives* (ed. Yuval Taylor; Chicago: Lawrence Hill, 1999), II.103–158.

76. Ibid., 151–152.

77. Ibid., 151.

78. Ibid., 154.

79. Ibid.

80. Ibid.

81. Collins, *The Apocalyptic Imagination*, 215.

82. On the first "Christian" emperor, Ramsey MacMullen has this to say: "The empire had never had on the throne a man given to such bloodthirsty violence as Constantine" (*Christianizing the Roman Empire: A.D. 100-400*, New Haven, Conn.: Yale University Press, 1984, 50).

83. The theme of this conference is not human judgment, because when human judgment attempts to interfere (that is, when it attempts to mask itself as God's judgment) then not only do we hear the religious rhetoric of the war on Iraq or the devastation of the Twin Towers, but also when human judgment attempts to interfere there is an attempt to exclude rather than include. Such human interference always goes awry as it only disguises itself, as Womanist ethicist Joan M. Martin remarks, "in anti-affirmative action attacks, in so-called welfare reform and workfare, in anti-immigration legislation, in privatization of public education, and in the lack of political will to provide anything other than drugs and prisons for those who are structured out of the common good" ("A Sacred Hope and Social Good: Womanist Eschatology," in *Liberating Eschatology: Essays in Honor of Letty M. Russell,* Louisville: Westminster John Knox, 1999, 224).

84. James Cone, *The Spirituals and the Blues* (Maryknoll: Orbis, 1972), 85.

THE UNITY OF JUDGMENT AND LOVE

RANDALL C. ZACHMAN

The discussion of the judgment of God in the contemporary church is marked by a curious dichotomy, seen in both the conservative and liberal communities. On the one hand, the church has no trouble at all speaking about the justice and judgment of God standing over against those with whom it disagrees. This is most easily discerned in more conservative Christians, when they claim that God does not hear the prayers of the Jews or proclaim that the destruction of the World Trade Center is the judgment of God on America for the sins of our culture, or when they state definitively that homosexuality is contrary to Scripture, tradition, and natural law, and hence that those who practice it are not welcome in the church or at least in its ordained ministry. Such behavior on the part of conservative Christians, reaching its virtual caricature in the annual celebration of Matthew Shepherd's reception into hell, confirms the sense among liberal Christians that a focus on the judgment of God leads inexorably to becoming judgmental oneself. However, liberal Christians have no difficulty in speaking about the judgment of God against others, even if it is not clear to them that this is in fact happening. The call for social justice, rooted in prophets like Amos and Isaiah, is a clear indication of the importance of divine judgment. Liberal Christians have no difficulty pronouncing divine judgment on those they consider to be sexist, racist, classist, ageist, Eurocentric, militaristic, or homophobic. Liberal Christians cannot tolerate those they deem to be intolerant, any more than they can tolerate those who tolerate injustice against others. What is clear from all this is that both conservative and liberal Christians have no difficulty invoking the judgment of God against their opponents. They fall completely silent, however, when it comes to the judgment of God against themselves.

There are several real and legitimate pastoral difficulties confronting the church when it comes to speaking about the judgment of God against itself. There is the fear of sounding manipulative by using the fear of hell to scare people into believing. We have all seen those pamphlets that proclaim the love of God for sinners, saying all we have to do to be saved is believe, but which then end by

The Unity of Judgment and Love

threatening us with eternal wrath in hell if we do not believe. There is also the fear of sounding judgmental, especially when one has encountered those whose hearts have been permanently seared by the divine condemnation pronounced on them by others. There is the fear of sounding like one is blaming the victims, as when AIDS is seen to be divine retribution against homosexual men, or the Holocaust is said to reveal yet again God's wrath against the Jews. Finally, there is the anxiety of confirming people's worst fears about God, namely that God is a wrathful and capricious Judge who delights in punishing human beings.

As a consequence the message the church preaches to itself is one from which the judgment of God has been eliminated, being reserved only for those with whom the church disagrees. God is said to love sinners unconditionally, meaning that there is nothing you can do to keep God from loving you, just as there was nothing you did which made God love you. God is said to accept everyone just as they are, however that might be, so that one need not fear rejection or condemnation, even as Jesus ate with tax collectors and sinners. God is definitely not the cause of calamities in this world, for God does not cause evil. And the evils of this world are most definitely not signs of the wrath of God. Finally, God is love and mercy, not judgment and wrath; the latter attributes belong to the one we have come to call "the OT God," which we may thankfully consign to the dustbin of history.

In many ways the situation we face today with regard to the judgment of God echoes the problems that arose within the church from the very beginning of its existence. Marcion, who worked around 140 C.E., used a very keen form of dialectics rooted in the letters of Paul to distinguish between love and judgment, forgiveness and condemnation, mercy and wrath. The result was the confident declaration that the God of the law in the OT is not the same as the God of Jesus Christ in the NT. The God of Israel is a wrathful and capricious Judge who delights in punishing and destroying, whereas the God of Jesus Christ is a God of mercy and love who delights in forgiving and saving. The God of Jesus Christ saves us from the illusion of thinking that the God of Israel is the true God. It is one of the tragedies of the Christian tradition that Marcion was seen as much more of a threat in the Eastern Greek church than in the Western Latin church. The theology of Greek fathers like Origen and Gregory of Nyssa was formulated in large part against the position of Marcion and was designed to demonstrate that the mercy and love of God are one with the judgment and wrath of God. The much-maligned allegorical method was designed in large part to give a more salutary meaning to those passages which seemed to confirm Marcion's worst fears, such as the prayer that they would be blessed who would take the infants of Babylon and smash them against the rock (Ps 137:9), or the command of God to kill every man, woman, child, and animal in the Canaanite city of Jericho (Josh 6:21). According to Origen and Gregory the punishment and wrath of God is never an end in itself but is always as expression of the goodness of God and is meant to turn sinners from sin to seek their true goal in God. The Greek fathers would never allow themselves to discuss the judgment and wrath of God in isolation from God's goodness and love, since they were at pains to show that these apparent opposites were in fact united in the one true God, over against the way Marcion divorced them from one another.

The Latin tradition, on the other hand, did not feel the force of Marcion's position and, therefore, allowed itself to speak of the manifestation of God's judgment and wrath in isolation from God's love and mercy. Thus Augustine could claim that handing sinners over to eternal destruction properly revealed the justice of God, even as saving the elect sinners from sin and wrath so that they might be eternally happy in God manifested God's mercy. The Reformation only intensified the dichotomy between judgment and mercy by means of Luther's dialectic of the law and the gospel, which is nicely summarized by Calvin. "In the precepts of the Law, God is but the rewarder of perfect righteousness, which all of us lack, and conversely, the severe judge of evil deeds. But in Christ his face shines, full of grace and gentleness, even upon us poor and unworthy sinners" (*Inst.* II.vii.8). One must first be humbled by the awareness of sin and wrath revealed by the law before one can believe in the love and mercy of God towards sinners revealed in the Gospel. The advantage of this position is that it makes it necessary for all the godly to pass through the judgment of God to come to faith in mercy. The liability of this position is that it can make faith sound like enlightened self-interest, as the means by which to free oneself from wrath and condemnation. It can also perpetuate the dichotomy between love and judgment. The Reformation perpetuated Augustine's view of the distinct manifestations of justice and mercy. Those who believe in the love of God have been elected by mercy, whereas those who do not believe have been either passed over or even reprobated by judgment. The clear thrust of this theological trajectory is that the judgment of God reveals sin and wrath, whereas the love of God reveals forgiveness and mercy.

It is important to remember that the move away from the judgment and wrath of God to the love of God began as a criticism of this Reformation position. Schleiermacher's remarkable sermon on the wrath of God is an explicit criticism of Luther and Calvin's claim that faith is made possible only once the conscience of the sinner has been terrified by the revelation of sin and wrath so that one seeks comfort in the mercy and love revealed in the gospel. One sees a similar criticism emerging earlier in figures such as Jonathan Edwards and Nicholas Ludwig, Count von Zinzendorf, both of whom have strong suspicions of a faith that seeks to escape wrath by taking refuge in love. Moreover, the move away from the law/gospel dialectic was accompanied by the emergence of the insight that the nature and essence of God is above all else love, and not, as in the previous tradition, goodness, which in the West still allowed for the dichotomy between judgment and love. The consensus that God is love came to be widely shared by theologians as diverse as Søren Kierkegaard and G. W. Hegel and was further developed in the twentieth century by Roman Catholic theologians such as Karl Rahner and Hans Urs von Balthasar, as well as Protestant theologians such as Karl Barth and Eberhard Jüngel.

Moreover, it was the genius of Kierkegaard—as well as the source of his life-long torment—to realize that nothing judges the human being more radically or pervasively than the love that is God. If the church is going to speak clearly and responsibly about the judgment of God today, it cannot seek to correct the modern focus on the love of God with a counterbalancing emphasis on the judgment of God, i.e., by repristinating the theology of Augustine or Luther and Calvin. Rather, the task is to show the church that it cannot believe in the love that is God without simultaneously submitting itself to the radical judgment of God. One does not escape the judgment of God by fleeing to the love of God; rather, one is never more thoroughly known and judged than when one allows oneself to be loved by God.

The unity of love and judgment is clearly seen in the defining event of Israel's life, in which the nature of God is definitively revealed. While the Israelites are languishing in Egypt, God hears their cry on account of their taskmasters, knows their sufferings, and comes down to deliver them by freeing them from the hand of the Egyptians and by bringing them to the land promised to Abraham, Isaac, and Jacob (Exod 2:23–25; 3:7–10). These actions are the archetypal manifestation of the love of God for the Israelites. Thus, in the psalms the faithful ask God to hear their cry, to look upon their affliction, to come down and free them from the hand of their oppressors, and to bring them to a place of peace: "I will exult and rejoice in your steadfast love, because you have seen my affliction; you have taken heed of my adversities, and have not delivered me into the hand of the enemy; you have set my feet in a broad place" (Ps 31:7). The hope that God will hear and deliver is the basis of the prayers of the faithful in the midst of their affliction. The psalmist prays, "I call upon you, for you will answer me, O God; incline your ear to me, hear my words. Wondrously show your steadfast love, O savior of those who seek refuge from their adversaries at your right hand" (Ps 17:6–7). Thus the love of God is manifested in the life of Israel when God hears their cry, sees their affliction, delivers them from their adversaries, and brings them peace, as happened in a definitive way in the exodus from Egypt.

However, the love of God revealed in the exodus from Egypt also brings about the revelation of the sin of the Israelites in the wilderness. My students are always appalled by the behavior of the patriarchs in Genesis, and especially by their deception of others, as when Abram asks Sarai to lie, or Jacob deceives his father to obtain his brother's blessing. But I tell them that there is no sin where there is not first the manifestation of God's love in the exodus. The litanies of the sins of

Israel in Scripture always begin after God has delivered the people out of Egypt by the power of God's love. "Both we and our ancestors have sinned; we have committed iniquity, have done wickedly. Our ancestors, when they were in Egypt, did not consider your wonderful works; they did not remember the abundance of your steadfast love, but rebelled against the Most High at the Red Sea" (Ps 106:6–7). The love of God manifested in the deliverance of Israel from Egypt brings about the judgment of the people as they rebel against that love by their sin. The law of God revealed at Sinai is an essential aspect of this judging character of the love of God, for the people redeemed by the love of God must now yield the entirety of their lives to God, as God's own treasured possession. God tells them, "You have seen what I did to the Egyptians, and how I bore you on eagles' wings and brought you to myself. Now therefore, if you obey my voice and keep my covenant, you shall be my treasured possession out of all the peoples" (Exod 19:4–5). This may be why Ezra links the giving of the law with the exodus from Egypt, for the love expressed in these events simultaneously brings about the disclosure of the sin of the people. In Neh 9:16–17 Ezra complains, "But they and our ancestors acted presumptuously and stiffened their necks and did not obey your commandments; they refused to obey, and were not mindful of the wonders that you performed among them; but they stiffened their necks and determined to return to their slavery in Egypt."

If the exodus and Sinai reveal the essential unity of love and judgment so that the love that redeems also discloses the rebellion of the people against that love, then God's response to their sin and rebellion reveals the essential unity of judgment and love. On the one hand, precisely because Israel is called in love to be God's treasured possession, dedicated to God alone, God cannot and will not tolerate the violation of that love in faithlessness and betrayal. Thus, when Israel can wait no longer for Moses to come down from Sinai and has Aaron make gods for them, God's saving love manifests itself in the blazing wrath of rejection: "The Lord said to Moses, 'I have seen this people, how stiff-necked they are. Now let me alone, so that my wrath may burn hot against them and I may consume them; and of you I will make a great nation'" (Exod 32:9–10). The love of God that makes Israel the treasured possession of God does not spare it from judgment and wrath but rather exposes it to the radicality of such judgment so that it is threatened with destruction at the hands of God, just as Pharaoh and his army had been destroyed. On the other hand, Moses responds to this threat by appealing to the unity of the love of God with the judgment of God. Since the judgment of God is an expression of the love of God, when that judgment expresses itself in wrath, one must intercede by appealing to the love that remains even in the midst of wrath in the hope that God will repent of the wrath and show mercy. Moses prays to God, "Turn from your fierce wrath; change your mind and do not bring disaster on your people" (Exod 32:12). Moses explicitly appeals to the goodness of God, over against the evil reputation God would gain by destroying God's people, and he appeals to God's faithfulness to the promises made to Abraham, Isaac, and Jacob. However, lying behind these explicit appeals is the confidence that the judgment and wrath of God is one with the love and mercy of God so that even in the midst of wrath one can appeal to mercy.

This insight into the nature of God is confirmed by the vision of God Moses is shown on Sinai, as God proclaims God's name before Moses: "The Lord passed before him, and proclaimed, 'The Lord, the Lord, a God merciful and gracious, slow to anger, abounding in steadfast love and faithfulness, keeping steadfast love for the thousandth generation, forgiving iniquity and transgression and sin, yet by no means clearing the guilty, but visiting the iniquity of the parents upon the children and the children's children, to the third and fourth generation'" (Exod 34:6–7). Calvin rightly claimed that there is no other passage of Scripture that so clearly portrays the nature of God to the life, as in a living image. The proclamation of the name before Moses confirms what Moses already knew when he interceded before God on behalf of the sinful people. The wrath of God is an expression of the love of God, which remains even in the midst of wrath, and the love of God that forgives iniquity and transgression and sin also judges and punishes sin. It is not surprising, therefore, that when the people again rebel against the love of God by seeking to return to Egypt at the border of Canaan, Moses explicitly appeals to the proclaimed name of God to intercede on behalf of the people: "And now, therefore, let the power of God be great in the way that you promised when you spoke, saying, 'The Lord is slow to anger and abounding in steadfast love, forgiving iniquity and transgression, but by no means clearing the guilty, visiting the iniquity of the parents upon the children to the third and fourth generation'" (Num 14:17–18). Because Moses knows that the power and wrath of God are one with the steadfast love of God, he can appeal for forgiveness even at the apex of God's judgment and wrath. On the other hand, precisely because it is the love of God that judges and condemns sin, God not only forgives the people, but also punishes them so that the generation that rebelled against God will not enter the Promised Land, except for Caleb and Joshua (Num 14:19–23).

The unity of love and judgment, of judgment and love, is revealed once again during the time of the prophets before the Assyrian and Babylonian exiles. The love of God is manifested most remarkably in two of the promises made by God in reference to Jerusalem. On the one hand, in response to David's desire to build God a house in which to dwell, God promises to make a house of David's descendants. Moreover, in contrast to Saul, from whom the love of God eventually departed, God promises never to take God's love away from David's son: "I will be a father to him, and he will be a son to me. When he commits iniquity, I will punish him with a rod such as mortals use, with blows inflicted by human beings. But I will not take my steadfast love from him, as I took it from Saul, whom I put away from before you" (2 Sam 7:14–15). The love of God for David and his sons does not exclude judgment, but the judgment will never eclipse the love of God towards the sons of David.

The radical nature of this promise is revealed in the way God responds to the sin of David in contrast to the sins of Saul. When Saul sins by reserving the best of the animals of the Amalekites, Samuel finally brings him to a confession of his sin. Saul follows the lead of Moses and appeals to the mercy of God in the midst of his acknowledgement of sin and judgment: "Saul said to Samuel, 'I have sinned; for I have transgressed the commandment of the Lord and your words, because I feared the people and obeyed their voice. Now therefore, I pray, pardon my sin, and return with me, so that I may worship the Lord'" (1 Sam 15:24–25). Far from pardoning his sin, however, Samuel declares that God has rejected Saul from being king over Israel. This point is brought even more poignantly and tragically home in the last days of Saul's life. When God refuses to answer Saul in his distress, he summons Samuel from the dead, only to hear these chilling words: "Why then do you ask me, since the Lord has turned from you and become your enemy?" (1 Sam 28:16). On the other hand, when David sins by committing adultery with Bathsheba and having her husband Uriah the Hittite killed after he learns she is pregnant, the response of Nathan is very different: "David said to Nathan, 'I have sinned against the Lord.' Nathan said to David, 'Now the Lord has put away your sin; you shall not die. Nevertheless, because by this deed you have utterly scorned the Lord, the child that is born to you shall die'" (2 Sam 12:13–14). David is clearly punished both by the loss of the child he conceived with Bathsheba and by the rebellion of his son Absalom against him, showing the unity of judgment with love; but the love of God is not taken away from David, as it was from Saul.

God makes a similarly radical promise in response to the building and dedication of the temple in Jerusalem by Solomon. In response to the prayer of dedication made by Solomon, God says, "I have heard your prayer and your plea, which you have made before me; I have consecrated this house that you have built, and put my name there forever; my eyes and my heart will be there for all time" (1 Kgs 9:3). The promise of God to dwell in the temple forever has direct consequences for the city of Jerusalem, for it means that God will fight to defend the city against its enemies, even when all hope seems to be lost: "God is in the midst of the city; it shall not be moved; God will help it when the morning dawns" (Ps 46:5). The love of God revealed in the promise to David is further buttressed by the promise to dwell in the temple forever. Thus, when Solomon sins by following the gods of his many wives, God punishes him by taking the northern kingdom from him: "Yet for the sake of your father David I will not do it in your lifetime; I will tear it out of the hand of your son. I will not, however, tear away the entire kingdom; I will give one tribe to your son, for the sake of my servant David and for the sake of Jerusalem, which I have chosen" (1 Kgs 11:12–13).

Given these remarkable promises to David and Jerusalem, it is easy to understand why the inhabitants of Judah and Jerusalem would be tempted to think that such love would preclude the judgment of God altogether. Given the unconditional nature of these promises, it would not matter what the king or the citizens did; God would maintain their cause and defend them against all their adversaries on the basis of God's love. In light of such presumption the prophets are sent to proclaim yet again the essential unity of God's love and judgment. Thus Isaiah accuses the people of Jerusalem of wanting the love and peace of God without God's righteousness and judgment: "For they are a rebellious people, faithless children, children who will not hear the instruction of the Lord; who say to the seers, 'Do not see'; and to the prophets, 'Do not prophesy to us what is right; speak to us smooth things, prophesy illusions, leave the way, turn aside from the path, let us hear no more about the Holy One of Israel'" (Isa 30:9–11). Even the hope that Isaiah holds out for the people if they return to God reveals the unity of love and judgment: "Therefore the Lord waits to be gracious to you; therefore he will rise up to show mercy to you. For the Lord is a God of justice; blessed are all those who wait for him" (Isa 30:18).

One sees the same dynamic even more dramatically in the prophet Micah. It is clear to him that the people of Jerusalem want God only to love them, reserving God's judgment only for their enemies. In this way they can live their lives without fear of being held to account by God, for God has promised always to be with them. Micah says, "Hear this, you rulers of the house of Jacob and chiefs of the house of Israel, who abhor justice and pervert all iniquity, who build Zion with blood and Jerusalem with wrong! Its rulers give judgment for a bribe, its priests teach for a price, its prophets give oracles for money; yet they lean upon the Lord and say, 'Surely the Lord is with us! No harm shall come upon us'" (Mic 3:9–11). Such an attempt to sever love from judgment results in the apparent withdrawal of love with the destruction of the temple in which God promised to dwell: "Therefore because of you Zion shall be plowed as a field; Jerusalem shall become a heap of ruins, and the mountains of the house a wooded height" (Mic 3:12). One sees the same indictment of such presumption in the prophet Jeremiah. The people of Jerusalem clearly think that the love of God can be divorced from the judgment of God so that they can behave however they wish, knowing that God will always love and protect them. "Here you are, trusting in deceptive words to no avail. Will you steal, murder, commit adultery, swear falsely, make offerings to Baal, and go after other gods that you have not known, and then come and stand before me in this house, which is called by my name, and say, 'We are safe!'—only to go on doing these abominations?" (Jer 7:8–10). The threat is the same as with Micah—God will do to the temple in Jerusalem what was done to the shrine at Shiloh. The attempt to sever the love of God from the judgment of God results in the emergence of the judgment and wrath of God to the apparent exclusion of love and mercy: "Therefore thus says the Lord God: My anger and my wrath shall be poured out on this place, on human beings and animals, on the trees of the field and the fruit of the ground; it will burn and not be quenched" (Jer 7:20). Jeremiah is even forbidden to intercede for the people and cannot, therefore, appeal to the love and mercy of God now deeply concealed beneath God's judgment and wrath. God tells him, "As for you do not pray for this people, do not raise a cry or prayer on their behalf, and do not intercede with me, for I will not hear you" (Jer 7:16). The reason given is even more chilling—God has taken away from the people God's steadfast love: "For thus says the Lord: Do not enter the house of mourning, or go to lament, or bemoan them; for I have taken away my peace from this people, says the Lord, my steadfast love and mercy" (Jer 16:5). When the people of Jerusalem want love without judgment, God reveals to them in a frightening way God's judgment and wrath without love.

The destruction of Jerusalem and the exile of the people to Babylon should always remind the church that the love of God can never be severed from the judgment of God. The attempt to preserve the love of God for ourselves, while reserving the judgment of God for our enemies, has the result of placing ourselves under radical judgment so that the love of God seems to be utterly lost to view. On the other hand, no matter how radical the judgment of God shown toward God's people, God's love is always present with them, even if it is deeply hidden from view. In Isa 54:7–8 God says, "For a brief moment I abandoned you, but with great compassion I will gather you. In overflowing wrath for a moment I hid my face from you, but with everlasting love I will have compassion on you, says the Lord, your Redeemer." So remarkable is the exhibition of God's love in the return from Babylon that the prophets suggest it even eclipses the exodus: "Therefore, the days are surely coming, says the Lord, when it shall no longer be said, 'As the Lord lives who brought the people of Israel up out of the land of Egypt,' but 'As the Lord lives who brought the people of Israel up out of the land of the north and out of all the lands where he had driven them'" (Jer 16:14–15). However, the manifestation of God's love after a time of wrath does not mean that the judgment of God is no longer present. Even as love is being shown to those who have been under judgment, they are reminded that such love still holds them to account, even as it delivers them from captivity and exile. Exiles are told, "Seek the Lord while he may be found, call upon him while he is near; let the wicked forsake their way, and the unrighteous their thoughts; let them return to the Lord, that he may have mercy on them, and to our God, for he will abundantly pardon" (Isa 55:6–7). Thus, even as Ezra and Nehemiah help to rebuild the temple and the city in which God would return to dwell, they are also concerned to read and teach the law to the people so that they might devote the entirety of their lives to the God who had redeemed them out of love (Neh 8:1–8).

The Unity of Judgment and Love

Moreover, when the Jews in Jerusalem suffer persecution and death at the hands of Antiochus IV Epiphanes, they recognize that the appearance of the judgment of God is not contrary to God's love but is rather a form of love which is meant to discipline them. Those whom God loves are willing to suffer under the judgment and apparent wrath of God, believing that these are in fact inseparable.

> In fact it is a sign of great kindness not to let the impious alone for long, but to punish them immediately. For in the case of the other nations the Lord waits patiently to punish them until they have reached the full measure of their sins; but he does not deal in this way with us, in order that he might not take vengeance on us afterward when our sins have reached their height. Therefore he never withdraws his mercy from us. Although he disciplines us with calamities, he does not forsake his own people. (2 Macc 6:13–16)

The love of God that had been known by freeing the Israelites from their adversaries is now known in the midst of their affliction, which might otherwise appear to them to be a sign of God's wrath. Thus the mother and her seven sons console one another with the love and compassion of God, even as they prepare to be tortured and killed for the sake of their obedience to the law.

> The smoke from the pan spread widely, but the brothers and their mother encouraged one another to die nobly, saying, "The Lord God is watching over us and in truth has compassion on us, as Moses declared in his song that bore witness against the people to their faces, when he said, 'And he will have compassion on his servants.'" (2 Macc 7:5–6)

In Rom 5:8 the apostle Paul describes the death of Jesus as being the superlative expression and pledge of the love of God for both Israel and the Gentiles: "But God proves his love for us in that while we were yet sinners Christ died for us." However, the death of Jesus contains within itself the complete coincidence of the judgment and love of God, demonstrating how inseparable they are to one another. On the one hand, the death of the only Son of God is the clear manifestation of the self-giving love of God for humanity. "If God is for us, who is against us? He who did not withhold his own Son, but gave him up for all of us, will he not with him also give us everything else?" (Rom 8:31–32). On the other hand, the death of Jesus reveals the judgment of God against human sin by the fact that Christ takes the place of sinners under judgment and wrath. "Christ redeemed us from the curse of the law by becoming a curse for us—for it is written, 'Cursed is everyone who hangs on a tree'" (Gal 3:13). The love that liberates sinners from sin and wrath manifests itself as the condemnation of sin in the death of Christ. "For God has done what the law, weakened by the flesh, could not do: by sending his own Son in the likeness of sinful flesh, and to deal with sin, he condemned sin in the flesh" (Rom 8:3). The event that reveals more than any other the love of God for Jews and Gentiles also reveals like no other the judgment and wrath of God against sin. "We are convinced that one has died for all; therefore all have died" (2 Cor 5:14).

The lives of the faithful mirror this coincidence of wrath and love seen in the death of Christ. On the one hand, faith has as its object the love of God in the death of Christ. Paul writes, "And the life I now live in the flesh I live by faith in the Son of God, who loved me and gave himself for me" (Gal 2:20). In Rom 8:38–39 the death of Christ is the pledge to Paul that nothing will separate him from God's love, surpassing even as it fulfills the promises of God to David and the temple: "For I am convinced that neither death, nor life, nor angels, nor rulers, nor things present, nor things to come, nor powers, nor height, nor depth, nor anything else in all creation, will be able to separate us from the love of God in Christ Jesus our Lord." On the other hand, the faithful, like Jesus, appear to be handed over in judgment to the wrath of God, for they suffer the afflictions thought to be the punishments of sinners. In 2 Cor 6:8–10 Paul writes, "We are treated as impostors, and yet are true; as unknown, and yet are well known; as dying, and see—we are alive; as punished, and yet not killed; as sorrowful, yet always rejoicing; as poor, yet making many rich; as having nothing, and yet possessing everything." The faithful believe that nothing in all creation will separate them from the love of God, even as they experience all the signs of being abandoned by God in judgment and wrath, as attested in 2 Cor 1:8–9: "We do not want you to be unaware, brothers and sisters, of the affliction we experienced in Asia; for we were so utterly crushed that we despaired of life itself. Indeed, we felt that we had received the sentence of death."

The full extent of the love of God in the death of Christ both frees the faithful from condemnation and becomes the standard by which the whole of their lives are to be judged. On the one hand, Paul claims that "there is now no condemnation for those who are in Christ Jesus" (Rom 8:1), so that he can boldly ask, "Who will bring any charge against God's elect? It is God who justifies. Who is to condemn?" (Rom 8:33). On the other hand, faith in Christ involves the lifelong awareness that we must render an account of our lives to Christ himself. "For all of us must appear before the judgment seat of Christ, so that each may receive recompense for what has been done in the body, whether good or bad" (2 Cor 5:10). The judgment does not simply look at the deeds visible to others but reveals the most secret thoughts and affections of our hearts that are not only concealed from others, but might even be hidden from ourselves. Paul speaks of this as happening "on the day when, according to my gospel, God, through Jesus Christ, will judge the secret thoughts of all" (Rom 2:16). Since the eschatological judgment of God will take place through Jesus Christ, we can confidently hope that the love of God will prevail in the midst of judgment, even as that judgment finally removes all within us that opposes the love of God. "If the work is burned up, the builder will suffer the loss; the builder will be saved, but as through fire" (1 Cor 3:15). As this is the only hope the faithful can have before the judgment of God's love, so it is the only hope they can have for the world.

However, there is a real sense in which this judgment searches out the faithful every day of their lives, for the God who loves them so completely in Christ also knows them better than they know themselves. "For now we see in a mirror dimly, but then we will see face to face. Now I know only in part; then I will know fully, even as I have been fully known" (1 Cor 13:12). The message that reveals to us the love of God also reveals our hearts to ourselves so that we might begin to know ourselves even as we are already fully known by God in Christ. "Indeed, the word of God is living and active, sharper than any two-edged sword, piercing until it divides soul from spirit, joints from marrow; it is able to judge the thoughts and intentions of the heart. And before him no creature is hidden, but all are naked and laid bare to the eyes of the one to whom we must render an account" (Heb 4:12–13). Calvin describes the conscience as that power within us by which we judge ourselves the way God judges us. The love of God cannot but awaken the power of the conscience in a way much more radical than the judgment of God taken in isolation; for God already sees and knows everything hidden within our hearts, and yet loves us nonetheless. Hence we cannot but open ourselves more and more to the judging light of God's love so that we come to know and judge ourselves the way God knows and judges us. Such knowledge does not leave us complacent, as does the view that God accepts all of us as we are, but rather summons us forth to continual transformation. "And all of us, with unveiled faces, seeing the glory of the Lord as though reflected in a mirror, are being transformed into the same image from one degree of glory to another; for this comes from the Lord, the Spirit" (2 Cor 3:18).

Moreover, the standard by which we are judged is not the judgment of God abstracted from God's love, but is the very love of God for us in Christ. Even as Christ did not consider equality with God something to be used for his own advantage, but emptied himself, taking on the form of a slave, so we are both condemned in our selfish preoccupation with ourselves and our own interests, even as we are continually summoned to "do nothing from selfish ambition or conceit, but in humility regard others as better" than ourselves (Phil 2:3). As Christ, though rich, yet made himself poor in order to enrich us, so we ought to do all we can with what we have to help those who are in want (2 Cor 8:9). As Christ took upon himself our sins and the curse of God in order to bring us the righteousness and blessing of God, so we ought to bear one another's burdens, and so fulfill the law of Christ (Gal 6:2). Most importantly for the theme of this paper, we who know that we are continually summoned to give an account of our lives to the God who has so thoroughly loved and known us in Jesus Christ will not spend our days judging and condemning others. "Why do you pass judgment on your brother or sister? Or you, why do you despise your brother or sister? For we will all stand before the judgment seat of God. For it is written, 'As I live, says the Lord, every knee shall bow to me, and every tongue shall give praise to God.' So then, each of us will be accountable to God. Let us therefore no longer pass judgment on one another" (Rom 14:10–13). Those whose hearts have been opened and illumined by the light of the love of God will not think of judging and condemning others, for they will be too busy judging themselves before God. "But if we judged ourselves, we would not be judged" (1 Cor 11:31).

  The love of God manifested in the life of Jesus exhibits the same unity of love and judgment we see in his death. On the one hand, we see the love of God in his utter devotion to the needs of others, to the utter neglect of his own interests. We see his pursuit of sinners in his willingness to sit at table with tax collectors and sinners, and to have his feet washed with the tears of a prostitute. We see his exercise of authority and power by the way he makes himself a servant and slave of others. We see his utter devotion to God by his willingness to drink the cup that God handed to him, even though it means being abandoned by God on the cross. And we see his utter dedication to the welfare and salvation of his followers, even though they leave him alone in his distress in the night and abandon him when he is in the greatest need.

  However, the very actions that reveal to us the astonishing love of God in Christ also stand over against us to judge us. We are not simply to admire his devotion to others but are also called to sell all our possessions and give them to the poor so that we might follow him. We are not only to be moved and impressed by his willingness to eat with tax collectors and sinners, but we are to transform our own dinner tables so that we no longer use them as means to obtain patronage, but to feed those who will not be able to do anything for us in return. We are not only to admire his dedication to God and the kingdom by suffering at the hands of others, but we ourselves are to suffer persecution for the sake of his name, even to the point of being isolated and forsaken in the world, even as we bless, pray for, and forgive those who persecute us. The human life of Jesus therefore not only mirrors the love of God for us in all its richness, but it also judges us for clinging to our possessions, excluding those not from our class from our dinner tables, using our power and authority to lord it over others, conforming our lives to the expectations of others so that we will not be ostracized or rejected by others for the sake of Christ, and failing to pray for, bless, and forgive those who seek to hurt or destroy us.

  There is no way to plumb the depths of the love seen in this life any more than there is any way to satisfy the judgment that it brings to everything we are. If Christians paid any attention to the one they are called to follow and really took seriously what it means to be a disciple, they would have no time to look around for others to judge and condemn, for they would be far too busy feeling the judgment of Christ in their own hearts and consciences. "Do not judge, so that you may not be judged. For with the judgment you make you will be judged, and the measure you give will be the measure you get. Why do you see the speck in your neighbor's eye, but do not notice the log in your own eye?" (Matt 7:1–2).

    The love of God is so mysterious, and the judgment it brings upon our lives is so complete and radical, that it appears to surpass anything of which we are capable. Since we all know in our heart of hearts that our lives would be condemned were God to judge us by the standard of God's love, without also upholding and forgiving us by the same love, we relieve ourselves of the pressure of knowing and judging ourselves by the light of the gospel by pointing out to others how far they fall short of the requirements God holds before us. We first need to find a passage of Scripture that clearly condemns the behavior we wish to judge, such as homosexuality or social injustice. We then have to find a group to which we do not ourselves belong, and have no desire to belong, and then bring the judgment of God down upon this group, showing them that they really are condemned by God, even as we assure ourselves God loves us unconditionally. But judging others of whom we disapprove is not even remotely the same as being known and judged by the love of God revealed in Israel and Jesus Christ. Indeed, by acting in this way we bring even greater judgment upon ourselves. We will only learn to speak responsibly about the judgment of God when we first of all see more clearly than we do that the judgment of God is rooted in the love of God and cannot be separated from it, and secondly, when we allow ourselves to be known and judged by the light of that love so that the inmost thoughts and affections of our hearts begin to be revealed. Only one who is continually illumined and upheld by the intimate judgment of love in her heart and conscience can speak of the judgment of God without becoming judgmental, for she knows that we are all summoned to give an account of our affections, thoughts, and deeds to the God who is love. "Therefore you have no excuse, whoever you are, when you judge others; for in passing judgment on another you condemn yourself, because you, the judge, are doing the very same things" (Rom 2:1).

A GOAT'S PERSPECTIVE: MATTHEW 25:31–46

PAUL SCOTT WILSON

When the Son of Man comes in his glory, and all the angels with him, then he will sit on the throne of his glory. All the nations will be gathered before him, and he will separate people one from another as a shepherd separates the sheep from the goats, and he will put the sheep at his right hand and the goats at the left. Then the king will say to those at his right hand, "Come, you that are blessed by my Father, inherit the kingdom prepared for you from the foundation of the world; for I was hungry and you gave me food, I was thirsty and you gave me something to drink, I was a stranger and you welcomed me, I was naked and you gave me clothing, I was sick and you took care of me, I was in prison and you visited me." Then the righteous will answer him, "Lord, when was it that we saw you hungry and gave you food, or thirsty and gave you something to drink? And when was it that we saw you a stranger and welcomed you, or naked and gave you clothing? And when was it that we saw you sick or in prison and visited you?" And the king will answer them, "Truly I tell you, just as you did it to one of the least of these who are members of my family, you did it to me." Then he will say to those at his left hand, "You that are accursed, depart from me into the eternal fire prepared for the devil and his angels; for I was hungry and you gave me no food, I was thirsty and you gave me nothing to drink, I was a stranger and you did not welcome me, naked and you did not give me clothing, sick and in prison and you did not visit me." Then they also will answer, "Lord, when was it that we saw you hungry or thirsty or a stranger or naked or sick or in prison, and did not take care of you?" Then he will answer them, "Truly I tell you, just as you did not do it to one of the least of these, you did not do it to me." And these will go away into eternal punishment, but the righteous into eternal life. (NRSV)

I have no idea how my preaching students at the University of Toronto refer to me when I am not present. If a student in preaching class signs up to preach on a certain day and shows up without a sermon, I don't say "Hey that's cool," or "No problem," or "Do it whenever." They may call me an old goat, and today, at least, I would not mind. When I hear Jesus speak about the day of judgment in Matt 25, I feel like a goat, I hear it like a goat, and so I have to preach it as a goat, which is not all that difficult—but not just any goat, a goat in sheep's clothing.

At some time in the future, Jesus says, all of the nations will gather before the Son of Man in all the colors of the rainbow. It will be like on the playing field for sports, and everyone will be divided into two teams. The good team on the right will be called the Sheep, and the bad team on the left will be called the Goats. The captain doing the choosing is Jesus Christ, the captain of our souls, and folks are selected not on the basis of their athletic ability, or their earthly success, or even on their doctrinal beliefs, but on their kindness. Everyone wants to be on the sheep team because he says to them, "Inherit the kingdom prepared for you from the foundation of the world; for I was hungry and you gave me food, I was thirsty and you gave me something to drink, I was a stranger and you welcomed me, I was naked and you gave me clothing, I was sick and you took care of me, I was in prison and you visited me." These acts were not one act occurrences or occasional events; they point toward a disposition or attitude towards life. And Jesus says to the unrighteous goats, "Depart from me into the eternal fire prepared for the devil and his angels; for I was hungry and you gave me no food, I was thirsty and you gave me nothing to drink, I was a stranger and you did not welcome me, naked and you did not give me clothing, sick and in prison and you did not visit me." Both groups are amazed and respond in identical fashion, "Lord, when was it that we saw you hungry or thirsty or a stranger or naked or sick or in prison and did not take care of you?" And to both he says, "Truly I tell you, just as you did [or did not] do it to one of the least of these, you did [or did not do] it to me." In one way of thinking, judgment day happens not only at the end of time but every occasion we refuse to acknowledge Christ in a neighbor. There is no court of appeal because this is the court of appeal, the last court, the supreme court, supreme court justice. There are no degrees of guilt: sheep right; goats left. At least that is how Jesus' words have been understood.

Jesus' words are such good news for so many people. Twenty-five hundred black people are dying each week in the Darfur region of Sudan because of genocide and the effects of disease and violence. What good news is there for them, if it is not that this life is not all that there is, that the guilty will not escape, and that punishment will be dispensed? What good news is there for the parents in Beslan, Russia, if justice is not part of it? Terrorists, rapists, murderers, racists, and pillagers of the earth around the globe and in our land, beware: every life you damaged is precious in God's sight. We want justice and Jesus says that soon it is tally time. The account is due; time to pay up. You are going to the checkout counter, the capital 'C' checkout counter. Every sin has a price. Every deed will be scanned. You might have thought you could bank your *good* deeds, but you won't be able to pay the price. You don't have a wallet fat enough, and you won't be able to pay the price. You don't have enough bonus points on your charge cards, and you won't be able to pay the price. You don't have enough rich relatives, and you won't be able to pay the price. You don't have enough property to mortgage, and you won't be able to pay the price. You don't have friends upstairs to help you out, and you won't be able to pay the price. It is sweet news for the sheep and gruff news for the goats. Justice will be done. Right will be done. God's will will be accomplished. Let the people say, "Hallelujah." Let the people say, "All right." And let the people say, "Amen."

I am busily cheering with everyone else, and then I remember that I am a goat and not proud of it. Before any of us get too excited at the sweet prospect of others getting their due, let us just remember that we will all stand before God's judgment at that big checkout counter in the sky. There is only one lineup: no separate express lane for those with 13 sins or less; no friendly cashiers who will ignore the odd sin here or there; and no special queue for terrorists, murderers, thieves, and rapists. We will all be in the same line. We will all be looking around at each other's shopping baskets to see what is in there: You have that? You did that? We may not have done something criminal, but I know that when my own sins are scanned, truth be told, I will not be able to pay the price. That is why I was wondering why you were all cheering so much. We hope we have been good, but I know that I have willingly passed by some folks sitting on street corners with an inverted cap in front of them on the sidewalk, people who needed water, food, or shelter. And it did not even occur to me that that was Christ sitting there. When I passed by the federal penitentiary, I haven't always taken the freeway exit in order to go make a visit to Christ behind bars. By the definition of our text, I am a goat. We are all goats.

Here is the problem: if every sin has a price, when the check out register tallies what we owe, none of us will be able to go home. If all of the nations are divided into sheep and goats, the teams are not going to be even. There will be a multitude of goats on the goat side, and over on the sheep side there will be one lone sheep. There will be only one who is innocent, not many, and that one will be Jesus Christ, the only one who is truly a sheep, the Lamb of God. One sheep and many goats—the odds are not good.

As a goat, I figure that Jesus already knew the composition of the teams when he told this parable. No sooner does Jesus finish telling it than he turns to his disciples and announces that the Son of Man will be crucified within the week (Matt 26:1–2). In other words, he is going to the cross to die. But he is not just going to the cross to die, he is going to die for the goats. As Jesus says earlier in Matthew to the Pharisees, "Those who are well have no need of a physician, but those who are sick. Go and learn what this means, 'I desire mercy, not sacrifice.' For I have come to call not the righteous but sinners" (9:12–13). Jesus came to save the sinners. He died for the goats. He died to save the goats. He rose again to sit at the right hand of God on behalf of the goats. He is God's judge. He is God's judgment. He is God's payment for our sins. He is the one who pays for us when we come up short at the checkout counter. He comes over to us as we are vainly patting our pockets and purging our purses looking for the means to pay, and he says, "I see you are a goat. Goat, I love you. I love *you*. Let me pay for *you*. I desire mercy, not sacrifice. Won't you let me offer you my cloak that you might share in my innocence and glory?" And to all of us who want to follow his ways he drapes over our shoulders his sheep's cloak that we might not only look like sheep but be counted as sheep by our God. We are goats in sheep's clothing. One hundred per cent pure Lamb's wool.

I heard a woman named Jane Glaves tell her inspiring story this week, and I have her permission to share the story. She lives in Brantford, Ontario. When she reached sixty-five, she had raised her family and followed her career. She felt she still had a lot to give, so she applied to be a missionary. She was refused. They said her teaching certificate was too old and so was she. She was accepted as a volunteer at an orphanage in Malawi where she tended to two-year old twin boys who were badly malnourished. They climbed in bed with her to sleep because that was the custom in that country. She got scabies from them, and she gave them health. When the children's father remarried, he came to get the boys, hoping to be able to care for them. She did not see them for several months, and then, not able to wait any longer, one month before leaving she wrote to the father to see if she could see them. They reached out to her with love, but something was gone, hope was gone, and they were in danger of dying. Their stomachs were bulging from malnutrition. The father expressed his hope that she would take his sons with her when she returned to Canada. So at sixty-six, with the help of many people, she managed to get the necessary papers, not just for them but also for the five-year-old girl she had also cared for. She brought them all back with her. Her family thinks she is crazy. Whatever she is, she is most certainly a sheep.

We may not be able to go so far. All we need do is to offer a cup of water, bread, shelter, and company. Be kind. Be kind. Be generous, not to become a sheep, for you are that already by God's grace. In our baptism we have already tasted through faith the judgment day that lies ahead. Rather, be kind because you love Jesus and you love doing God's will, and nothing about the future need cause you fear.

ANNOTATED BIBLIOGRAPHY ON JUDGMENT*

Almond, Philip C. *Heaven and Hell in Enlightenment England.* Cambridge: Cambridge University Press, 1994. Almond offers a picturesque account of ideas about life after death and changing concepts of heaven and hell in English thought from 1650 to 1750. Of particular import are the discussions of the day of judgment by English thinkers like Browne, Hobbes, and Milton.

Balabanski, Vicky. *Eschatology in the Making: Mark, Matthew and the Didache.* Cambridge: Cambridge University Press, 1997. This study questions both the idea that the delay of Christ's return was the primary factor shaping the development of eschatological expectation in the early church and the linearity of the models used to understand the development of early Christian eschatology.

Bauckham, Richard. *The Climax of Prophecy: Studies on the Book of Revelation.* Edinburgh: T. & T. Clark, 1993. Bauckham's work is a model of thoroughness, clarity, and helpfulness. This volume is an extensive collection of Bauckham's previously released articles on the book of Revelation. This is an excellent volume for background on apocalyptic literature, historical context, and symbolism in Revelation.

———. *The Theology of the Book of Revelation.* Cambridge: Cambridge University Press, 1993. Bauckham explains how Revelation's imagery conveyed meaning in its original context and how the book's theology is inseparable from its literary structure and composition. This work grounds our understanding of the theology and function of Revelation in its original context and also allows it to speak to the contemporary church. This is an excellent brief overview for pastors.

Benoît, Pierre, and Roland Murphy, eds. *Immortality and Resurrection.* New York: Herder and Herder, 1970. This is a collection of essays by Catholic scholars discussing the Christian notion of life after death, particularly as it relates to the understanding of the immortality of the soul and the nature of resurrected life.

Bernstein, Alan E. *The Formation of Hell: Death and Retribution in the Ancient and Early Christian Worlds.* Ithaca, N.Y.: Cornell University Press, 1993. The first two-thirds of this extensive work analyzes the Greek and Roman understandings of the netherworld and the understanding of the afterlife in ancient Judaism. Bernstein then discusses the treatment of hell in the NT and the doctrinal tensions in early Christian thought that result from a focus on judgment.

Boyd, Gregory. *Satan and the Problem of Evil: Constructing a Trinitarian Warfare Theodicy.* Downers Grove, Ill: InterVarsity, 2001. Boyd challenges the well accepted "blueprint view" of God's sovereignty so that every occurrence in human history fits into God's sovereign blueprint and brings the discussion of spiritual warfare to the forefront.

---

*This bibliography is based on contributions and suggestions made by the participants of the symposium and was augmented, compiled, and annotated by James Amadon and Lars Stromberg, to whom sincere thanks is heartily expressed.

Chapter 12, "Hell, *das Nichtige*, and the Victory of God," deals with questions of God's sovereignty in the realities of judgment and hell. This is a refreshing voice in the judgment discussion.

Brandon, S. G. F. *The Judgment of the Dead: The Idea of Life After Death in the Major Religions.* New York: Charles Scribner's Sons, 1967. Brandon provides important material for comparison and as background for theological discussion of judgment. He provides an overview of various understandings of the afterlife in the major religions throughout history. Included are chapters on ancient Egypt, ancient Mesopotamia, Hebrew religion, Greco-Roman culture, Christianity, Islam, Iran, Hinduism, Buddhism, and Japanese thought.

Braun, Jon E. *Whatever Happened to Hell?* Nashville: Thomas Nelson, 1979. Braun studies historical, theological, and biblical treatments of hell for the sake of the contemporary culture, which throws around "hell" vocabulary and imagery with frightening regularity.

Brueggemann, Walter. *Theology of the Old Testament: Testimony, Dispute, Advocacy.* Minneapolis: Fortress, 1997. Issues related to the judgment of God appear in several places within this large volume, especially in "metaphors of governance," but also in scattered discussions of Yahweh's hiddenness, ambiguity, negativity, and partnership with Israel and the nations.

Bryan, Steven M. *Jesus and Israel's Traditions of Judgement and Restoration.* Society for New Testament Studies Monograph Series 117. Cambridge: Cambridge University Press, 2002. This book examines the eschatology of Jesus by evaluating his appropriation of sacred traditions related to Israel's restoration. It addresses the way in which Jesus' future expectations impinged upon his understanding of key features of Jewish society.

Cameron, Nigel M. de S., ed. *Universalism and the Doctrine of Hell.* Grand Rapids: Baker, 1992. This book surveys the debate concerning the doctrine of hell among various evangelical scholars and brings together contributions from Britain, France, the United States, South Africa, and Australia. Of particular interest is John Wenham's "The Case for Conditional Immortality."

Chapman, Stephen B. "Reading the Bible as Witness: Divine Retribution in the Old Testament." *PRSt* 31 (2004): 171–190. Chapman argues that in order for Brevard Childs to do full justice to his own approach he needs to maintain greater openness about what constitutes a "witness." In doing so, he examines the theological issues involved in understanding divine retribution in the OT. Using 2 Sam 12 as a sample text, Chapman describes the complex interplay between "intrinsic" (act-consequence) and judicial forms of divine retribution.

Charette, Blaine. *The Theme of Recompense in Matthew's Gospel.* Journal for the Study of the New Testament Supplement Series 79. Sheffield: Sheffield, 1992. Charette traces the theme of recompense in Matthew by examining the OT covenantal background (both the covenants of Abraham and Sinai) on which Matthew's thought rests. On that basis the Matthean teaching on reward and punishment is examined. Charette emphasizes that grace is presupposed for Matthew and that Matthew seeks to elicit faith and obedience.

Charles, R. H. *A Critical History of the Doctrine of a Future Life: In Israel, in Judaism, and in Christianity.* London: Adam and Charles Black, 1899. A classic work that examines and compares the eschatology of the OT, apocryphal and apocalyptic literature, and the NT.

Cooper, John W. *Body, Soul, and Life Everlasting: Biblical Anthropology and the Monism-Dualism Debate.* Grand Rapids: Eerdmans, 1989. Is human nature constructed in such a way that at death the conscious personal being continues to exist while the physical organism does not? Cooper discusses this question through study of OT and NT anthropology and through the thought of the Christian church. For those interested in the anthropology and psychology underlying the theological discussions of judgment and hell, this study is a must.

Crockett, William, ed. *Four Views on Hell*. Grand Rapids: Zondervan, 1992. This book uses easily accessible language and presents the view of four scholars on the nature of hell. John Walvoord argues for the literal view, William Crockett contends for the metaphorical view, Zachary Hayes defends the purgatorial view, and Clark Pinnock puts forth the conditional view. After each presentation the other authors provide a critique.

Dixon, Larry. *The Other Side of the Good News: Confronting the Contemporary Challenges to Jesus' Teaching on Hell*. Wheaton, Ill.: Victor, 1992. Is it better to stress a kinder, gentler theology, or an eternal conscious punishment? Dixon answers that question by emphasizing Jesus' teaching on the destiny of the wicked. He seeks to keep the good and "very bad" news of the Gospel in balance for the sake of theological discussion.

Duff, Paul B. *Who Rides the Beast? Prophetic Rivalry and the Rhetoric of Crisis in the Churches of the Apocalypse*. Oxford: Oxford University Press, 2001. The book of Revelation has long been understood as an encouragement to the churches to stand firm despite Roman persecution. Duff argues like Adela Yarbro Collins and Leonard Thompson that, not only was there no present Roman persecution during the writing of the book, but that Revelation is a rhetorically sophisticated response to leadership crises in the apocalyptic churches.

Elliott, Mark Adam. *The Survivors of Israel: A Reconsideration of the Theology of Pre-Christian Judaism*. Grand Rapids: Eerdmans, 2000. Much of this massive work is an examination of the relevant texts to discern the eschatology of Judaism prior to the Christian movement. Elliott seeks to demonstrate that many in pre-Christian Judaism held to a soteriological dualism, a destruction-preservation soteriology, i.e., they expected many in Israel to be rejected and destroyed by God while others would be among the elect.

Filson, Floyd Vivian. *St. Paul's Conception of Recompense*. Untersuchungen Zum Neuen Testament 21. Liepzig: Hinrichssche, 1931. This is a classic examination of Pauline literature on the topic of judgment and reward, one that seeks to do justice both to grace and to human accountability. Though dated, it is still a helpful analysis.

Fretheim, Terence. "God and Violence in the Old Testament." *WW* 24 (2004): 18–28. Fretheim posits that "God chooses to become involved in violence so that evil will not have the last word. In everything, including violence, God seeks to accomplish loving purposes."

_____. "'I Was Only a Little Angry': Divine Violence in the Prophets." *Interpretation* 58 (2004): 365–375. Fretheim traces the connections between God's involvement in relationships with human beings and God's association with violence. His discussion of God's use of human agents is especially pertinent to the understanding of divine judgment in Jeremiah.

_____. *Jeremiah*. Smyth and Helwys Bible Commentary. Macon, Ga.: Smyth and Helwys, 2002. This commentary is an extended theological exposition of Jeremiah as a book addressed to exiles. According to Fretheim, in Jeremiah God mediates or facilitates the consequences of human sin but does not punish Israel, Babylon, or the other nations.

_____. *The Suffering of God: An Old Testament Perspective*. Philadelphia: Fortress, 1984. Fretheim places "God as Judge" in perspective by focusing on God's relationship with the world. God is a God who suffers because of, with, and for creation.

_____. "Theological Reflections on the Wrath of God in the Old Testament." *HBT* 24 (2002): 1–26. Fretheim argues that the wrath of God is both an important biblical theme and valuable for our reflection about God. He seeks to keep together various dimensions that are often driven apart: personal and natural; personal and political; wrath and grief; emotion and reason; covenant and creation; historical and eschatological.

Fudge, Edward William. *The Fire That Consumes: A Biblical and Historical Study of Final Punishment.* Houston: Providential, 1982. This book seeks to exegete fairly the texts concerning the notion of final punishment in the OT, NT, and intertestamental literature. He provides a serious argument for conditional immortality and annihilation.

_____, and Peterson, Robert A. *Two Views of Hell: A Biblical and Theological Dialogue.* Downer's Grove, Ill.: InterVarsity, 2000. A debate between two evangelical scholars concerning the nature of hell. Both base their arguments in Scripture. Fudge makes the case for conditionalism (hell has an end) while Peterson makes the case for traditionalism (hell consists of conscious punishment forever).

Gerstner, John. *Jonathan Edwards on Heaven and Hell.* Grand Rapids: Baker, 1980. Gerstner gives an extensive survey of the doctrines of both heaven and hell from the sermons and writings of Jonathan Edwards. From his obvious admiration for Edward's theological positions he tries to redeem Edward's voice in the modern discussions of the nature, locale, and rationale of heaven and hell.

Girard, René. *I See Satan Fall Like Lightning.* Translated by James G. Williams. Maryknoll, N.Y.: Orbis, 2001. This work of comparative religion shows Girard at his clearest and most brilliant as he compares the Gospel readings of violence to mythological interpretations that conceal the role mimetic desire plays in our conflicts. Especially revealing is a late chapter on "the concern for victims," the absolute value of modern culture. In the book's final pages Girard finally postulates the existence of a power superior to violent corruption.

Gorringe, Timothy. *God's Just Vengeance.* Cambridge: Cambridge University Press, 1996. This book examines the relationship between the theologies of atonement and criminal law. The author argues that atonement theology, particularly "satisfaction theory," helped shape policies that favor retributive justice. By looking at biblical texts, thinkers such as St. Anselm, and eighteenth and nineteenth-century British social history, Gorringe makes his case and contends that there needs to be a shift to biblical conceptions of redemption and reconciliation.

Griffin, William, ed. *Endtime: The Doomsday Catalog.* New York: Collier, 1979. Griffin compiles and edits what famous writers and illustrators have to say about living and dying in the endtime. He includes selections that deal with rapture, tribulation, millennium, judgment, heaven, and hell. Selections in the judgment section include works from Gregory of Nazianzus, Martin Luther, Augustine, Thomas à Kempis, C. S. Lewis, and Jacques Ellul to name a few.

Griffiths, John Gwyn. *The Divine Verdict: a Study of Divine Judgement in the Ancient Religions.* Studies in the History of Religions 52. Leiden: Brill, 1991. This is a comparative study of the future life and its impact on ethics in ancient religions.

Heschel, Abraham J. *The Prophets.* New York: Harper & Row, 1962. Heschel's seminal work on the prophets is an important study for anyone trying to understand the seers of the Hebrew Scriptures and how they comprehend and communicate God's judgment.

Howard-Brook, Wes, and Anthony Gwyther. *Unveiling Empire: Reading Revelation Then and Now.* Maryknoll, N.Y.: Orbis, 1999. This in-depth study treats a broad range of topics pertinent to interpreting Revelation, including apocalyptic literature, historical context, time and space in Revelation, violent language, the new Jerusalem, liturgy and worship, the myth of Rome, and empire today. This is a scholarly work, and its treatment of important themes ought not be neglected. A significant bibliography is included.

Johnston, Phillip. *Shades of Sheol: Death and Afterlife in the Old Testament.* Downers Grove, Ill.: InterVarsity, 2002. Johnston provides a thorough examination of death and the afterlife in ancient Israel. In addition to treating the pertinent texts of the Hebrew Bible, he also investigates archaeological remains. He argues that the Israelites were not preoccupied with the underworld. Their faith in Yahweh as the God of the living, coupled with the belief that Sheol meant being cut off from God, led eventually to the hope of a positive afterlife.

Kelley, Page H. *Judgment and Redemption in Isaiah: Studies in Isaiah 1–12 and 40–55.* Nashville: Broadman, 1968. This brief treatment of key passages in Isaiah is intended to help pastors and laymen in their understanding of the book's message of judgment and redemption. This book is helpful for sermon preparation, Sunday School curricula, and personal study.

Kohler, Kaufmann. *Heaven and Hell in Comparative Religion with Special Reference to Dante's Divine Comedy.* New York: MacMillan, 1923. Kohler presents a study of comparative religions to show the development of the concepts of heaven, hell, and purgatory which influenced Dante.

Küng, Hans. *Eternal Life? Life After Death as a Medical, Philosophical, and Theological Problem.* Translated by Edward Quinn. New York: Crossroads, 1996. Küng offers nine lectures dealing with the difficult questions of life after death. As usual, he is candid and thoughtful.

Kuck, David W. *Judgment and Community Conflict: Paul's Use of Apocalyptic Judgment Language in 1 Corinthians 3:5–4:5.* Leiden: Brill, 1992. This exegetical study seeks to shed light on the nature of the problems in the Corinthian congregation and Paul's response to them in order to get a clearer picture of what early Christians thought about the end. The author includes a survey of previous scholarship on Paul's use of eschatological language and also traces the concept of divine judgment in Greco-Roman and Jewish sources.

Kvanvig, Jonathan L. *The Problem of Hell.* New York: Oxford University Press, 1993. Kvanvig asserts that the problem of hell is a quite general problem for a variety of religious perspectives. At the heart of his argument is the fundamental role of evil in the world, which artfully convinces the reader that the problem of hell, though largely irresolvable, must not be ignored.

Leclerc, Thomas L. *Yahweh is Exalted in Justice: Solidarity and Conflict in Isaiah.* Minneapolis: Fortress, 2001. Leclerc traces how the three major parts of Isaiah emphasize justice differently and yet find unity in an overarching vision of justice rooted in Yahweh's character and purposes. This book is accessible to students, pastors, and scholars and includes an analysis of Isaiah passages that appear in the lectionary readings.

Léon-Dufour, Xavier. *Life and Death in the New Testament: The Teaching of Jesus and Paul.* Translated by Terrence Prendergast. San Francisco: Harper & Row, 1979. This comprehensive study of life and death in the NT explores how Jesus and Paul approached their own death and the deaths of others. Topics include the afterlife and judgment, among others.

Lewis, C. S. *The Problem of Pain*. London: Collins, 1957. This classic work by one of the most prominent voices of the twentieth century still holds great value for the modern reader. Lewis' discourses on divine omnipotence, divine goodness, heaven, and hell hold particular merit in the ongoing discussion of judgment. Lewis reminds us that "in all discussions of Hell we should keep steadily before our eyes the possible damnation, not of our enemies nor our friends but of ourselves. This chapter is not about your wife or son, nor about Nero or Judas Iscariot; it is about you and me."

MacCulloch, J. A. *The Harrowing of Hell: A Comparative Study of an Early Christian Doctrine*. Edinburgh: T. & T. Clark, 1930. MacCulloch analyzes the sources of the early Christian doctrine of the Lord's descent into Hades and its results. He shows by a preliminary study of related beliefs that this doctrine answered to a widespread desire of the church and to its questions.

Maier, Harry O. *Apocalypse Recalled: The Book of Revelation after Christendom*. Minneapolis: Fortress, 2002. Maier provides a refreshing voice in the study of Revelation, one that helps people see that the book is more than a set of apocalyptic endtime scenarios that glorify a God of violent judgment. Pastors will particularly appreciate Maier's emphasis on personal application and his commitment to viewing Revelation as a powerful and important message for Christians today.

Marshall, Christopher D. *Beyond Retribution: A New Testament Vision for Justice, Crime, and Punishment*. Grand Rapids: Eerdmans, 2001. Marshall considers what is entailed in thinking through a Christian position on crime, punishment, judgment, and vengeance, while raising questions about the extent to which the NT speaks to such issues. Marshall artfully poses questions for readers about their own methods of judgment and offers a dynamic model for forgiveness.

Martin, James Perry. *The Last Judgment in Protestant Theology from Orthodoxy to Ritschl*. Grand Rapids: Eerdmans, 1963. Martin chronicles the method and rapidity by which Protestant theology has been shorn of its eschatology and in doing so raises the question whether the last judgment ever occupied an essential place in relation to justification by faith. Martin seeks to allow the scriptural teaching concerning the last judgment to have its rightful place.

McConville, J. Gordon. *Judgment and Promise: An Interpretation of the Book of Jeremiah*. Leicester: Apollos, 1993. McConville faithfully treads the waters between the two major scholarly views of the book of Jeremiah: the tradition coming largely from the work of the prophet himself and the tradition as a "Deuteronomistic" production. Those interested in themes of judgment raised in Jeremiah will find this work is a good synthesis of the message of Jeremiah for God's people.

Mealy, J. Webb. *After the Thousand Years: Resurrection and Judgment in Revelation 20*. Sheffield: Sheffield, 1992. An exegetical study that seeks a solution to problems of interpretation that have plagued scholars throughout Christian history. Special emphasis is given to the contextual network of the final chapters of Revelation as an aid in interpreting the end of the book with fresh eyes.

Miller, Patrick D., Jr. *Sin and Judgment in the Prophets: A Stylistic and Theological Analysis*. Chico, Calif.: Scholars, 1982. Miller looks at how sin and judgment correlate in prophetic oracles and narratives, paying attention to both stylistic and theological dimensions to see how the two are united together. Each prophetic book is treated, followed by sections that examine the source and setting of the correspondence pattern and that set forth a classification of that pattern. The concluding chapter offers a reflection on the theology of judgment.

     ———. "Slow to Anger, The God of the Prophets." Pages 39–56 in *The Forgotten God: Perspectives in Biblical Theology*. Edited by A. Andrew Das and Frank G. Matera. Louisville: Westminster John Knox, 2002. Miller uses the OT prophetic literature to characterize God as a God of justice and righteousness, rather than as an angry God of judgment. He shows God's willingness to relent, his grief over sin and judgment, and his purpose of using punishment to reshape the people for renewed relationship.

Milne, Bruce. *The Message of Heaven and Hell: Grace and Destiny*. Downers Grove, Ill.: InterVarsity, 2002. Milne argues that we are all the poorer for being so unheavenly minded that we lose sense of earthly good and the gravity of life in the present. His work guides the readers from Genesis to Revelation through key texts that illumine the destiny of humanity, the nature of heaven and hell, and the glory of life everlasting.

Moltmann, Jürgen. *The Coming of God: Christian Eschatology*. Minneapolis: Fortress, 1996. Moltmann is noted for several important works on eschatology, and this one provides a serious study of judgment. Of particular interest is his section on the last judgment, which includes a lengthy discussion of the nature of judgment and Jesus as judge.

Moore, David George. *The Battle for Hell: A Survey and Evaluation of Evangelicals' Growing Attraction to the Doctrine of Annihilationism*. Lanham, Md: University Press of America, 1995. Moore explains the current evangelical thinking about hell and the recent tendency toward theories of annihilation. His work reappraises common understandings of hell and would be useful for theological discussion in churches.

Morgan, Christopher W., and Robert A. Peterson, eds. *Hell under Fire: Modern Scholarship Reinvents Eternal Punishment*. Grand Rapids: Zondervan, 2004. This collection of essays from prominent conservative churchmen and theologians explores the complex topic of hell from various angles while still upholding the authority of Scripture. Contributors include Douglas Moo, Gregory Beale, R. Albert Mohler, J. I. Packer, and Robert Yarbrough.

Morris, Leon. *The Biblical Doctrine of Judgment*. Grand Rapids: Eerdmans, 1960. In this brief study Morris examines the most frequently used words for judgment in the OT and also examines judgment in the NT as both a present reality and future certainty. Throughout is the conviction that judgment is first and foremost an activity of God.

Nielsen, Kirsten. *Yahweh as Prosecutor and Judge*. Journal for the Study of the Old Testament Supplement Series 9. Sheffield: JSOT, 1978. This study of the prophetic lawsuits where God is prosecutor and judge summarizes previous scholarship, exegetes specific instances of prophetic lawsuit in Isaiah, Hosea, and Ps 50, argues that the *Sitz im Leben* of the prophetic lawsuit is the Israelite New Year's Festival, and concludes with a treatment of God's roles within the lawsuits.

Paternoster, Michael. *Thou Art There Also: God, Death, and Hell*. London: SPCK, 1967. Although somewhat dated, Paternoster offers a highly readable biblical and historical overview of the theological questions pertaining to death and hell. He deals with the unpleasant reality of death, but views it "as the only gateway to more abundant life."

Pinnock, Clark H., and Robert C. Brow. *Unbounded Love: A Good News Theology for the 21st Century*. Downers Grove, Ill.: InterVarsity, 1994. In the difficult discipline of doing theology on an individual and communal level it is easy to lose focus on the Word of God proclaiming his love and desire for fellowship with his creation. Pinnock and Brow attempt to refocus the interpretative methods that can cloud our fellowship with God. Chapters six and seven are concerned with the issues of judgment and hell respectively and are beneficial for those who want a healthy understanding of God as both loving and judging.

Polkinghorne, John. *The God of Hope and the End of the World.* New Haven, Conn.: Yale University Press, 2002. This book is accessible for lay people and combines scientific insights, cultural expectations, biblical resources, and theological reflection to build an argument that embraces hope for the life to come. Though there is only a brief section on judgment, the other themes and sections are directly related and will be helpful.

Powys, David. *Hell: A Hard Look at a Hard Question—The Fate of the Unrighteous in New Testament Thought.* Carlisle: Paternoster, 1997. Powys provides a helpful effort to take account of this doctrinal challenge.

Raitt, Thomas M. *A Theology of Exile: Judgment/Deliverance in Jeremiah and Ezekiel.* Philadelphia: Fortress, 1977. Raitt deals both with oracles of judgment and oracles of deliverance and sheds light on the theological questions surrounding the Babylonian exile. Both prophets are seen as prophets of doom and prophets of salvation.

Reiser, Marius. *Jesus and Judgment: The Eschatological Proclamation in Its Jewish Context.* Translated by Linda M. Maloney. Minneapolis: Fortress, 1997. Reiser investigates the theme of judgment in the preaching of Jesus, but also includes material on John the Baptist and Second Temple Judaism. He shows that judgment is a central feature of Jesus' message and that Jesus cannot be understood apart from this theme. This is an excellent study which deserves the attention of both scholars and pastors.

Roetzel, Calvin J. *Judgement in the Community: A Study of the Relationship Between Eschatology and Ecclesiology in Paul.* Leiden: Brill, 1972. Much Roman Catholic and Protestant scholarship on the theme of judgment in Paul has focused on justification by faith, often insisting on the importance of work for salvation. Roetzel proposes a new attempt to see the relationship between judgment and other themes and purposes in Pauline literature. Of particular interest is his study of the effect of Jewish apocalyptic thought on Paul's understanding of judgment.

Rowell, Geoffrey. *Hell and the Victorians: A Study of the Nineteenth-Century Theological Controversies Concerning Eternal Punishment and the Future Life.* Oxford: Clarendon, 1974. This investigation of the extensive nineteenth-century writings focuses on the "four last things" of Christian theology: heaven, hell, death, and judgment. The work includes discussions of the contribution of the Unitarians, future blessedness, and the bounds of purgatory.

Schillebeeckx, Edward, and Boniface Willems, eds. *The Problem of Eschatology.* New York: Paulist, 1969. This collection of essays from Catholic scholars includes a biblical study of "The Judgment of God" by Augustin George. This essay looks at the predictions of divine judgment found in the prophets and Jesus and what meaning was attributed to them. The author finds that at the root of prophetic preaching on judgment is not just a focus on the end of time but a summons to live faithfully in the present.

Schleiermacher, Friedrich. "The Wrath of God." Pages 152–165 in *Servant of the Word: Selected Sermons of Friedrich Schleiermacher.* Translated by Dawn de Vries. Minneapolis: Fortress, 1987. This 1830 sermon from a classic theologian helps the reader who struggles with a Christian understanding of God's wrath. Schleiermacher posits that Paul gives us no reason to dwell on the idea of God's wrath and that perhaps the more we occupy ourselves and others with this notion, "the further we depart from the true Spirit of Christianity."

Schüssler Fiorenza, Elisabeth. *The Book of Revelation: Justice and Judgment.* Philadelphia: Fortress, 1985. This work champions the move in recent Revelation scholarship toward a literary-historical paradigm of interpretation. Schüssler Fiorenza studies this paradigm shift through theological perspectives, the early Christian context, and literary vision and composition.

Schuurman, Douglas James. *Creation, Eschaton, and Ethics: The Ethical Significance of the Creation-Eschaton Relation in the Thought of Emil Brunner and Jürgen Moltmann.* American University Studies. Series VII, Theology and Religion 86. New York: Lang, 1991. This study concerns the ways in which theological claims about creation's original and final perfection shape social ethics. Schuurman concludes that "continuity between creation and eschaton is necessary if Christian social ethics is to avoid dualistic understandings of love and justice, personal and impersonal values, church and world, revolutionism and conservatism."

Schwarz, Hans. *Beyond the Gates of Death: A Biblical Examination of Evidence for Life After Death.* Minneapolis: Augsburg, 1981. This book is a good, "textbook" overview of thinking on the afterlife and, in addition to its focus on biblical texts, compares and contrasts the biblical documents with current science and near-death experiences. Schwarz takes into account evidence from ESP, clairvoyance, telepathy, recognition, psychokinesis, and hypnosis. He seeks to find what is compatible with the Christian faith.

Segal, Alan F. *Life after Death: A History of the Afterlife in Western Religion.* New York: Doubleday, 2004. This comprehensive study of the afterlife in western religion draws together the contribution of various sacred scriptures to provide an overview of positions held. Segal deals with the literary, sociological, philosophical, and historical dimensions to compare visions of the afterlife in the various western religions and to make connections between these visions and the communities that produced them.

Snodgrass, Klyne. "Justification by Grace—to the Doers: An Analysis of the Place of Romans 2 in the Theology of Paul." *NTS* 32 (1986): 72–93. This article surveys the attempts to understand—or avoid— Rom 2 and its focus on judgment according to works in relation to Paul's teaching on justification by faith. The OT and Jewish teaching on judgment according to works is investigated, as is judgment more generally in Paul's letters, which more often than not is focused on judgment of Christians.

Tasker, R. V. G. *The Biblical Doctrine of the Wrath of God.* London: Tyndale, 1951. This short treatise was written to remind Christians of the necessity of God's wrath. Tasker argues that God's wrath is consistent with God's love and that the doctrine of the wrath of God safeguards the essential distinction between Creator and creature.

Toon, Peter. *Heaven and Hell: A Biblical and Theological Overview.* Nelson Studies in Biblical Theology. Nashville: Nelson, 1986. In this relatively compact work Toon gives an overview of understandings on heaven and hell in each NT book. He also gives a very helpful overview of Christian interpretation throughout the centuries which provides insight concerning the formation of Christian creeds and doctrines.

Towner, W. Sibley. *How God Deals with Evil.* Philadelphia: Westminster, 1976. Towner exegetes biblical passages, both OT and NT, that help form a theology of judgment. He concludes that there are undeniable biblical grounds on which to understand God's judgment as retribution, though retribution theology is only one answer to the problem of evil. Towner then argues for a movement toward a nonretribution lifestyle.

Walker, D. P. *The Decline of Hell: Seventeenth-Century Discussions of Eternal Torment.* Chicago: University of Chicago Press, 1964. Those interested in the development of the doctrine of hell will find this work informative on both a historical and a theological level. Why did the doctrine of hell remain almost unchallenged for nearly a century and a half, and what brought about major challenges to this doctrine in the seventeenth century? Several enlightening answers are provided.

Walls, Jerry L. *Hell: The Logic of Damnation*. South Bend, Ind.: University of Notre Dame Press, 1992. By the use of philosophical theology the author defends traditional understandings of hell from the charges of immorality and unintelligibility. This is done by examining categories such as the divine attributes, the nature of human freedom, and the process of character formation.

Weems, Renita. *Battered Love: Marriage, Sex, and Violence in the Hebrew Prophets*. Minneapolis: Fortress, 1995. This study of the images and symbols used by the biblical prophets examines the violence against women often incorporated in these images and warns against the power that they carry. Weems explores the capacity of these sexist metaphors and images to legitimize and authorize sexist human power and calls her readers to an honest and critical reading of the tradition.

Westermann, Claus. "God's Judgment and God's Mercy." Pages 276–297 in *The Flowering of Old Testament Theology*. Edited by Ben C. Ollenburger, Elmer A. Martens, and Gerhard F. Hasel. Winona Lake, Ind.: Eisenbrauns, 1992. This essay examines the nature of sin as a human limitation that necessitates judgment, the role of Israelite prophecy in pronouncing judgment, and God's compassion, mercy, and forgiveness in spite of human sin.

Wilmore, Gayraud S. *Last Things First*. Philadelphia: Westminster, 1982. Wilmore writes from an African-American perspective and presents an eschatology not rooted just in future realities after death but which is a source of meaning and mission in the world.

Witherington, Ben, III. *Jesus, Paul and the End of the World: A Comparative Study in New Testament Eschatology*. Downer's Grove, Ill.: InterVarsity, 1992. The author examines the eschatology of Jesus and Paul on such topics as imminence, the dominion of God, the community of Christ, the Israel of God, the day of the Lord, and the resurrection of the dead. Special focus is given to countering the writings of Albert Schweitzer regarding Jesus' and Paul's understanding of eschatological timing.

Yinger, Kent L. *Paul, Judaism, and Judgment According to Deeds*. Society for New Testament Studies Monograph Series 105. Cambridge: Cambridge University Press, 1999. Why does "judgment according to deeds" produce no discernable theological tension for Paul's understanding of justification by faith? Yinger examines second temple Judaism and the relevant Pauline texts. In doing so he shows the Jewishness of Paul's theology and the role of judgment according to works.

Zenger, Erich. *A God of Vengeance? Understanding the Psalms of Divine Wrath*. Louisville: Westminster John Knox, 1996. Zenger posits that the Psalms of Divine Wrath, which can so often be seen as contradictory to the new covenant and Jesus' command to love one's neighbor, are actually laments that cry out against violence and injustice in the world. Pastors and students will find new insight as to the relevance of violent biblical passages and may even learn how to pray through them.

NORTH PARK THEOLOGICAL SEMINARY

SYMPOSIUM ON THE THEOLOGICAL INTERPRETATION OF SCRIPTURE

SEPTEMBER 23–25, 2004

JUDGMENT

THE PRESENTERS

RICHARD BAUCKHAM
    University of St. Andrews (New Testament)

STEPHEN LONG
    Garrett-Evangelical Theological Seminary (Theology)

GORDON McCONVILLE
    University of Gloucestershire (Old Testament)

JOHN PHELAN
    North Park Theological Seminary (New Testament)

CLARK PINNOCK
    McMaster Divinity College (Theology)

EMERSON POWERY
    Lee University (New Testament)

PAM SCALISE
    Fuller Theological Seminary—Northwest (Old Testament)

PAUL SCOTT WILSON
    Emmanuel College, University of Toronto (Preaching)

RANDALL ZACHMAN
    University of Notre Dame (History)

THE RESPONDENTS

D. LYLE DABNEY
    Marquette University

TERENCE FRETHEIM
    Luther Seminary

BOAZ JOHNSON
    North Park University

L. EDWARD PHILLIPS
    Garrett-Evangelical Theological Seminary

GRANT OSBORNE
    Trinity Evangelical Divinity School

KLYNE SNODGRASS
    North Park Theological Seminary

MICHAEL VAN HORN
    Trinity Church, Livonia, Mich. and University of Detroit Mercy (Adjunct)

PAUL SCOTT WILSON
    Emmanuel College, University of Toronto

NORTH PARK THEOLOGICAL SEMINARY

SYMPOSIUM ON THE THEOLOGICAL INTERPRETATION OF SCRIPTURE

SEPTEMBER 23–25, 2004

JUDGMENT

PERSONS IN ATTENDANCE

James Amadon	David Kersten
Phil Anderson	Karl Klockars
Richard Bauckham	Paul Koptak
Linda Belleville	Brent Laytham
Robert Boehm	Karen Lichlyter-Klein
Margaret Brady	Stephen Long
Paul Bramer	Gordon McConville
Karen Brewer	Don Meyer
Guylla Brown	Mary Miller
James Bruckner	Yumi Murayama
Phil Cannon	James Nelson
Richard Carlson	Monty Newton
Mary Chase-Ziolek	Carol Norén
Michelle Clifton-Soderstrom	David Nystrom
Paul Corner	Amanda Olsen
D. Lyle Dabney	Grant Osborne
Jo Ann Deasy	Nathan Pawl
Rebekah Eklund	Adria Pearson
James H. Erickson	Deborah Penny
Terence Fretheim	John Phelan
Stephen Graham	L. Edward Phillips
Robert Hubbard	Clark Pinnock
Everett Jackson	Dorothy Pinnock
Joyce Jackson	Emerson Powery
Boaz Johnson	Pam Scalise
Ryan Johnson	Klyne Snodgrass
Tim Johnson	Jon Stock
Todd Johnson	Lars Stromberg

Robin Swieringa
Michael Van Horn
Melissa Wall
John Weborg
Lois Weborg
Jonathan Wilson
Paul Scott Wilson
John Wipf
Randall Zachman
Joan Zetterlund